THE FUTURE OF U.S. FOREIGN POLICY

Edited by

ROBERT JERVIS
LOREN KANDO

THE ACADEMY OF POLITICAL SCIENCE
NEW YORK

Published by
The Academy of Political Science
475 Riverside Drive, Suite 1274
New York, NY 10115

Cover design: Loren Morales Kando

Cover credits: U.S. Air Force, U.S. Marine Corps, and U.S. Department of Defense photos

Library of Congress Cataloging-in-Publication Data

The future of U.S. foreign policy / edited by Robert Jervis, Loren Kando.
    p. cm.
  Summary: "Discusses the development and implementation of U.S. foreign policy by examining theories that inform U.S. strategy, responses to U.S. military and geopolitical power, and the role of human rights and civil liberties"—Provided by publisher.
   ISBN 978-1-884853-07-4 (pbk.)
  1. United States—Foreign relations—21st century. 2. World politics—21st century. 3. International relations. 4. Security, International. I. Jervis, Robert, 1940- II. Kando, Loren Morales, 1975-

JZ1480.F88 2008
327.73—dc22

                                                   2008029307

Printed in the United States of America
p 5 4 3 2 1

Contents

Preface and Acknowledgements

This book is one of a series of special publications published by the Academy of Political Science on topics of particular importance in public and international affairs. *The Future of U.S. Foreign Policy* brings together in one volume essays with material that explores recent developments in American foreign relations. In addition to examining the conditions that inform U.S. strategy, the book discusses international reactions to U.S. military and geopolitical power. A concluding section addresses the role of human rights and civil liberties in the construction and implementation of U.S. policies. We hope the book, with an introduction by Robert Jervis, will enlighten the ongoing debate over the future direction of American foreign policy.

The Academy of Political Science is a nonpartisan, nonprofit organization founded in 1880 with a threefold mission: to contribute to the scholarly examination of political institutions, processes, and public policies; to enrich political discourse and channel the best social science research in an understandable way to political leaders for use in public policy making and the process of governing; and to educate members of the general public so that they become informed participants in the democratic process. The major vehicles for accomplishing these goals are its journal, *Political Science Quarterly*, Academy conferences, books, and other publications.

Published continuously since 1886, *PSQ* is the most widely read and accessible scholarly journal on government, politics, and policy, both international and domestic. Dedicated to objective analysis based on evidence, *PSQ* has no ideological or methodological slant and is edited for both specialists and general readers who have a serious interest in public and foreign affairs.

I thank the authors of the essays in this collection. It is a pleasure for me in my capacity as Editor of *PSQ* that their contributions were originally unsolicited submissions to the *Quarterly*. As is normal, the views expressed are those of the authors and not of the institutions with which they are affiliated.

I am especially grateful to Robert Jervis, a long-term member of *PSQ*'s editorial board, not only for organizing this book and writing an introductory chapter, but also for having over the years provided all kinds of valued assistance and advice. Others on our small staff at the Academy who warrant my warm thanks are Marylena Mantas, *PSQ*'s managing editor, and Katherine Soverel, my research assistant. Loren Morales Kando, Vice President for Operations and Executive Director of the Academy, continues to use her excellent talents by getting deeply involved in the organization, editing, and production of this kind of volume, for which she is appropriately listed as coeditor. Ms. Kando also designed the book's cover.

DEMETRIOS JAMES CARALEY
President, The Academy of Political Science
Editor, *Political Science Quarterly*

Introduction

ROBERT JERVIS

Most eras appear to be unsettled to those who are living through them, but I suspect that ours will appear so even in retrospect. For all its dangers and surprises, the Cold War had a clear logic and soon settled down to a pattern of some stability. An observer who went to sleep in 1950 would not have been surprised at the scene 30 years later. The end of the Cold War, welcome as it was, produced great uncertainty about the policies the United States should follow and, as a cause and an effect of this, generated confused and changing configurations of world politics. It was far from clear what the major menaces to American interests were or what the United States would or should do. This is true again, despite the past eight years of misguided clarity.

September 11, 2001 brought the first post-Cold War era to an end and produced a distinct line of American foreign policy and a new set of international cleavages. Many people in the United States, and more outside it, found the policies unfortunate if not reprehensible, but at least they understood them. Terrorism, ignored by the George W. Bush administration in its first nine months in office, was defined as the central threat to America. More specifically, the danger was seen as arising from the nexus between terrorism, nuclear weapons, and tyrannical regimes, which made a perfect storm. September 11 was bad enough, but, as the refrain went, "Imagine 9/11 with nuclear weapons." For the Bush administration, this fear was made especially vivid by rumors that a nuclear bomb had been planted in Washington.[1] The anthrax attacks shortly thereafter may have removed whatever doubts remained that this danger constituted an existential threat. Because weapons of mass destruction (WMD), especially nuclear weapons, are extremely difficult to develop, it is unlikely that terrorists could get them without the assistance of a government. Almost by definition, the only states that might do this were "rogues"

---

[1] George Tenet with Bill Harlow, *At the Center of the Storm: My Years at the CIA* (NY: Harper-Collins, 2007), 170.

ROBERT JERVIS is Adlai E. Stevenson Professor of International Politics at Columbia University and former president of the American Political Science Association. He is author, most recently, of *System Effects: Complexity in Political and Social Life* and *American Foreign Policy in a New Era*.

that disregarded the rules of international behavior and were prone to reck-
lessness, in part because they were so cut off from the rest of the world. These
states also were tyrannical, and for the Bush administration, as for many
Americans throughout its history, it seemed obvious that the states that most
disturbed the international system were those that tyrannized and terrorized
their own people.

This diagnosis pointed to obvious prescriptions. Tyrannies had to be over-
thrown, both for the intrinsic benefit this would provide for the people involved and to protect the United States. If this was impossible, or would be
long delayed, strenuous efforts at counter-proliferation were necessary. Iran
had to be prevented from gaining nuclear weapons or even nuclear material,
and the North Korean program had to be rolled back. But in neither case
should the United States be willing to make major concessions, because this
would be rewarding evil and setting a bad precedent. Security guarantees were
to be resisted, because although they might produce some cooperation, they
would also increase the longevity of the regimes and so would at best postpone
the day of reckoning.

This analysis and the resulting policies were controversial from the start,
especially when it became clear that they implied the overthrow of Saddam
Hussein's regime. But the approach was remarkably coherent, at least in comparison to most strategies. Ordinarily, policy is a compromise and composite
that grows out of conflicting goals and values, multiple considerations, and
divergent domestic interests and beliefs. These were not absent after September 11, but at first, the Bush administration was able to impose an unusual
degree of intellectual and political discipline over policy.

It is doubtful that this could have been maintained even under the most
favorable circumstances. The shock of September 11 diminished with time,
and whether the policy would have been invigorated or undermined had there
been subsequent attacks is an intriguing but unanswerable question. The normal workings of domestic politics led to more-vocal opposition and the ar-
ticulation of multiple interests. On top of this, and perhaps sufficient to
undermine support for the policy by themselves, were the multiple failures
in North Korea, Iran, and especially Iraq. Not only supporters of the policy,
but most critics as well, were shocked to find that Saddam did not have active
WMD programs. This not only opened the administration to the charge of having politicized intelligence and lied to the American people, but it removed the
main justification for the invasion. The administration, and particularly the
President, responded not only by claiming that Saddam still had been a men-
ace because of his malign intentions, but by stressing even more the goal of
establishing democracy in Iraq and the region. This was always one element
of Bush's policy, and it had significant popular appeal.

The American public, and much of the policy elite, had never been comfortable with the realist approach to international politics that downplayed
morality and values and argued that whether or not a state was a democracy

was much less important in determining its foreign policy than was the international setting. This bleak outlook cut against much American tradition and self-image, and so Bush's crusading Wilsonianism had a degree of immediate popularity. It did not and I think could not provide stable foundations for policy, however, because it ran afoul of powerful realities in the world. Bush soon found that it was too risky to press autocratic but friendly governments, like those in Egypt and Saudi Arabia, to democratize. Even more important, and partly a cause of the failures elsewhere, was the trajectory in Iraq. Although the final chapters have yet to be written, the costs of the American effort are much higher than the administration estimated, and the best conceivable outcome falls far short of recognizable democracy. With the initial justification for the war as necessary to meet a pressing threat having been demolished, the failure to establish a functioning democracy was especially powerful in casting doubt on the wisdom of pursuing similar adventures elsewhere.

If all but a few die-hards recognize the fact of failure in Iraq, there is more dispute over its causes and nature. The debate is not academic, or not merely academic, because it has important implications for what the United States should now do, and the disagreement is one of the reasons why the lines of future policy are unclear. One group of analysts, largely conservatives and neo-conservatives, blames the administration for the incompetent implementation of its policy. The United States was simply unready for the post-war situation. Little planning was done, the number of troops was inadequate, counter-insurgency tactics were ignored for too long, and the domestic politics within Iraq was mishandled. Many of the most vocal members of this group claim that the fundamental error was in not turning over power to Ahmed Chalabi, who had been a favorite of the neoconservatives. Another school of thought agrees that the implementation of the policy was incompetent but denies that even a better designed policy would have succeeded. In this view (which I share), installing democracy is difficult. Even the successes in post-war Germany and Japan were not foreordained, and the smooth transitions to democracy in Eastern Europe after the Cold War should not mislead us, as perhaps we should have learned from the Russian experience. The prognosis is especially grim for countries that are poor, display deep social divisions, and lack a democratic tradition. Furthermore, when the new regime is brought in by an outside power, nationalism and the reaction to a foreign imposition are likely to further reduce its prospects.

Although this debate is academic in the sense that it draws on and seeks to further our general understanding of the conditions under which democracy can be established and thrive, it has important implications for the future of American foreign policy. If the first school of thought is correct, the main thrust of Bush's policy can and should be preserved. "All" that is required is to develop a greater degree of competence: with skill and effort, we could overthrow the malign regime in Iran and establish a peaceful and democratic state in its place. But if the second view is correct, the Bush policy must be rejected root and branch. Although the United States can and should do what it can to encourage and build democracies, its expectations and efforts must be limited. The United States simply cannot transform the world, and instead must concentrate on furthering a narrower set of vital interests. These include limiting if not stopping nuclear proliferation and, if possible, increasing the respect for human rights around the world. But the United States must exercise self-restraint against the temptations to become excessively involved around the world in a way that will not only dissipate American energies, but will also be self-defeating in producing backlashes (including more terrorism) and allowing others to shirk their responsibility to build a better world.

AMERICAN WAYS OF FOREIGN POLICY AND FOREIGN RESPONSES

As Christopher Hemmer argues, part of the reason why American policymakers adopted such an expansive view of the threat and the remedies was that they drew an analogy between the attacks of 11 September 2001 and 7 December 1941. (Those interested in more quirky historical parallels should read President Franklin D. Roosevelt's speech of 11 September 1941, in which he misleadingly describes the German attacks on American destroyers in the North Atlantic and urges a policy of preemption.) Both were terrible surprises, although they should not have been, and led many to believe that waiting on events was dangerous and that a too-narrow conception of American interests would eventually degrade American power and security. The attempt to understand September 11 in this way contributed to overreaching in terms of goals and overstretching in terms of resources, however. The fascist threat required the sort of all-out effort that followed from Pearl Harbor; seeing terrorism in these terms misunderstands the situation and so generates a set of inappropriate policies.

Jeffrey Cavanaugh advances a parallel argument, although he places more emphasis on the Bush administration's strategic use—and misuse—of evidence than on an honest misreading of the situation. In the conflict with Iraq, as in a series of other cases since 1945, the administration systematically exaggerated the threat in order to generate support for its preferred policy. Cavanaugh's discussion raises what is perhaps the central question for the United States and countries throughout the world: what is the magnitude of the threat posed by terrorism? There have been too many attacks, let alone attempted ones, for anyone to dismiss the dangers. But the world is full of menaces, and even more full of terrible things that we can imagine happening. Bush has stressed the crucial nature of the nexus between terrorists and nuclear weapons, and here he has a great deal of company. Without nuclear material, while terrorists can cause individual tragedies, they cannot threaten the fabric of our societies. But since it is extraordinarily difficult to find evidence bearing on the likelihood of terrorists being able to acquire nuclear weapons, people are thrown back on their instincts. Full scope is given to those who would exaggerate the threat for political purposes and to those who have very active imaginations.

Other states seem less preoccupied by the danger of nuclear-armed terrorists than the United States is. They have reacted in various ways, not only to terrorism, but to the American response to it. Although no superpower has emerged to challenge the United States, Seth Jones argues that there has been a striking increase in the extent to which European defense companies have cooperated with each other. Encouraged by their governments, these companies see not only economic incentives to work together, but also the fundamental political purpose of reducing the reliance on the United States. Countries of course generally seek to reduce their dependence on others, but there are special reasons to do so when the other country is both extremely strong and lacking in good judgment.

THE NEOCONSERVATIVE HERITAGE AND ITS FLAWS

As it moves forward, the United States cannot escape the heritage of Bush's policy and neoconservative ideas. For many observers, these constitute a major burden on the country and the world. Piki Ish-Shalom looks at the roots of the neoconservative promotion of democracy in the Middle East and notes that while some of them are unique to this small if important group of thinkers, parts of their vision are more widely shared and have continuing appeal. The very contradiction within neoconservative thought between skepticism about "social engineering" and support for the democratization project, and between the fear of unchecked power domestically and the use of unchecked American power abroad both allows the policies to appeal to a wider audience and may permit a new policy to adopt some of the threads of the old one while turning in a more productive direction.

Another continuity is a deep concern for the credibility of American threats to adversaries and promises to allies, as Christopher Fettweis explains. Cold War thinking was characterized if not dominated by worries about falling dominos. Although much ridiculed in the years after Vietnam, in fact the concern with credibility and reputation is common in international politics and indeed in much of social life. Thus, people and states often act in a particular way not because of the direct effects that are expected but in order to produce the desired impression on a range of audiences. During the Cold War, American decision makers often believed that they could not back down or make concessions over issues of little intrinsic importance because others would infer that the United States lacked resolve and so could be pushed around on more-important questions. Some analysts and members of the policy elite came to doubt this view, and in any event thought that with the end of the Cold War the question had become one of historical interest only. But it reemerged after September 11. Clearly, one reason for invading Iraq was to impress Iran, North Korea, and other rogue states. A related motive was to impress and discourage terrorists. We lack a definitive answer as to whether force works in this way, but the question is central both to what the United States has done over the past several years and to how it should act in the future.

Human Rights and Civil Liberties

The war on terror has influenced human rights abroad and civil liberties at home. As John Dietrich notes, concern for human rights has been part of the American consciousness and policy from the earliest days. During the Cold War, human rights policies episodically reinforced anti-Soviet policies and conflicted with them. With the demise of the Soviet Union, some of the inhibitions against promoting human rights disappeared, but others, especially the importance of bilateral ties and the desire for stability, remained. The perceived threat of terrorism reinforced multiple and conflicting imperatives. On the one hand, promoting human rights is seen as part of facilitating democracy and combating terrorism. On the other hand, some of the staunchest foes of terrorism violate the rights of their own people.

The worst human rights violation is genocide, and the two most obvious recent cases are Rwanda and Darfur. Eric Heinze explores them, noting that while the administration of Bill Clinton was careful to avoid labeling the events in Rwanda as genocide in order to reduce the pressure to do something about them, the Bush administration did label the events in Darfur as genocide. But far from spurring effective action, the rhetoric substituted for it. Although everyone in the United States deplores ethnic violence and massive killing, the question of how it can be stopped and whether the United States should make this a priority at the expense of other goals has yet to be answered, or even fully addressed. The United States, and indeed the entire world, seems to have made little progress in deciding how to deal with these situations. They are likely to recur, and unfortunately, there is little reason to expect more-coherent or effective responses.

Human rights is not only a question of helping others. The war on terror has sharply raised the question of the permissibility of torture, a question that many of us thought would never arise. By any normal definition, the United States has tortured terrorist suspects, and many accounts claim that doing so has yielded important information that has prevented further attacks. Even if this latter claim is correct, it leaves many of us with grave doubts and bad consciences. Jerome Slater argues that there is no easy way out of the dilemma, and that the infliction of bodily harm is sometimes necessary but must be carefully regulated and controlled to see that it is done only as a last resort.

All of these issues will confront the new administration. It will have to decide whether and how to seek democracy abroad, how to set priorities among competing foreign policy goals, how much the counter-terrorism agenda should drive American foreign policy, how to deal with human rights abuses abroad, and what to do about prisoners currently held at Guantanamo Bay or captured in the future. Constructing a coherent and effective policy will be a challenge as great as those the country faced in 1945 and failed to meet in 2001–02.

Part I:
AMERICAN WAYS OF FOREIGN POLICY AND FOREIGN RESPONSES

The Lessons of September 11, Iraq, and the American Pendulum

CHRISTOPHER HEMMER

In a seminal 1974 article, Michael Roskin argued that U.S. policy toward interventions overseas has varied depending on the central historical lessons that different generations of policymakers had derived from recent historical events.[1] Since it has been over a generation since Roskin's article appeared, it is worth revisiting his approach for insights regarding America's current and future foreign policy. The Vietnam generation that Roskin saw as coming to the fore in the mid-1970s and supplanting the World War II generation has had its era, and today the lessons of Vietnam are being increasingly challenged by lessons derived from the terrorist attacks of 11 September 2001. The purpose of this article is to document the lessons that policymakers in the George W. Bush administration have learned from September 11, argue that those lessons were a necessary cause of the administration's decision to invade Iraq in 2003, and explore what the continued applications of those lessons could mean for the future of American foreign policy.

In an irony that Roskin surely would have anticipated, the lessons of September 11 bear a striking similarity to the earlier lessons of World War II (including the lessons of Pearl Harbor and Munich). As President Bush put it, "The events of September the 11th were as decisive as the attack on Pearl Harbor and the treachery of another September in 1939. And the lesson of all those events is the same: aggression and evil intent must not be ignored or appeased; they must be opposed early and decisively."[2] It was this lesson that

---

[1] Michael Roskin, "From Pearl Harbor to Vietnam: Shifting Generational Paradigms and Foreign Policy," *Political Science Quarterly* 89 (Fall 1974): 563–588.

[2] George W. Bush, "Remarks to the People of Poland," Krakow, 31 May 2003. This and all cited presidential statements are available from www.whitehouse.gov and were accessed on 12 February 2004.

CHRISTOPHER HEMMER is an associate professor of international security studies at the Air War College and is the author of *Which Lessons Matter? American Foreign Policy Decision Making in the Middle East, 1979-1987*.

helped lead America to war with Iraq in 2003. Thus, instead of a revolution,[3] the Bush administration's foreign policy may represent a restoration—a swing of the pendulum back to an interventionist policy more characteristic of the post-World War II generation than the post-Vietnam generation.

Intervention in the affairs of other states is more a matter of degree than a simple binary choice of whether to intervene or not. To yield or withhold diplomatic recognition, for instance, is by itself a kind of intervention. This type of intervention, however, is a far cry from using a state's military forces to invade another country, evict a particular regime, and install another one. Thus, in looking at the pattern of American interventions overseas, it is important to look at the scale and purpose of these interventions and not just the basic question of whether the United States decided to intervene or not. For example, although the United States conducted a number of military interventions in the eighties and nineties, these interventions were limited in size (Grenada and Panama), goals (Libya and Bosnia), blood and treasure the United States was willing to expend (Lebanon and Somalia), or some combination of these (Haiti and Kosovo). Indeed, many of these interventions and the difficulties they presented, especially Lebanon and Somalia, served to reinforce the lessons of Vietnam and to further limit America's appetite for bold interventions overseas.

In the case of Iraq specifically, enforcing the no-fly zones, supporting United Nations sanctions, and aiding opponents of Saddam Hussein's regime were American interventions in Iraqi politics that had been ongoing since the 1990–1991 Gulf War. Indeed, regime change in Iraq has been an official policy goal of the United States at least since President Bill Clinton signed the Iraq Liberation Act in 1998. These interventions, however, were strictly limited, in keeping with Presidents George H.W. Bush's 1991 decision not to use the full power of the U.S. military to evict Saddam Hussein from power by marching on Baghdad following Iraq's expulsion from Kuwait, a decision that was in part driven by fears of a Vietnam-type quagmire if the United States were to get involved in an Iraqi civil war.[4] The no-fly zones produced no American casualties, the sanctions were more focused on containment of Iraq's military capabilities than regime change, and the amount of support given to Iraqi opposition groups was paltry. It was these limits, however, that the George W. Bush administration decided to ignore in the aftermath of September 11, opting instead for a policy of immediate, largely unilateral, and forcible regime change.

---

[3] See Ivo H. Daalder and James M. Lindsay, *America Unbound: The Bush Revolution in Foreign Policy* (Washington DC: Brookings Institution Press, 2003). For a view that stresses more continuity (but some change), see Melvyn P. Leffler, "9/11 and American Foreign Policy," *Diplomatic History* 29 (June 2005): 395–413.

[4] Yuen Foong Khong, "Vietnam, The Gulf, and U.S. Choices: A Comparison," *Security Studies* 2 (Autumn 1992): 74–95.

The following section explains the analogical approach to American foreign policy used in this article. Then, the article discusses the specific lessons that members of the Bush administration have derived from September 11 and the similarities of those lessons to the lessons of Munich and Pearl Harbor, and argues that those lessons were a necessary but not sufficient cause of the administration's decision to invade Iraq. The subsequent section explores some alternative explanations for the Bush administration's actions and their relationship to the analogical explanation offered here.

Making a conclusive case that the lessons of September 11 are going to have a generational-type effect on American foreign policy similar to the lessons of Munich or Vietnam is obviously impossible at this point. By necessity, any definitive argument along those lines will only be possible after the cohort of policymakers who experienced September 11 have had more time in power. While this article does attempt to document the individual learning that has taken place as a result of September 11 within the Bush administration and its impact on U.S. policy toward Iraq, there is an unavoidable gap between this and a fully demonstrated generational argument.[5] Thus, the generational portion of my argument here is necessarily prospective. The evidence presented here on the Bush administration, as well as debates within Congress over the lessons of September 11, is, I argue, suggestive that a generational shift may be in the offing and that, therefore, it is worth exploring what a continued application of these lessons could mean for the future of American foreign policy. This is the purpose of the final section before the conclusion, which looks at America's earlier attempts to apply the lessons of Munich and Pearl Harbor during the Cold War to explore how the lessons of September 11 might similarly inform and, more worrisomely, could potentially misinform American policymakers if applied indiscriminately.

HISTORICAL ANALOGIES AND THE AMERICAN PENDULUM

When faced with foreign policy problems, decisionmakers often turn to historical analogies for guidance.[6] Historical analogizing consists of using a

---

[5] On the distinctions between individual, organizational, governmental, and generational learning, see Jack S. Levy, "Learning and Foreign Policy: Sweeping a Conceptual Minefield," *International Organization* 48 (Spring 1994): 287–289, 303–304.

[6] Ernest May, *"Lessons" of the Past: The Use and Misuse of History in American Foreign Policy* (New York: Oxford University Press, 1973); Robert Jervis, *Perception and Misperception in International Politics* (Princeton, NJ: Princeton University Press, 1976), 217–282; Yuen Foong Khong, *Analogies at War: Korea, Dien Bien Phu and the Vietnam Decisions of 1965* (Princeton, NJ: Princeton University Press, 1992); Richard Neustadt and Ernest May, *Thinking in Time: The Use of History for Decision Makers* (New York: The Free Press, 1986); Christopher Hemmer, *Which Lessons Matter? American Foreign Policy Decision Making in the Middle East, 1979-1987* (Albany: State University of New York Press, 2000); Jeffrey Record, *Making War, Thinking History: Munich, Vietnam, and Presidential Uses of Force from Korea to Kosovo* (Annapolis, MD: Naval Institute Press, 2002); Alex

previous political event to help interpret a new situation. Whether others judge the lessons policymakers derive from historical events to be accurate or inaccurate, perceptive or superficial, applicable or not applicable is irrelevant for understanding their behavior. If policymakers hold certain lessons to be applicable, it will affect their foreign policy behavior regardless of what anyone else sees to be the insightfulness or shallowness of those lessons.[7] A policymaker who interprets a challenge from abroad as similar to the one posed by Hitler in the 1930s is far more likely to favor an activist policy than one who interprets a challenge from abroad as similar to the one posed by Vietnam in the 1960s.

In looking at the broad sweep of U.S. foreign policy, many analysts have characterized America's approach to the world as susceptible to dramatic shifts, with policies alternating between extremes, like the swing of a pendulum. The terminology used to describe these extremes varies. Some speak of an alternation between realism and idealism, or isolationism and internationalism, or more recently, America as the internally focused promised land versus America as the externally focused crusader state.[8] While these distinctions highlight different facets of American foreign policy, they all center around one core concern: how actively engaged does the United States need to be in shaping events overseas? America's answer to this question has tended to be

Roberto Hybel, *How Leaders Reason: U.S. Intervention in the Caribbean Basin and Latin America* (Cambridge, MA: Blackwell, 1990); James Goldgeier, *Leadership Style and Soviet Foreign Policy: Stalin, Khrushchev, Brezhnev, and Gorbachev* (Baltimore, MD: The Johns Hopkins University Press, 1994); Michael Fry, ed., *History, the White House and the Kremlin: Statesmen as Historians* (New York: Pinter Publishers, 1991); Dan Reiter, *Crucible of Beliefs: Learning, Alliances, and World Wars* (Ithaca, NY: Cornell University Press, 1996); and William Jarosz and Joseph Nye, "The Shadow of the Past: Learning From History in National Security Decision Making" in Philip Tetlock, Charles Tilly, Robert Jervis, Jo L. Husbands, and Paul C. Stern, eds., *Behavior, Society and International Conflict*, vol. 3 (New York: Oxford University Press, 1993), 126–189.

[7] For example, historians and political scientists have long questioned how much the purported lessons of Munich are based on an accurate reading of events leading up to World War II. For two recent examples, see Jeffrey Record, *The Specter of Munich: Reconsidering the Lessons of Appeasing Hitler* (Dulles, VA: Potomac Books, 2007); Daryl G. Press, "The Credibility of Power: Assessing Threats During the 'Appeasement' Crises of the 1930s," *International Security* (Winter 2004/5): 136–169. For a general argument on separating issues of learning from any accuracy criterion, see Levy, "Learning and Foreign Policy," 291–294.

[8] Henry Kissinger, *Diplomacy* (New York: Simon and Schuster, 1994), 29–55; Stanley Hoffman, *Gulliver's Troubles, Or the Setting of American Foreign Policy* (New York: McGraw Hill, 1968), 190–208; Dexter Perkins, *The American Approach to Foreign Policy* (Cambridge, MA: Harvard University Press, 1962), 135–155; Thomas M. Magstadt, *An Empire If You Can Keep It: Power and Principle in American Foreign Policy* (Washington DC: Congressional Quarterly Press, 2004); Walter A. McDougall, *Promised Land, Crusader State: The American Encounter with The World Since 1776* (Boston, MA: Houghton Mifflin, 1997); H.W. Brands, *What America Owes The World: The Struggle for the Soul of American Foreign Policy* (Cambridge, UK: Cambridge University Press, 1998); and Walter Russell Mead, *Special Providence: American Foreign Policy and How it Changed The World* (New York: Alfred A. Knopf, 2001).

cyclical, with disappointment over the results of one approach leading the pendulum to swing toward its opposite.

Michael Roskin's contribution was to link these pendulum swings in U.S. foreign policy with salient historical events that shaped the thinking of an entire generation of leaders. For example, the rush to war in 1914 and the horrific results of World War I led the next generation of policymakers to give diplomacy more time to work in future crises. This determination was in part responsible for the attempts at appeasement prior to World War II. The failure of appeasement then swung the pendulum back toward activism and pre-disposed the next generation of leaders to see all challengers as potential Hitlers that needed to be confronted immediately. In 1974, Roskin foresaw a passing of the torch from the Munich generation to a Vietnam generation. For this Vietnam cohort, new Hitlers were not the major thing to worry about; that is what, in part, got the United States into its difficulties in Vietnam. Instead, what the United States needed to worry about was overextension, quagmires, and the danger of getting pulled into peripheral conflicts.[9] The subsequent decades largely confirmed Roskin's predictions regarding the impact that the lessons of Vietnam would have on American foreign policy.[10] The central insight of Roskin and other discussions of generational learning[11] does not depend on any one-to-one correlation between birth year and policy pref-erences. Instead, the central insight of this literature focuses on the overall im-pact that dramatic events can have in shaping how policymakers think about the problems they confront, and thus the policies they should pursue.

The lessons of Vietnam are now being challenged by lessons drawn from September 11. Moreover, rather than representing a completely new set of historical lessons, the lessons of September 11 being drawn by current Ameri-can policymakers are remarkably similar to the lessons their counterparts drew from Pearl Harbor and the failure of appeasement in the 1930s. Similarly, critics of current American foreign policy have warned that events in Iraq today could potentially lead the United States into a new Vietnam. Thus, while the names may have changed (from the lessons of Munich and Pearl Harbor to the lessons of September 11 and from the lessons of Vietnam to the lessons of Iraq), the core of current debates regarding American interventions overseas is remarkably similar to earlier debates during the Cold War.

---

[9] Roskin, "From Pearl Harbor To Vietnam," especially 576–580.

[10] Record, *Making War, Thinking History*, 79–128.

[11] Richard Ned Lebow, "Generational Learning and Conflict Management," *International Journal* 40 (Autumn 1985): 555–585; Jervis, *Perception and Misperception*, 249–271; Ole Holsti and James Rosenau, "Does Where You Stand Depend on When You Were Born? The Impact of Generation and Post-Vietnam Foreign Policy Beliefs," *The Public Opinion Quarterly* 44 (Spring 1980): 1–22; and Howard Schuman and Cheryl Reiger, "Historical Analogies, Generational Effects and Attitudes toward War," *American Sociological Review* 57 (June 1992): 315–326.

THE LESSONS OF SEPTEMBER 11 AND THE DECISION TO INVADE IRAQ

In an apt image, Josef Joffe likened the terrorist attacks of 11 September 2001 to a lightning bolt rather than an earthquake. The attacks did not radically reshape the contours of international politics, but instead shined a bright but fleeting light on the already-existing landscape.[12] September 11 ushered in an ideational change in American foreign policy rather than a structural change. The attacks did not change the global balance of power, but they did bring about unexpected shifts in American foreign policy.[13] This section attempts to document the lessons that American foreign policymakers drew from that sudden bolt and how it has impacted the course of American foreign policy, especially the Bush administration's decision to invade Iraq in 2003.

In examining the lessons that President Bush and others in his administration have gleaned from the events of September 11, two recurring themes come to the fore. The first is the increased threat of devastating surprise attacks—of potential new Pearl Harbors with weapons of mass destruction. This increased sense of threat has pushed the administration toward a universal war on terror. As President Bush put it, "Here's what I took away from September the 11th, 2001—that any time a President sees a gathering threat to the United States, we must deal with it. We can't pick or choose like we used to .... In the old days oceans protected us from harm's way, and a President could stand back and say, well, maybe this gathering threat is an issue, maybe it's not. After September the 11th that complacency ... is no longer relevant."[14]

The second theme is the need to counter threats actively, to go on the offense and not rely on defense and deterrence. While increasing domestic security is an important part of the administration's overall war on terror, the attacks on New York and Washington have clearly pushed the Bush administration to favor an overseas offense over homeland defense. In short, according to the President, "The best way to secure America is to get the enemy before they get us.... I will not forget the lessons of September the 11th."[15]

Both of these lessons helped to push the United States to war against Iraq, the first by greatly increasing the Bush administration's perception of the threat that Saddam Hussein's Iraq posed and the second by offering the policy prescription of taking care of such threats early and decisively.[16] Even in the

---

[12] Josef Joffe, "Of Hubs, Spokes, and Public Goods," *The National Interest* 69 (Fall 2002), 17–20.

[13] Stephen Walt, "Beyond Bin Laden: Reshaping U.S. Foreign Policy," *International Security* 26 (Winter 2001/2002), 56–78.

[14] George W. Bush, press conference, Washington DC, 15 December 2003.

[15] George W. Bush, "President Bush, Secretary Rumsfeld Discuss Progress in Iraq: Remarks in Press Availability," Crawford, Texas, 8 August 2003.

[16] In Jack Levy's terms, the Bush administration engaged in both diagnostic learning (increased perception of threat) and causal learning (act decisively now to ward off future challenges). "Levy, Learning and Foreign Policy," 285.

absence of any direct link between Iraq and the September 11 attacks, those attacks moved Saddam Hussein's regime from being a second-tier irritant to be contained with sanctions and no-fly zones to being an immediate danger that had to be removed by military force.[17] Prior to September 11, Condoleezza Rice argued that there need be no sense of panic about states like Iraq and that even if Baghdad were to acquire weapons of mass destruction, America's policy should be one of deterrence and defense.[18] That was no longer the case after September 11. In explaining his case for a preemptive (more properly, preventive) war against Iraq, President Bush asked, "After 11 years of living with this problem, why do we need to confront it now?" His answer was that because "we've experienced the horrors of September the 11th.... Before that tragic date we had only hints of al-Qaeda's plans and designs. Today in Iraq, we see a threat whose outlines are more clearly defined, and whose consequences could be far more deadly."[19] Prior to September 11, the Bush administration was thinking about how sanctions could be better crafted to contain Iraq, but after September 11, according to the President, "the doctrine of containment just doesn't hold any water."[20]

Seeing the damage done by a group of hijackers armed primarily with box-cutters, and extrapolating from that what other enemies of the United States could do with more-advanced weapons, especially weapons of mass destruction, the President's perception of the threat posed by Saddam Hussein increased markedly after September 11. "Imagine those 19 hijackers with other weapons and other planes—this time armed by Saddam Hussein. It would take one vial, one canister, one crate slipped into this country to bring a day of horror like none we have ever known. We will do everything in our power to make sure that day never comes."[21] Post-mortems conducted in both the United States and Great Britain regarding the failure to find the expected large arsenal of weapons of mass destruction in Iraq have stressed that the raw intelligence produced on Iraq did not change after September 11, but estimates of how threatening that intelligence was did change. As British Prime Minister Tony Blair put it, "What has changed is not the pace of Saddam Hussein's weapons of mass destruction programs, but our tolerance of them post 11 September."[22]

---

[17] See Bob Woodward, *Plan of Attack* (New York: Simon and Schuster, 2004), 3–5, 12–16, 27, 421; and Tommy Franks with Malcolm McConnell, *American Soldier* (New York: Regan Books, 2004), 197, 200.

[18] Condoleezza Rice, "Promoting the National Interest," *Foreign Affairs* 79 (January/February 2000): 45–62.

[19] George W. Bush, "President Bush Outlines Iraqi Threat, Remarks by the President on Iraq," Cincinnati, OH, 7 October 2002.

[20] George W. Bush, "President Bush Meets with Prime Minister Blair," Washington DC, 31 January 2003.

[21] George W. Bush, "President Delivers 'State of the Union,'" Washington DC, 28 January 2003.

[22] The Rt Hon The Lord Butler of Brockwell, *Review of the Intelligence on WMD: Report of a Committee of Privy Counsellors (The Butler Report)* (London: The Stationery Office, 2004), 70,

Given the similarities between the lessons President Bush has derived from September 11 and the lessons some of his predecessors derived from the failure of appeasement against Germany and Japan's surprise attack against Pearl Harbor, it is not surprising that Bush has drawn attention to the parallels. Indeed, his diary entry on September 11 asserts, "The Pearl Harbor of the 21st century took place today."[23] Indeed, one of the recurring images in the President's rhetoric on terrorism and Iraq is to equate America's current enemies with the enemies of World War II and the Cold War.[24]

The imperative for America today, according to the President, is to avoid the mistakes that France, Britain, and the United States made in the 1930s by failing "to recognize, much less confront the aggressive evil in plain sight."[25] If al Qaeda or Saddam Hussein's Iraq are the equivalent of imperial Japan or Nazi Germany, President Bush is determined to play the role of Winston Churchill, a bust of whom he keeps in the Oval Office.[26] Who is Neville Chamberlain in this schema? They are President Bush's predecessors in office, who, under the caution induced by the failure in Vietnam, were hesitant to use force abroad. As the President put it, "For the generation leading up to September 11th, 2001, terrorists and their radical allies attacked innocent people in the Middle East and beyond without facing a sustained and serious response. The terrorists became convinced that free nations were decadent and weak. And they grew bolder."[27]

National Security Advisor and now Secretary of State Condoleezza Rice has drawn a similar set of lessons from the attacks of September 11.[28] In discussing the lessons of September 11, Rice stresses five points, all of which indicate an increased perception of threat and the conviction that these threats must be confronted aggressively and overseas. First, Rice argues that the attacks demonstrate the acute vulnerability of the United States. Her second

---

34–35, 63, 105, accessed at http://www.butlerreview.org.uk/report.pdf, 5 April 2007. For the U.S. side, see U.S. Senate Select Committee on Intelligence, *Report on the U.S. Intelligence Community's Prewar Intelligence Assessments on Iraq*, 108th Cong., 2d sess., 2004, 31, 363.

[23] Woodward, *Plan of Attack*, 24.

[24] George W. Bush, "President Pays Tribute at Pentagon Memorial," Arlington, VA, 11 October 2001; George W. Bush, "President: We're Fighting To Win—And Win We Will, Remarks By the President on the USS Enterprise on Pearl Harbor Day," Norfolk, VA, 7 December 2001; George W. Bush, "President Speaks on War Effort to Citadel Cadets," Charleston, SC, 11 December 2001; George W. Bush, "President Bush Delivers Graduation Speech at West Point," West Point, NY, 1 June 2002; and Bush, "President Delivers 'State of the Union.'"

[25] George W. Bush, "President Bush Discusses Iraq Policy," London, 19 November 2003.

[26] George W. Bush, "President Bush Discusses Importance of Democracy in Middle East, Remarks By the President on Winston Churchill and the War on Terror," Library of Congress, 4 February 2004. See also James Mann, *Rise of The Vulcans: The History of Bush's War Cabinet* (New York: Viking, 2004), 294, 300.

[27] George W. Bush, "President Addresses the Nation," Washington, DC, 7 September 2003.

[28] See for example, Condoleezza Rice, "Dr. Condoleezza Rice Speaks at Los Angeles Town Hall," Los Angeles, CA, 12 June 2003. Rice's statements are also available at www.whitehouse.gov, accessed 10 February 2004.

and third points are that while the attacks show the need to increase America's homeland defense efforts, no matter how much emphasis the United States puts on homeland security, protection will require activism abroad, because "the best defense is a good offense." Fourth, Rice argues that the proliferation of weapons of mass destruction presents a grave threat to the United States, and fifth, that the United States needs allies and coalition partners to execute the war on terror.[29] In explaining why the United States needed to go after Saddam Hussein, Rice gave perhaps the most succinct statement of the lessons of September 11: "Take care of threats early."[30]

The similarity between this and the lessons of Munich and Pearl Harbor is obvious to Rice, who also makes the comparison explicit. For Rice, September 11 is this generation's Pearl Harbor and it is time that the current crop of America's leaders act more like the post-World War II generation and not like the post-Vietnam generation. As Rice put it, "September 11th reintroduced America to a part of itself that some had forgotten or that some thought we no longer had. We have been reminded that defending freedom was not just the work of the greatest generation, but is the work of every generation."[31] What needs to be forgotten now, according to Rice, is the Vietnam-induced caution in American foreign policy, which only emboldened the terrorists.[32]

Turning from the White House to the civilian leadership in the Pentagon, one sees similar conclusions being drawn. When one senator asked Secretary of Defense Donald Rumsfeld why the United States had to go to war with Iraq now, Rumsfeld's response was, "What's different is 3,000 people were killed, I suggest that any who insist on perfect evidence are back in the 20th Century and still thinking in pre-9/11 terms."[33] To be more precise, Rumsfeld has nothing against twentieth-century thinking as long as you have the right decade; the 1930s and the 1970s are out, but the 1940s and 1950s are back. Facing early criticism that the war in Afghanistan was going too slowly, Rumsfeld offered his version of historical perspective, and all his examples came from World War II. When pressed further, he added the Cold War, Korea, and Desert Storm to the list, clearly passing over Vietnam.[34] Indeed,

---

[29] See Condoleezza Rice, "National Security Advisor Speaks at Texas A&M," 8 April 2002; and Condoleezza Rice, "Remarks by National Security Advisor Condoleezza Rice on Terrorism and Foreign Policy," 29 April 2002.

[30] Bob Woodward, *Bush At War* (New York: Simon and Schuster, 2002), 350.

[31] Rice, "National Security Advisor Rice Speaks"; Condoleezza Rice, "Remarks by Dr. Condoleezza Rice, International Institute For Strategic Studies," London, 26 June 2003; Condoleezza Rice, "Dr. Condoleezza Rice Discusses Iraq in Chicago," 8 October 2003.

[32] Condoleezza Rice, "National Security Advisor Dr. Rice, remarks to National Legal Center," 31 October 2003.

[33] John Newhouse, *Imperial America: The Bush Assault on the New World Order* (New York: Alfred A. Knopf, 2003), 47.

[34] "DoD News Briefing—Secretary Rumsfeld and General Myers," 1 November 2001. This and all Department of Defense statements are available at www.defenselink.mil. Accessed 13 February 2004.

Rumsfeld is positively scornful of those who suggest the possible relevance of America's Vietnam experience for policy today.

Given Rumsfeld's age, it is not surprising that World War II references should be prevalent in his statements. For the Secretary of Defense, failure to confront Saddam Hussein would be the equivalent of the League of Nations' failures to respond to the fascist challengers in the 1930s. To avoid a similar outcome today, America has to actively confront its enemies. As Rumsfeld asked:

> One wonders looking back on history, what might have happened if the world heeded Winston Churchill's warnings in the 1930s—if, instead of ignoring the growing evidence, free nations had united, and formed a coalition to intervene and stop Hitler .... Consider the lives that could have been saved if the world had faced up to the mounting evidence and the compelling logic of the case Churchill presented, instead of waiting for perfect evidence of his capabilities and intentions in the form of 25 million dead human beings. The historical record of appeasement is a sorry one. And in an age when terrorists and dictators are seeking nuclear, chemical, and biological weapons of mass murder, we need to consider the lessons of history. We can look to our experience on September 11th.[35]

Rumsfeld's then-deputy, Paul Wolfowitz, offered four lessons from the events of September 11 that also stressed the twin themes of American vulnerability to surprise attacks and the need for an activist foreign policy. The first lesson is that surprise is to be expected, the second is that America is vulnerable, the third is that America's enemy has changed from the Soviet Union to rogue states and terrorist groups, and finally, that even if America's foes have changed, they have the same goal of the tyrants America confronted in the past, which is to frighten the United States into isolationism.[36] For Wolfowitz, the attacks of September 11 made war against Iraq "a war of necessity, not a war of choice." Wolfowitz also draws the connection between September 11 and the lessons of World War II. "We learned in the last century that democracies cannot live peacefully and undisturbed in a world where evil people control whole nations and seek to expand their bloody rule. We may have forgotten the lesson in the euphoria over the end of the Cold War. The attacks of September 11th were a shocking wake-up call."[37]

The lessons of September 11, however, probably had the least impact on the thinking of people like Wolfowitz and other so-called neoconservatives in the Bush administration because many of those lessons are consistent with what the neoconservatives have been saying for years with regard to U.S.

---

[35] Senate Armed Services Committee, *Testimony on Iraq (as prepared)*, 108th Cong., 1st sess. 2003.

[36] Prepared Statement for the House and Senate Armed Services Committees, "Building a Military for the 21st Century," 3 and 4 October 2001.

[37] Paul Wolfowitz, "Conference on Iraqi Reconstruction, Mercatus Center, George Mason University," 4 November 2003. See also Paul Wolfowitz, "Statements to the Munich Conference on European Security Policy, as Prepared," 2 February 2002; and Woodward, *Plan of Attack*, 426.

foreign policy in general and Iraq in particular. Well before September 11, the neoconservatives had decried the Vietnam-induced caution in U.S. foreign policy and clearly preferred World War II analogies.[38] Thus, September 11 served more to confirm what the neoconservatives already believed, rather than to change their thinking. What September 11 did offer the neoconservatives was a political opportunity to more forcefully push their preexisting agenda. The lessons of September 11 made the rest of the administration, particularly the President, more open to many parts of the neoconservative agenda.[39]

Strikingly, even the domino theory has made a comeback in the post-September 11 world, with the deputy director of the policy planning staff arguing that "now we understand that a failed state in Central Asia, mistreatment of women under a perverse interpretation of Islam, the curriculum in religious schools in Indonesia, drug trafficking in the Andes, and a virus in the bloodstream of millions of Africans can set in place a string of dominos that, once set toppling, can touch our lives here in America in the most immediate ways imaginable."[40] Concerns regarding the lessons of Vietnam were now passé. As Richard Haass, then the director of the policy planning staff phrased it, prior to September 11, America "still lived with the messy 'lessons' of Vietnam, Somalia and Bosnia.... That changed on the morning of September 11th."[41]

The impact of the lessons of September 11 can also be seen in the Bush administration's *National Security Strategy* (NSS).[42] Seeking to prevent a potential September 11 with weapons of mass destruction, the administration identifies the gravest threat to the United States as the "crossroads of radicalism and technology." Also consistent with the lessons of September 11, the NSS calls for a proactive and universal response by the United States. It calls for the United States to actively spread its values overseas, it challenges the military to build "defenses beyond challenge," and, most famously, it

---

[38] Mann, *Rise of the Vulcans*, xv, 27, 81–83, 190–192, 294, 300; Stefan Halper and Jonathan Clarke, *America Alone: The Neo-Conservatives and The Global Order* (Cambridge, UK: Cambridge University Press, 2004), 11, 30–31, 36, 52, 56.

[39] See Robert Jervis, "Understanding the Bush Doctrine," *Political Science Quarterly* 118 (Fall 2003): 365–388; Nicholas Lemann, "The Next World Order," *The New Yorker,* 1 April 2002, 42–48; Elizabeth Drew, "The Neocons in Power," *New York Review of Books,* 12 June 2003; Joshua Muravchik, "The Neo-Conservative Cabal," *Commentary* 116 (September 2003): 26–33; and Max Boot, "Think Again: Neocons," *Foreign Policy* 140 (January/February 2004): 20–28.

[40] Donald K. Steinberg, "Foreign Policy Post-September 11: Learning the Right Lessons," 27 February 2003, accessed at http://www.state.gov/s/p/rem/2003/18762.htm, 12 February 2004.

[41] Richard Haass, "From Reluctant to Resolute: American Foreign Policy after September 11th," Remarks to the Chicago Council on Foreign Relations," 26 June 2002, accessed at http://www.state.gov/s/p/rem/11445.htm, 12 February 2004.

[42] The White House, *The National Security Strategy of the United States of America*, September 2002, accessed at http://www.whitehouse.gov/nsc/nss.pdf, 5 April 2007.

openly discusses the possibility of pre-empting (again, more properly, pre-venting) threats before they arise. Perhaps the most ambitious statement in the NSS comes from the President's speech at the National Cathedral during the memorial service for the victims of September 11, in which the President argued that "our responsibility to history is already clear: to answer these attacks and rid the world of evil."[43] Even Woodrow Wilson, who was in attendance that day, as his body is interred at the National Cathedral, must have marveled at the boldness of that agenda. An administration that had criticized its predecessor for having an "overly broad definition of America's national interest" and had argued that value-based interventions should be "exceedingly rare" had clearly been changed by the attacks of September 11.[44]

ALTERNATIVE EXPLANATIONS

To further explore the argument regarding the importance of the lessons of September 11 in the Bush administration's decision to invade Iraq, the purpose of this section is to explore two sets of alternative explanations for America's decision and their relationship to the analogical explanation offered here. The first set of explanations focuses on America's international position. The second set of explanations focuses on American domestic politics and the preexisting ideological agenda of neoconservatives in the Bush White House. What ties these latter two together is that both see references to the lessons of September 11 as mere propaganda designed to obscure other motives that members of the administration had in advocating an invasion of Iraq. While unipolarity and American domestic politics do provide important pieces of the puzzle, the argument of this section is that neither of these factors would have resulted in an invasion of Iraq had it not been for the lessons drawn from September 11.

Unipolarity

One possible argument is that America's actions can be explained solely by its position as the unipolar power. A realist could argue that America's interests expanded in line with its power, and in invading Iraq, the Bush administration was simply acting as a hegemon would be expected to by eliminating a long-standing irritant. The central problem with such an argument, however, is that it is an argument about opportunity, not motive. Indeed, predicting the specific behavior of the American unipole is likely to be a particularly difficult task for realists, because a hegemonic state faces few

[43] White House, *National Security Strategy*, v, 5, 13–16, 29.
[44] Rice, "Promoting the National Interest," 53–54.

international constraints and has a greater ability to ignore or attempt to overcome those that do exist.[45]

After Charles Krauthammer popularized the phrase *the unipolar moment*,[46] debates quickly ensued regarding what unipolarity meant, how long it could be expected to last, and what impact it might have on U.S. foreign policy.[47] Being a lone superpower means not having to worry that much about how other states may respond to your actions. This gives the United States more latitude in its foreign policy than it had under bipolarity or would have in a multipolar system. As a result of having a larger menu to choose from, however, predicting the specific choices the United States will make becomes more difficult. Unipolarity enables the United States to do more things, but has little impact on determining what things the United States will do.

The difficulties inherent in attempting to predict the behavior of the United States from its status as the world's preeminent power are evident in a number of recent attempts by realists to do so. For example, consider John Mearsheimer's offensive realism, which argues that anarchy offers states powerful incentives for expansion and that "survival mandates aggressive behavior." Given this, is America's decision to invade Iraq consistent with offensive realism? Looking at the full logic of Mearsheimer's argument, the answer is no. As a result of what he calls "the stopping power of water," Mearsheimer contends that global hegemony is beyond the capability of any state and that the best a state can hope for is to be a regional hegemon while preventing other regions from having a hegemon. Since this, he maintains, is the position of the United States today, an activist policy is no longer needed or desirable. Instead, Mearsheimer concludes that the United States should adopt a policy of disengagement and

[45] Shibley Telhami, "Kenneth Waltz, Neorealism, and Foreign Policy," *Security Studies* 11 (Spring 2002): 166–170.

[46] Charles Krauthammer, "The Unipolar Moment," *Foreign Affairs* 70 (1990/1991): 23–33; see also Charles Krauthammer, "The Unipolar Moment Revisited," *The National Interest* 70 (Winter 2002/2003): 5–17.

[47] See Joseph S. Nye, *The Paradox of American Power: Why The World's Only Superpower Can't Go It Alone* (Oxford, UK: Oxford University Press, 2002), 35–40; Samuel P. Huntington, "The Lonely Superpower," *Foreign Affairs* 78 (March/April 1999): 35–49; Stephen G. Brooks and William C. Wohlforth, "American Primacy In Perspective," *Foreign Affairs* 81 (July/August 2002): 20–33; Immanuel Wallerstein, "The Eagle Has Crash Landed," *Foreign Policy* 131 (July/August 2002): 60–68; Christopher Layne, "The Unipolar Illusion: Why New Great Powers Will Rise," *International Security* 17 (Spring 1993): 5–51; Charles Kupchan, *The End of the American Era: U.S. Foreign Policy and the Geopolitics of the 21ˢᵗ Century* (New York: Alfred A. Knopf, 2002), 29, 61–64; William C. Wohlforth, "The Stability of a Unipolar World," *International Security* 24 (Summer 1999): 5–41; Charles L. Glaser, "Structural Realism in a More Complex World," *Review of International Studies* 29 (July 2003): 403–414; G. John Ikenberry, ed., *America Unrivaled: The Future of the Balance of Power* (Ithaca, NY: Cornell University Press, 2003); Barry R. Posen, "Command of the Commons: The Military Foundations of U.S. Hegemony," *International Security* 28 (Summer 2003): 5–46; Robert Kagan, *Of Paradise and Power: America and Europe in the New World Order* (New York: Vintage Books, 2004); G. John Ikenberry, "Is American Multilateralism in Decline?" *Perspectives on Politics* 1 (September 2003): 533–550.

only insert itself into regional balances overseas if a potential regional hegemon arises that can only be stopped with U.S. assistance.[48]

Offering a different reading, Christopher Layne argues that offensive realism suggests that hegemons "must expand their power constantly. If they do not, they risk being knocked off their hegemonic perch by a rival."[49] While the American invasion of Iraq could be argued to be consistent with this form of offensive realism, Layne rejects the argument that America's international activism is being driven by these structural incentives. Instead, Layne believes that the United States, as a geographically insular power, would be wise to follow a strategy of offshore balancing. Structural incentives, as Layne reads them, point against any attempt to pursue primacy. "For the United States the logic of offshore balancing should trump the logic of offensive realism. The big question is why it has not."[50] To answer this question, Layne moves beyond structure and appeals to America's liberal ideology as the prime source of its behavior.[51]

Considering other realist approaches, Michael Mastanduno examines balance-of-power theory associated with the work of Kenneth Waltz and balance-of-threat theory associated with Stephen Walt and derives a set of predictions from each regarding America's current foreign policy choices.[52] None of the arguments he derives, however, can explain the U.S. decision to invade Iraq. In one sense, the very fact that these different realist approaches make competing predictions is evidence that international structural constraints are ambiguous and subject to different plausible interpretations.

With regard to balance-of-power theory, Mastanduno argues that unipolarity means that the United States will face fewer international constraints. While this follows logically from the definition of unipolarity, it offers little in the way of positive predictions regarding U.S. behavior. Indeed, Mastanduno uses what he characterizes as the haphazard and episodic nature of U.S. policy toward interventions overseas as evidence in favor of this prediction.[53] This is an argument about structural opportunities, not which opportunities the United States will pursue and which it will defer.

---

[48] John Mearsheimer, *The Tragedy of Great Power Politics* (New York: W.W. Norton & Company, 2001), 10–11, 21, 41–42, 360–402; and John Mearsheimer, "The Future of the American Pacifier," *Foreign Affairs* 80 (September/October 2001): 46–61.

[49] Christopher Layne, "The 'Poster Child for Offensive Realism': America as a Global Hegemon," *Security Studies* 12 (Winter 2002/3): 120–164.

[50] Layne, "Poster Child," 121, 164. See also Christopher Layne, "From Preponderance to Offshore Balancing: America's Future Grand Strategy," *International Security* 22 (Summer 1997): 86–124; and Christopher Layne,"Offshore Balancing Revisited, *The Washington Quarterly* 25 (Spring 2002): 233–248.

[51] Christopher Layne, *The Peace of Illusions: American Grand Strategy from 1940 to the Present* (Ithaca, NY: Cornell University Press, 2006), 118–133, 159–192.

[52] Michael Mastanduno, "Preserving The Unipolar Moment: Realist Theories and U.S. Grand Strategy after the Cold War," *International Security* 21 (Spring 1997): 49–88.

[53] Mastanduno, "Preserving the Unipolar Moment," 57.

With regard to balance-of-threat theory, Mastanduno argues that it predicts the United States will attempt to preserve unipolarity by working multilaterally with other status quo states, by reassuring undecided states that the United States is not a threat, and by containing states with revisionist aims. While Iraq could be argued to be a state with revisionist aims, the Bush administration explicitly rejected containment, and few would argue that the administration's actions were designed to be multilateral or reassuring to other states. Moreover, in offering these predictions, Mastanduno has had to move beyond structure and bring in distinctions with regard to state motives. While it could be argued that as the preeminent state in the system, the United States is likely to be a status quo power, this is not inevitable. It is also possible that the state at the top of the hierarchy would like to take advantage of its position by remaking the world in its image. One need only consider the calls for the United States to radically reshape the Middle East in a more democratic direction to see the possibility of the preeminent power in the system having far-reaching revisionist aims.[54] Indeed, Mastanduno explicitly warns against the danger of the arrogance of power and the temptation for the hegemon to dictate to and impose its values on others.[55] This warning is indicative of a final reason to conclude that the American decision to invade Iraq was not based solely on realist considerations regarding the international balance of power, which is that it was the realists themselves who were among the most out-spoken opponents of the war, something that would not be expected if the United States were simply responding directly to the incentives of the inter-national system. Even if Iraq had developed weapons of mass destruction in a bid for regional influence, John Mearsheimer and Stephen Walt argued, the best policy for the United States would be containment and deterrence, not invasion.[56]

Kenneth Waltz probably captured best the most that can be said with regard to how unipolarity is likely to impact the behavior of the United States. "Structures shape and shove; they do not determine the actions of states. A state that is stronger than any other can decide for itself whether to conform to structural pressures and whether to avail itself of the opportunities that structural change offers."[57] While the structure of the international system can explain the opportunity America had to invade Iraq and is thus part of the explanation for the invasion, it does not provide a motive. That motive, as argued above, was provided by the lessons the Bush administration drew from

---

[54] Walter Russell Mead, *Power, Terror, Peace, and War: America's Grand Strategy in a World at Risk* (New York: Alfred A. Knopf, 2004), 59–60.

[55] Mastanduno, "Preserving The Unipolar Moment," 88.

[56] See John J. Mearsheimer and Stephen M. Walt, "An Unnecessary War," *Foreign Policy* 134 (January/February 2003): 51–59. See also "War with Iraq is Not in America's National Interest," *New York Times*, 26 September 2002. (This ad was also signed by a number of scholars who would not consider themselves realists.)

[57] Kenneth Waltz, "Structural Realism after the Cold War," *International Security* 25 (Summer 2000): 24.

September 11. The international distribution of power did not fundamentally change between 10 September and 12 September 2001. Nor did the objective threat posed by Saddam Hussein's Iraq. Instead, what changed was America's perception of that threat and of the best way of responding to it, once that threat was viewed through the prism of September 11.

Domestic Politics, the Neoconservative Agenda, and September 11 as Propaganda

Another potential explanation for the Bush administration's decision to attack Iraq focuses on the domestic incentives for the invasion rather than the international ones. Here the argument is that President Bush launched the war in Iraq hoping to bolster his own political prospects or those of the Republican Party by creating a crisis in Iraq that could lead to a rallying effect behind the President or simply to focus attention on an issue (security) upon which the electorate tends to trust the Republicans more than the Democrats.[58] Another potential explanation is that the decision to invade Iraq flowed directly from the long-standing ideological agenda of some in the White House and would have been arrived at with or without September 11.[59]

What both these explanations share is a belief that the frequent invocations of the lessons of September 11 by the administration were made purely for propaganda purposes to sell a policy that had been decided upon for other reasons. For example, Stefan Harper and Jonathan Clarke argue that the linkage of Iraq to September 11 was a "great conjuring trick" that was used as part of the administration's discursive strategy to persuade the public to accept a war in Iraq.[60] In this view, it was not the lessons of September 11 that

[58] For general arguments regarding the diversionary theory of war, see Jacks S. Levy, "The Diversionary Theory of War: A Critique" in Manus I. Midlarsky, ed., *Handbook of War Studies* (Boston, MA: Unwin-Hyman, 1989): 259–288; and Christopher Gelpi "Democratic Diversions: Governmental Structure and the Externalization of Domestic Conflict," *Journal of Conflict Resolution* 41 (April 1997): 255–282. For the case of Iraq, in particular, see Dan Plesch, "Weapons of Mass Distraction," *Observer Worldview*, 29 September 2002, accessed at http://www.guardian.co.uk/usa/story/0,,801257,00.html, 1 May 2007; see also Chalmers Johnson, *The Sorrows of Empire: Militarism, Secrecy, and the American Republic* (New York: Metropolitan Books, 2004), 226–237; and Roger Burbach and Jim Tarbell, *Imperial Overstretch: George W. Bush and the Hubris of Empire* (London, UK: Zed Books, 2004), 3, 15–16, 149–151.

[59] See Halper and Clarke, *America Alone*, 4, 155–156, 183, 206–231; and Ron Suskind, *The Price of Loyalty: George W. Bush, the White House, and the Education of Paul O'Neill* (New York: Simon and Schuster, 2004), 70–87, 96–97, 129, 187–188, 204, 258, 278–280, 288, 305–307, 324–325.

[60] Halper and Clarke, *America Alone*, 138–139, 183, 192, 202, 206–231, 306, 325–326. See also Burbach and Tarbell, *Imperial Overstretch*, 125–163; James Bamford, *A Pretext for War: 9/11, Iraq and the Abuse of America's Intelligence Agencies* (New York: Doubleday, 2004), 253–269, 283–331, 333–338, 367–377; John Prados, *Hoodwinked: The Documents That Reveal How Bush Sold Us a War* (New York: The New Press, 2004); and Christopher Scheer, Robert Scheer, and Lakshmi Chaudhry, *The Five Biggest Lies Bush Told Us about Iraq* (New York: Seven Stories Press, 2004). For views that

convinced the Bush administration to commit the United States to war; instead, it was the Bush administration that used the lessons of September 11 to convince America to go to war, a war that it wanted for other reasons.

These alternative explanations point to a perennial difficulty in attempting to establish the impact that the lessons of history have on policy decisions. Do policymakers use the lessons of history to analyze the current situation and decide which policy they want to follow or do they use them merely as rhetorical devices to justify the policies they have already chosen? This section puts forward five main reasons for believing that the Bush administration used the lessons of September 11 for analysis and not just for public argument. This is not to deny that the lessons of September 11 were used to build public support for the war; instead, the argument is that in addition to these advocacy purposes, the Bush administration also used the analogy for analytical purposes, to figure out what threats they faced and what they should do about them.

First, the argument that policymakers use analogies purely for propaganda purposes leads to a logical contradiction. For the lessons of history to be effective rhetorical devices, they must influence policy preferences. If they did not, they would be useless as propaganda tools and there would be no point in invoking them. Ironically, the very argument that historical analogies are mere justifications used to drum up support implicitly assumes the point that is ostensibly being criticized, that analogies can influence policy preferences. To dismiss the linkage between the lessons of September 11 and the decision to invade Iraq as merely a neoconservative "conjuring trick" is to argue that historical analogies are irrelevant in determining the policy position of some people (neoconservatives), but important for determining the policy position of others (those in and out of the administration who were fooled by this rhetorical trickery). To dismiss discussion of the lessons of September 11 as only rhetorical garb to cloak the administration's domestic interests leads to a similar inconsistency: analogies influence the policy position of some people, but not of others. Instead, a more consistent position is to argue that historical analogies can influence the policy preferences of all decisionmakers and that policymakers use these analogies for both purposes, to analyze and to advocate.

This is not meant to imply that the presence of neoconservatives within the Bush administration was irrelevant to the decision to go to war against Iraq, only that the lessons of September 11 are also a necessary part of the explanation. As Jack Levy argues, the impact that different ideas have on foreign

---

stress misleading intelligence without accusing the administration of lying, see Chaim Kaufmann, "Threat Inflation and the Failure of the Marketplace of Ideas: The Selling of the Iraq War," *International Security* 29 (Summer 2004): 5–48; and Joseph Cirincione, Jessica T. Mathews, George Perkovich, and Alexis Orton, "Weapons of Mass Destruction in Iraq: Evidence and Implications," *Proliferation Brief* 7 (Washington DC: The Carnegie Endowment for International Peace, 2004).

policy depends on both political and intellectual factors.[61] Indeed, the combination of a President who was relatively inexperienced in foreign policy (as he put it during his first presidential campaign, "I am not going to play like a person who's spent hours involved with foreign policy"[62]) and the presence of strong proponents within the administration for the preexisting agenda of the neoconservatives undoubtedly helped to push the administration to a largely unilateral war against Iraq. The efforts by the neoconservatives to launch a war against Iraq, however, would not have gone very far had not the lessons of September 11 predisposed the rest of the administration, and the President in particular, toward accepting their arguments. Indeed, the same is true with regard to the administration's public relations campaign in support of the war. While their efforts undoubtedly had some impact on shaping public views, in many ways, the events of September 11 helped ensure that they were pushing on an open door.[63]

To better understand the relationship between these variables, consider the not-implausible counterfactual[64] that an Al Gore administration had occupied the White House during the attacks of September 11. While it is likely that a Gore administration would have pursued a war against Afghanistan and would even have launched a wider campaign against terrorism, it is very unlikely that a Gore administration would have launched a war against Iraq in 2003. Indeed, Gore was openly critical of the largely unilateral and military-focused approach taken by the Bush administration, arguing that it was needlessly increasing the costs the United States would have to pay in reconstructing Iraq.[65] What this counterfactual usefully points out is that historical analogies do not end all foreign policy debates; instead, they help shape those debates and help to determine who wins them. For example, both Al Gore and 2004 Democratic presidential candidate John Kerry largely accepted the conclusion that the Hussein regime in Iraq was a threat that needed to be removed and that greater exertions by the United States in that direction were called for. Their criticisms, therefore, focused not on ends, but on the administration's unilateral and military-focused means. In a post-September 11 environment of height-

---

[61] Levy, "Learning and Foreign Policy," 300.

[62] Quoted in Hendrick Hertzberg, "Manifesto," *The New Yorker*, 14 and 21 October 2002, 63.

[63] See Amy Gershkoff and Shana Kushner, "Shaping Public Opinion: The 9/11-Iraq Connection and the Bush Administration's Rhetoric," *Perspectives on Politics* 3 (September 2005): 535–537; Jon Western "The War Over Iraq: Selling War to the American Public," *Security Studies* 14 (January–March 2005): 99–130; Kaufmann, "Threat Inflation," 5–48, as well as the response by Ronald R. Krebs and the author's reply in *International Security* 29 (Spring 2005): 196–207.

[64] On the use of counterfactuals, see Philip E. Tetlock and Aaron Belkin, eds., *Counterfactual Thought Experiments in World Politics: Logical, Methodological and Psychological Perspectives* (Princeton, NJ: Princeton University Press, 1996).

[65] See Albert Gore, speech to the Commonwealth Club of San Francisco, San Francisco, CA, 23 September 2002, accessed at http://www.commonwealthclub.org/archive/02/02-09gore-speech.html, 20 March 2006.

ened threat perceptions, however, their call for more-patient multilateral diplomacy was fighting an uphill and ultimately unsuccessful battle. In essence, September 11 helped the neoconservatives to win the debate within the administration and the administration to win the debate with the public.

Second, one way to demonstrate that policymakers use the lessons of history to determine and not just to sell their policies is to look for consistency between the public and private record. An analogy that is used often in public but never in private is most likely a tool of propaganda, not analysis. Conversely, an analogy that appears often in internal debates is likely to be a tool of analysis and not just public window dressing.[66] Even given the recency of events covered in this article, some insider accounts of the administration's deliberations have already appeared. These accounts support the argument that the lessons of September 11 shaped the administration's decision to go to war with Iraq, as they stress how much of an impact the events of September 11 had on the thinking of the Bush administration, especially that of the President.[67] While the unavailability of a complete archival record necessarily makes this conclusion a preliminary one, the information that is currently available supports the conclusion that the lessons of September 11 helped to determine administration policy, not just to sell it.

Third, prior to the war, it was by no means clear that a war in Iraq in March of 2003 would advance the President's domestic interests. If the purpose was to help the President's reelection prospects, why launch what was expected to be a short war twenty months prior to the election, virtually guaranteeing that when those elections came, U.S. forces would be deeply enmeshed in less-popular occupation duties? Just as the Gulf War of 1990–1991 did not secure his father's reelection, even though it was seen as a great success at the time, why would we expect George W. Bush's administration to see taking on a far more challenging mission in Iraq as a ticket to domestic success? If weapons of mass destruction had been used to cause mass casualties, if American troops had become bogged down in a bloody urban campaign, or if, as in fact did happen, the United States discovered that the costs of occupation both in terms of life and treasure were far more than the administration expected, the war in Iraq might have proven more of a domestic handicap than an asset. Had the administration viewed the possibility of war with Iraq as creating the danger of

---

[66] Khong, *Analogies at War*, 64–68.

[67] See Woodward, *Plan of Attack*, 3–5, 12, 24, 27, 410, 421, 426, 438–439; Richard A. Clarke, *Against All Enemies: Inside America's War on Terror* (New York: The Free Press, 2004), 24, 30–32; Franks, *American Soldier*, 246, 308, 315, 355–356, 373–374, 537–564; David L. Phillips, *Losing Iraq: Inside the Postwar Reconstruction Fiasco* (Boulder, CO: Westview Press, 2005), 6, 13, 15, 56, 159; Bill Sammon, *Fighting Back: The War On Terrorism from Inside the Bush White House* (Washington DC: Regnery Publishing, 2002), 5–8; U.S. Senate, "Report on the U.S. Intelligence Community's Prewar Intelligence Assessments on Iraq," 31, 363; Suskind, *The Price of Loyalty*, 70–76, 85–87, 184–188. Suskind notes that policy toward Iraq changes only after September 11.

"another Vietnam" rather than potentially avoiding "another September 11," their domestic as well as their international calculations would have been far different.

Fourth, although an analysis of the administration's entire foreign policy is beyond the scope of this article, there is evidence that the lessons of September 11 are affecting American foreign policy beyond the specific case of Iraq. This more widespread impact supports the argument that the September 11 analogy represents an important ideational shift in American foreign policy and is not merely a rhetorical tool that was used to sell a particular war. The invasion of Afghanistan, the missile strike against suspected terrorists in Yemen, as well as more-hard-line policies toward countries like Syria, Iran, and North Korea, are all areas of American foreign policy that have been impacted by September 11 and the lessons drawn from it.

Consider, for example, U.S. policy toward the other members of the "axis of evil," North Korea and Iran. While a full comparison of U.S. policies toward Baghdad, Pyongyang, and Tehran is not possible here, a few brief comments are in order. Of the three members of the axis of evil, the Bush administration clearly opted to deal with Iraq first. This decision was probably driven by a number of considerations: invading Iraq was militarily less risky than an invasion of North Korea or Iran; a large number of United Nations Security Council Resolutions had already been passed against Baghdad; under Saddam Hussein, Iraq had twice invaded its neighbors; and Iraq had used weapons of mass destruction in the past.[68] However, while neither Iran nor North Korea has yet become a target for U.S. military-imposed regime change, U.S. policy toward both of these nations has changed in ways consistent with the lessons of September 11.[69]

As argued above, the lessons of September 11 affected U.S. policy toward Iraq by greatly increasing the Bush administration's perception of the threat that Saddam Hussein's Iraq posed and by offering the policy prescription of

---

[68] For administration statements regarding why Iraq needed to be dealt with before the other members of the axis, see, George W. Bush, "President Bush Outlines Iraqi Threat, Remarks by the President on Iraq," Cincinnati, OH, 7 October 2002; Donald H. Rumsfeld, "Remarks by Secretary of Defense Donald H. Rumsfeld," Atlanta, GA, 27 September 2002; and interview with Condoleezza Rice, in Stan Crock, "You Cannot Afford to Let Dangers Gather," *Business Week*, 13 September 2004, 40. See also Richard N. Haass, "Regime Change and Its Limits," *Foreign Affairs* 84 (July/August 2005): 70–73; and Mahmood Monshipouri, "U.S. Policy toward Iran in Post-war Iraq: Antagonism or Engagement?" *The Muslim World* 94 (October 2004), 576.

[69] On the impact of September 11 on U.S. policy toward North Korea, see Robert E. Hunter, "After 9/11: US Policy in Northeast Asia," *Asia-Pacific Review* 10 (May 2003): 1–19; Victor D. Cha, "Korea's Place in the Axis," *Foreign Affairs* 81 (May/June 2002): 79–92; and Jihwan Hwang, "Realism and U.S. Foreign Policy toward North Korea: The Clinton and Bush Administrations in Comparative Perspective," *World Affairs* 167 (Summer 2004): 25–27. On Iran, see Monshipouri, "U.S. Policy toward Iran in Post-war Iraq," 565–586. For a contrary view, see Kenneth Pollack, *The Persian Puzzle: The Conflict Between Iran and America* (New York: Random House, 2004), 343–374.

taking care of such threats with offensive actions rather than relying on defense and deterrence. These two facets of the September 11 analogy have also been in evidence with regard to U.S. policy toward Tehran and Pyongyang. In examining the Bush administration's assessment of the threat posed by North Korea's nuclear program, one analyst concluded, "Relying on sketchy data, the Bush administration presented a worst-case scenario as an incontrovertible truth and distorted its intelligence on North Korea (much as it did on Iraq), seriously exaggerating the danger."[70] With regard to going on the offense to counter challenges posed by the proliferation of weapons of mass destruction in rogue states, as Richard Haass has recently argued, "The Bush administration has consistently shown that it would rather resolve all of these challenges through regime change in Tehran and Pyongyang."[71] How much more aggressively the United States pursues regime change in Iran and North Korea, including the possibility of using military force, will depend both on whether there are more-significant terrorist attacks against the United States, especially those involving weapons of mass destruction, and of course on the outcome in Iraq.[72]

A final reason for not dismissing the administration's invocation of the lessons of September 11 as mere rhetoric designed to support the neoconservative political agenda or the President's domestic political agenda is the extent to which other political elites who did not share those agendas also invoked the lessons of September 11 to explain their support for a war against Iraq. For example, congressional debates over the war in Iraq are replete with discussions of the lessons of September 11. Since many of these invocations are from members who are neither neoconservatives nor Republicans, it is hard to dismiss such statements as part of a neoconservative conjuring trick or a plan to shore up Republican electoral prospects. Agreement on the lessons of September 11 across the political aisle indicates that those lessons can have a broader generational-type effect on American foreign policy and are not simply the product of the short-term political machinations of a single administration.

On 11 October 2002, the Senate voted 77-23 in favor of authorizing the use of military force against Iraq. The debate prior to the passage of that resolution is permeated with discussions of the lessons of September 11, and the senators

---

[70] Selig S. Harrison, "Did North Korea Cheat?" *Foreign Affairs* 84 (January/February 2005): 99–100.

[71] Haass, "Regime Change and Its Limits," 66–67.

[72] For arguments that North Korea and Iran might be the next targets for a U.S. invasion, see Bruce Cumings "Rising Danger in Korea," *Nation* 24 (March 2003): 5–6; and Bryan Bender, "Iran: The Axis, Part III," *National Journal,* 15 February 2003, 6–11. For an argument that the outcome in Iraq has already put the brakes on a more aggressive policy toward Iran and North Korea, see Robert S. Litwak, "Non-Proliferation and the Dilemmas of Regime Change," *Survival* 45 (Winter 2003/04): 7–32.

supporting the resolution draw lessons virtually identical to those within the administration. There is talk of how the world has changed since the attacks, worries that America is now increasingly vulnerable because geography no longer protects the United States from distant threats, arguments that the United States needs to be proactive in responding to such threats, recriminations that the United States responded too meekly to earlier terrorist challenges, and many linkages drawn between these lessons and the lessons of World War II.[73] For example, Senator Joseph Lieberman, then one of the strongest supporters of action against Iraq in the Democratic Party, argued that the events of September 11 had a "profound effect" on him and that just as the United States should have dealt with al Qaeda more forcefully prior to September 11, he thought that the United States should act more forcefully against Iraq.[74] Evan Bayh (D-IN), in his short remarks in support of the resolution, referred explicitly to the lessons of September 11 four separate times.[75] The Democratic Party's 2004 presidential candidate, John Kerry, supported the resolution and argued that "the most legitimate justification for war" was that "in the post-September 11 world the unrestrained threat of weapons of mass destruction in the hands of Saddam Hussein is unacceptable."[76]

The debate in the House was much the same.[77] For example, after expressing certain doubts about a potential war with Iraq, New York Democrat Eliot Engel ultimately decided that he would support the use-of-force resolution because "what is most important and what is the bottom line for me is that as a New Yorker, after September 11th, the equation changed."[78] Adam Schiff, a Democrat from California, similarly explained that he was supporting

[73] The following references are taken from the *Congressional Record*, 107th Cong., 2nd sess., vol. 148: On the Republican side, see the statements by Senators Bunning (S9934–S9935), Voinovich (S9944), Warner (S9947–S9950, S10237, S10066, S10073), Kyl (S10017–S10018), Stevens (S1022), Hatch (S10025–10026), Craig (S10071), Gregg (S10079–S10080), Brownback (S10092–10093), Burns (S10096), Nickles (S10102), Hutchison (S10149–S10150), Grassley (S10154–S10155), McCain (S10170, S10249, S10274), Roberts (S10181), Hutchinson (S10202), Thompson (S10204), DeWine (S10298), Specter (S10303), Ensign (S10312–S10314), Smith (NH) (S10317), Shelby (S10323), McConnell (S10328), Santorum (S10332), and Murkowski (S10332–S10333). On the Democratic side, in addition to the statements quoted below, see the statements by Senators Graham, who advocated a stronger resolution than the one eventually passed, (S9968–S9969, S10314–10315), Lieberman (S10064, S10073), Nelson (S10100), Clinton (S10289–S10290), Kohl (S10301), Schumer (S10302), Rockefeller (S10307–S10308), Dorgan (S10324), and Harkin (S10327).

[74] Ibid., S10105.

[75] Ibid., S10067–10069.

[76] Ibid., S10171–S10174.

[77] Given the size of the House and the frequency of the invocations of the lessons of September 11 in its debates, rather than fill pages of notes with individual references, I would refer the reader to the entire debate and the representative examples offered below. See the *Congressional Record*, 107th Cong., 2nd sess., vol. 148: H7178–H7186, H7189–H7247, H7268–H7301, H7309–H7345, H7375–H7410, H7413–H7442, H7706–H7735, and H7739–H7799.

[78] Ibid., H7215.

the resolution because "on September 10, the danger from terrorists was imminent, and we took no action. On September 11 we were devastated. Now it will forever be September 12."[79] Minority Leader Richard Gephardt, who co-sponsored the resolution in the House, explained, "September 11 has made all the difference."[80] Links were also drawn to the similar lessons of World War II, such as the argument by Tom Lantos (D-CA) that "just as the leaders and diplomats who appeased Hitler at Munich in 1938 stand humiliated before history, so will we if we appease Saddam Hussein today."[81]

Advocates of the September 11 analogy and its relevance to a potential war in Iraq did not have the field to themselves in these congressional debates. Again, even analogies with generational-type effects do not uniformly deter-mine the policy positions of all decisionmakers, they just help to shape the context within which foreign policy debates are conducted. Some of the opponents of the resolution questioned the applicability of the September 11 analogy to the situation in Iraq, and others suggested that America's failures in Vietnam might be the more appropriate analogy.[82] Such suggestions often elicited sharp responses. For example, when Representative Jim McDermott (D-WA) suggested that the House adjourn to visit the Vietnam Memorial, Representative Heather Wilson (R-NM) immediately countered by suggesting that the Holocaust Museum be remembered as well.[83] To those who had concerns that a war in Iraq could lead to another Vietnam-like quagmire, Senator James Inhofe (R-OK) asked, "Are they more concerned about a war that took place over 30 years ago, or the tragic events that took place on September 11?"[84] Judging by the frequency of its usage in the debates and the final vote tallies (the House also passed the use-of-force resolution by a more than 2-1 margin with a vote of 296-133), more of the senator's con-gressional colleagues were worried about another September 11 than about another Vietnam.

POTENTIAL PERILS OF THE LESSONS OF SEPTEMBER 11

Part of the reason for the cyclical nature of the influence of historical lessons that stress the danger of sudden aggression and the need for an activist foreign policy (Pearl Harbor, Munich, and September 11) versus historical lessons that

[79] Ibid., H7290.

[80] Ibid., H7778.

[81] Ibid., H7195.

[82] For the most thoughtful challenge to the argument linking the attacks of 11 September to the need to go to war against Iraq, see the comments of Wisconsin Senate Democrat Russell Feingold, *Congressional Record*, 107th Cong., 2nd sess., vol. 148: S10147–S10149. For references to Vietnam, see H7276, H7319, H7395–H7396, H7425, and H7744.

[83] Ibid., H7276 and H7282.

[84] Ibid., S10216.

stress the limits of power and the dangers of quagmires (World War I and Vietnam) is that both sets of lessons have enduring value. Policymakers are right to worry about surprise attacks and that aggression unanswered can lead to more-dangerous challenges. Policymakers are also right to worry about overstretch and being sucked into protracted and peripheral contests. Similar lessons would be unlikely to recur unless there was some utility in them. The rise and fall of these historical lessons also suggests, however, that they can lead policymakers astray if they are applied uncritically, without a proper appreciation of their limits and of the potentially dangerous tendencies their underlying assumptions could encourage. As Stanley Hoffman put it, "When we invoke Munich in order to exorcise appeasement anywhere, we forget that Munich itself was the product of a disastrous example of analogical thinking."[85] In part, it is because the World War I analogy was over-applied that Munich resulted, it is because the Munich analogy was over-applied that Vietnam resulted, and it is because the lessons of Vietnam were over-applied that September 11 resulted. Since the lessons of September 11 are taking a more prominent role in U.S. foreign policy, the purpose of this section is to explore the limitations of these lessons and the potential dangers for American foreign policy that could result from an over-application of these lessons.

As the lessons of September 11 are similar to the lessons of Pearl Harbor and Munich, and since a large literature already exists regarding how the World War II analogies were applied and misapplied by American foreign policymakers during the Cold War, this section looks at America's attempts to apply those lessons in order to better understand how attempts to apply the similar lessons of September 11 could potentially lead to future difficulties in American foreign policy. Thus, this section is more retrospective and prospective than current. This analysis stresses five potential pitfalls lurking within the September 11 analogy. These are the dangers of letting threats determine interests, treating enemies as a monolith, favoring immediate action over long-term strategy, preferring universal solutions to particular problems, and escalating credibility spirals. Each of these contributes to the central danger of an over-application of the September 11 analogy, which is one of strategic overreach. The hope is that in pointing out these potential dangers, some of the pitfalls associated with the World War II analogies can be avoided in America's future attempts to apply the similar lessons of September 11.

Letting Threats Determine Interests

Before figuring out what threats exist and are imminent, a state has to first answer the question of a threat to what? What are a state's irreducible interests

---

[85] Hoffman, *Gulliver's Troubles*, 137.

and what is required to secure those interests? A state's determination of its interests, therefore, should come prior to a state's assessment of the threats it faces. One of the dangerous aspects of the Munich and the September 11 analogies, however, is that if over-applied, they can reverse that logical sequence and allow threats to determine interests. If a challenge unanswered is merely an invitation for additional and more serious challenges down the road, then every challenge must be answered, even if the political stakes in the immediate crisis are low. By assuming that one is facing an implacable threat whose resources and ambitions expand with each success, the mere fact that an object is threatened is enough to make protecting that object an important interest, regardless of how insignificant that object may be in itself. To give a concrete example, consider the U.S. decision to intervene in the Korean War. After publicly implying that it would not fight for Korea—and privately planning not to do so—the United States did decide to fight when North Korean forces attacked the South. Why? Not because Korea was important in and of itself. Instead, in the developing context of the Cold War in Asia, and interpreting any attack as a challenge similar to the one posed by Hitler in the 1930s, Korea became vastly more important to the United States after it was attacked. In this way, to a large extent, America let threats determine its interests.[86]

This should be an especially important worry in the future, given a task as broad as a global war on terror. The danger to be on the lookout for is allowing the terrorists to determine and expand America's conception of its interests simply by what they choose to threaten. As many have pointed out, terrorism is simply a tactic and "choosing one's enemies on the basis of their tactics alone has little to recommend it."[87] Just as not all third-world nationalist movements may have presented a threat to the United States during the Cold War, not all terrorists may pose a threat to the United States today. There is no doubt that al Qaeda represents a threat, but is the same true of Basque separatists, the Tamil Tigers, or the Real IRA? In prosecuting the war on terror, the United States needs to make clear distinctions between groups that have political agendas that threaten the United States and those that do not. The lessons of September 11, however, like the lessons of Munich before them, can blur that crucial distinction by encouraging policymakers to conclude that any use of terrorism is necessarily a threat to U.S. interests.

The Bush administration has, in part, recognized the importance of such distinctions. For example, its *National Strategy For Combating Terrorism* distinguishes between groups that operate purely on a national level, those that

---

[86] See John Lewis Gaddis, *Strategies of Containment: A Critical Appraisal of Postwar American National Security Policy* (Oxford, UK: Oxford University Press, 1982), 89–126 (especially page 98); and Alexander L. George and Richard Smoke, *Deterrence in American Foreign Policy: Theory and Practice* (New York: Columbia University Press, 1974), 144–157.

[87] Greenville Byford, "The Wrong War," *Foreign Affairs* 81 (July–August 2002): 34.

operate on a regional level, and those that operate on a global level.[88] The experience with the Munich analogy during the Cold War suggests, however, the difficulty of maintaining such distinctions, especially in the face of universalizing rhetoric. The lessons of September 11 could lead to a conclusion similar to the contention of National Security Council Report 68 that "a defeat of free institutions anywhere is a defeat everywhere."[89] Indeed, the *National Strategy For Combating Terrorism* approaches such a conclusion in its argument that the smaller, state-level terrorist groups "may expand geographically if their ambitions and capabilities are allowed to grow unchecked."[90] Just as during the Cold War it might not have been in America's interest to defend everyone claiming that they were threatened by communist subversion, it might not be in America's interests today to defend everyone claiming to face the threat of terrorism.

Treating Enemies as a Monolith

A second potentially dangerous aspect of the Munich and September 11 analogies is their tendency to minimize differences between enemies. The Munich analogy makes no distinctions between German, Italian, or Japanese aggression; instead, it merges all three into one totalitarian axis. During the Cold War, this encouraged American policymakers to treat communism as a monolithic threat, which minimized the chances of exploiting fissures between communist states and drove those states closer together.

The same danger exists in the September 11 analogy. When the Bush administration speaks about America's enemies today, it puts forward an extensive list of terrorist groups, rogue states, failed states, and proliferators of weapons of mass destruction.[91] To be sure, each of these groups does represent a threat to the United States that must be addressed. It is important, however, not to over-apply the September 11 analogy and treat each of these groups and individual members of these groups as identical threats. Just as Ho Chi Minh was no new Hitler, not all terrorists and rogue states are necessarily new al Qaedas.

Consider the differences between terrorist groups and rogue states. While certain terrorist organizations may be undeterrable, rogue states are not, which makes the former a far more dangerous threat than the latter. Similarly,

---

[88] The White House, *National Strategy for Combating Terrorism*, February 2003, 8, available at http://www.whitehouse.gov/news/releases/2003/02/counter_terrorism/counter_terrorism_strategy.pdf, 5 April 2007.

[89] *Foreign Relations of the United States 1950*, vol. 1 (Washington DC: U.S. Government Printing Office, 1977), 240.

[90] *National Strategy For Combating Terrorism*, 8.

[91] See Jeffrey Record, *Bounding the Global War on Terrorism* (Carlisle, PA: Strategic Studies Institute, U.S. Army War College, 2003), 13–19; and Jeffrey Record, "Threat Confusion and Its Penalties," *Survival* 46 (Summer 2004): 51–72.

failed states and proliferators represent a threat primarily to the extent that they enable potentially nondeterrable terrorist groups to target the United States. Strategic choice entails setting priorities, not conflating them. Just as the United States adopted a Germany-first strategy in World War II, similar choices need to be made in the war on terror. Also, just as the United States had to ally with a totalitarian Soviet Union to defeat Nazi Germany, the United States still has to consider such alliances of convenience today rather than pushing America's enemies together by treating them as a monolith.

Again, in some ways, the Bush administration has recognized the need for such distinctions. When Director of Central Intelligence George Tenet told President Bush that the United States faces a sixty-country problem, the President's response was, "Let's pick them off one at a time."[92] Similarly, the administration has recognized the need to work with states such as Syria in the campaign against al Qaeda, even though Syria still maintains its connections with Palestinian and Lebanese terrorist groups. The September 11 analogy, if over-applied, however, can make distinctions like these harder and harder to stick by if all terrorist groups, rogue states, failed states, and weapons of mass destruction proliferators are seen as potential al Qaedas. If those distinctions are lost, however, America will be in danger of losing its focus on the most dangerous threats and potentially making enemies of groups or states that America will need in prosecuting the campaign against those most serious threats.

Favoring Immediate Action over Long-term Strategy

One of the central lessons contained in both the Pearl Harbor and the Munich analogies is the need to confront threats immediately. The Pearl Harbor analogy warns against the danger of sudden attacks, and the logic of the Munich analogy suggests that if challenges go unpunished, foes will just become stronger and more ambitious. These lessons can lead policymakers astray, however, if applied in situations where a challenger does not have a political agenda that threatens the interests of a particular country or if a challenge, in the long term, will not add up to an appreciable difference in the balance of power. Vietnam is probably the best example of this during the Cold War. It is not clear that Ho Chi Minh's largely nationalist agenda threatened the United States or that a communist Vietnam would have represented an increase in power for the Soviet Union.

The September 11 analogy's stress on the importance of confronting threats early contains the same potential to push the United States to confront threats that may not exist. The failure to find evidence for an extensive and growing Iraqi arsenal of weapons of mass destruction is a good example of how

---

[92] Woodward, *Bush at War*, 33.

the lessons of September 11 have already pushed the United States into action based on an inflated threat assessment. Indeed, according to George Tenet, one of the reasons that the U.S. intelligence community overstated the threat posed by Saddam Hussein's Iraq was its failure to provide adequate warning before September 11.[93] The administration did not cynically use the September 11 analogy to intentionally mislead the American people about the threat posed by Iraq's weapons of mass destruction program; instead, by over-applying the September 11 analogy, the Bush administration deceived itself.

In the war on terror, the tension between the need to act in the short term and the need to plan for the long term can be seen in the Bush administration's dual convictions that time is not on America's side, but history is. The administration is adamant that America's enemies need to be confronted immediately and that delay only increases the danger, while at the same time, it is also convinced that in the long term, American ideals and values will be vindicated and that terrorists and their supporters will end up "in history's unmarked graves of discarded lies."[94] These two convictions pull in different directions. The first encourages a sense of panic and the need to focus on short-term responses, while the second encourages a sense of confidence and the need to focus on long-term strengths. For example, one of the key supports for George Kennan's strategy of containment during the Cold War was his conviction that there was no need to attack the Soviet Union directly, because in the long term, the system would collapse under its own weight.

The need to balance between the short and the long term is a perpetual problem that has no single solution. What the experience of the Cold War suggests, however, is that an over-application of the lessons of World War II encouraged short-term actions and potentially unnecessary overreactions. To prevent American policymakers from similarly misusing the lessons of September 11, it would be wise to heed the advice Kennan gave at the outset of the Cold War, that ultimately it is the task of the United States to

> create among the peoples of the world generally the impression of a country which knows what it wants, which is coping successfully with the problems of its internal life and with the responsibilities of a world power, and which has the spiritual vitality capable of holding its own among the major ideological currents of the time. To the extent that such an impression can be created and maintained, the aims of Russian Communism must appear sterile and quixotic.[95]

By simply replacing "Russian Communism" in that last sentence with "al Qaeda" or the name of any terrorist organization that threatens the

---

[93] Woodward, *Plan of Attack*, 438–439.

[94] George W. Bush, "Address to A Joint Session of Congress and the American People," 20 September 2001.

[95] Mr. X (George Kennan), "The Sources of Soviet Conduct," *Foreign Affairs* 25 (July 1947), 566–582.

United States, you will have an excellent description of America's task in the war on terror.

Preferring Universal Solutions to Particular Problems

One of the reasons that policymakers turn to analogies is to seek policy prescriptions.[96] If any analogy, whether to Pearl Harbor, to Munich, to Vietnam, or to September 11, becomes predominant in the thinking of a nation's foreign policy decisionmakers, it raises the potential danger of offering those policymakers a universal solution to what are invariably particular problems. In thinking about the war on terrorism, the United States must guard against mistakenly concluding that the lessons of September 11 hold the solutions to all terrorist threats.

For example, consider America's counterinsurgency policies during the Cold War. One of the problems with the U.S. response to guerrilla war was the assumption that all insurgencies stemmed from similar causes and were, therefore, susceptible to similar solutions. Seeing insurgency merely as a communist tactic, what the United States sought was a counter-tactic.[97] Since terrorism is also a tactic, the danger today is that the United States will simply seek a universal counter-tactic, seeing all terrorists as motivated by the same goals that drove al Qaeda and as susceptible to the same pressures.

The danger is less that the September 11 analogy will encourage the United States to ignore the root causes of terrorism and more that it will cause the United States to find only one root cause. What motivates a terrorist group in Afghanistan is likely to be far different from what motivates a terrorist group in Indonesia, Europe, or the United States. Any counterterrorism policy that ignores the local circumstances that give rise to particular terrorist groups is bound to fail.[98] Unfortunately, it is universal solutions that dominant analogies like September 11 encourage.

Escalating Credibility Spirals

At the heart of both the Munich and September 11 analogies are concerns about credibility: do other actors believe that a state has the capability and the will to defend itself? In the Munich analogy, the failure of the democracies to stand up to Germany early enough encouraged further aggression. In the September 11 analogy, America's failure to respond decisively to

---

[96] Khong, *Analogies at War*, 10, 20–21.

[97] D. Michael Shafer, *Deadly Paradigms: The Failure of U.S. Counterinsurgency Policy* (Princeton, NJ: Princeton University Press, 1988), 104–132.

[98] See Zbigniew Brzezinski, *The Choice: Global Domination or Global Leadership* (New York: Basic Books, 2004), 31–59.

earlier attacks encouraged the terrorists to escalate. While there is a material side to credibility (does a state have the physical capability to respond?), it is the will side that takes center stage in both the lessons of Munich and the lessons of September 11. If you fail to respond to small challenges, others will conclude that you lack the will to do so and will be further emboldened to act.

Although a state's credibility can be an important asset to protect, there is a danger that concerns about credibility and commitment can feed on themselves. As U.S. policymakers discovered during the Cold War, "diplomatic commerce in the coin of credibility was inherently inflationary."[99] Again, Vietnam presents the paradigmatic case. It was only because the United States made a commitment to South Vietnam that it was vulnerable in South Vietnam. Further, the more the United States invested to protect its credibility in Vietnam, the more its credibility was on the line.[100] Indeed, it was precisely the power of concerns about credibility to ensnare a great power in a quagmire that led to the rise of the Vietnam analogy in the first place.

As Roskin phrased it, both the Vietnam and the Munich analogies have "a built-in self-destruct mechanism" if over-applied.[101] It is the possibility of escalating credibility spirals that is the most likely self-destruct mechanism for the September 11 analogy. America's commitment to the reconstruction of Iraq and the building of a democracy in Baghdad has already stirred a debate between those looking to cut America's losses versus those dedicated to staying the course. Avoiding a credibility sinkhole in Iraq or anywhere else should be a principal worry of current American foreign policymakers, even if it means paying heed to the lessons of Vietnam that, at times, positions may need to be abandoned and goals made more modest if they prove to be untenable.

Taken together, these five perils all raise the risk of strategic overstretch. Combining the limited international checks that a unipolar system imposes on the United States with a September 11–driven activist foreign policy can provide the perfect recipe for overextension. This is not meant to imply that the United States does not have security interests that may require an engaged foreign policy. Instead, just as Thucydides warned the Athenians against assuming that their strength was equal to all of their hopes,[102] today America must not similarly assume that its strength will be equal to all of its September 11–inspired fears.

[99] Frank Ninkovich, *The Wilsonian Century: U.S. Foreign Policy Since 1900* (Chicago, IL: University of Chicago Press, 1999), 190.

[100] For Vietnam, see Gaddis, *Strategies of Containment*, 237–273; for the wider Cold War context, see Robert H. Johnson, *Improbable Dangers: U.S. Conceptions of Threat in the Cold War and After* (New York: St. Martin's Press, 1994), especially 89, 141–146.

[101] Roskin, "From Pearl Harbor to Vietnam," 576.

[102] *History of the Peloponnesian War*, translated by Rex Warner (New York: Penguin Books, 1972), 303 (Book IV: 65).

CONCLUSION

The long-term impact, both positive and negative, that the lessons of September 11 will have on future American foreign policy remains to be determined. Much will depend on the course of events, especially with regard to whether there are any more mass casualty terrorist attacks as well as the results of America's war in Iraq. September 11 has so far, fortunately, been a singular event. Although there were terrorist attacks before and after that date, none of these were on such a large scale. Should September 11 prove to be an anomaly, or a statistical outlier,[103] it is possible that the impact of its lessons on American foreign policy could fade. Similarly, if America's state-building efforts in Iraq fail or become exorbitantly costly, the impact of the lessons of September 11 could ebb. Indeed, a costly failure in Iraq could complete another analogical cycle, as critics of the invasion are increasingly likely to see difficulties in Iraq as indicative of a new Vietnam and of having delivered a deathblow to many of the strategic tenets associated with the lessons of September 11.[104]

On the other hand, if the United States succeeds in Iraq or even simply muddles through, and more importantly, if another mass terror attack hits the United States, the September 11 analogy can be expected to grow in influence and further impact U.S. policy. The reelection of President Bush and subsequent cabinet changes have also reinforced the hold that adherents to the lessons of September 11 have on power. The ongoing debate over whether the Bush administration's decision to invade Iraq was strategically wise or foolish is a sign that today neither the September 11/Munich analogies nor the Iraq/Vietnam analogies are going unchallenged. The coming years are likely to see continued struggles between the advocates of these different analogies for control over American foreign policy. If that debate is able to temper the extremes associated with the over-application of either of these sets of lessons, then America and the world will benefit.

The future direction of global politics will depend a great deal on how well the United States conducts itself as the world's preeminent power. To allow the United States to fulfill its role effectively, American policymakers must be able to heed the wisdom that does lie in the lessons drawn from September 11, while also recognizing their limitations and the dangers inherent in

---

[103] John Mueller, "Harbinger or Aberration? A 9/11 Provocation," *The National Interest* 69 (Fall 2002): 45–50.

[104] Jeffrey Record and W. Andrew Terrill, *Iraq and Vietnam: Differences, Similarities and Insights* (Carlisle, PA: Strategic Studies Institute, 2004); G. John Ikenberry, "The End of the Neo-Conservative Movement," *Survival* 49 (Spring 2004): 7–22; Moisés Naím, "Casualties of War: The Ideas That Died in Iraq," *Foreign Policy* 144 (September/October 2004): 95–96; and Francis Fukuyama, "The Neoconservative Moment," *The National Interest* 76 (Summer 2004): 57–58. For a more optimistic appraisal of the U.S. experience in Vietnam and U.S. prospects in Iraq, see Melvin R. Laird, "Iraq: Learning the Lessons of Vietnam," *Foreign Affairs* 84 (November/December 2005): 22–43.

their over-application. If history need not be destiny, then certainly the lessons of history need not be destiny. If the United States is to navigate the international balance of power effectively, it must first balance the American pendulum and prevent the lessons of September 11 from leading to a hyperactive and ultimately counterproductive foreign policy.*

*The author would like to thank the following for their useful comments on earlier drafts: Tim Borstelmann, Mary Hampton, Peter Katzenstein, Christoph Kunkel, Christopher Layne, Jeffrey Record, Stephen Wright, and the anonymous reviewers from *PSQ*. The views expressed here are those of the author alone and do not reflect the official policy or position of the United States Air Force, the Department of Defense, or the U.S. Government.

From the "Red Juggernaut" to Iraqi WMD: Threat Inflation and How It Succeeds in the United States

JEFFREY M. CAVANAUGH

Of the powers entrusted by the people of the United States to their government, few are as important as the directive to "provide for the common defense." The Constitution, however, leaves the door open to significant principal–agent problems by vesting national security decision-making power into the hands of one person and his handpicked assistants. Symptoms of these problems are intelligence "failures" of the type seen in the run-up to the U.S. overthrow of Saddam Hussein in 2003. Although of significant concern in and of itself, this incident is merely one episode in a larger pattern of executive branch threat inflation and policy manipulation since 1945. This essay discusses three instances of threat inflation: early estimates of the Soviet threat; the escalation of the Vietnam War; and the aforementioned case of Iraq. These cases are key because beyond their obvious importance, they were instances in which an administration had to make a substantive case on foreign policy to the people and Congress on national security grounds. They are examples of manipulation because the information presented stood in marked contrast to information held privately, giving the impression that administration policies stood a good chance of success or that alternatives were dangerous and impractical.

I theorize that the failure of Congress to challenge inflated threats is due to four factors. First, the relative ignorance of the average voter leaves the public, and therefore Congress, vulnerable to manipulation by the administration and its surrogates in civil society. This is especially problematic when doves are unable to use the mass media or when popular values are resistant to dove messages. Second, the bureaucracy has incentives to cooperate when an ad-

JEFFREY M. CAVANAUGH is an assistant professor of political science and public administration at Mississippi State University. His current research focuses on U.S. foreign policy and the dynamics of patron–client networks in the interstate system.

ministration exaggerates threats, thus choking off a vital source of information to opponents. The third factor at work is the importance of trigger events that induce a "rally-'round-the-flag" effect and push the public into prospect theory's domain of losses. Fourth, the politicization of national security makes it difficult to challenge administration claims.

I am not arguing that intelligence on these threats was wrong, inaccurate, or ambiguous. This may have been the case, but problematic intelligence was often further compounded by extensive, systematic exaggeration when it was conveyed to the public. Thus, I argue that intelligence was presented publicly in a manner that either flatly contradicted what the intelligence community reported or did not relay any significant doubts that the community may have had. These cases, therefore, are instances in which administrations selectively released information in order to manipulate the public. They are important institutional failures because they represent a break in the link between a controlling principal and an agent responsible for carrying out the principal's wishes, which calls into question the system of checks and balances upon which the United States and other democracies function.

As such, threat inflation poses serious challenges that can potentially undermine U.S. values and security. It is doubtful, for instance, that foreign policy will reflect the will of the citizenry if it is the result of manipulation. While this is in itself undesirable, the possibility is raised that choices made by those determining policy will be incorrect and detrimental to U.S. interests. Psychologists, for instance, report that when decision-making power is kept within too small a body, "groupthink" can quickly set in, while rational-choice scholars note that small decision-making bodies face greater likelihood of reaching incorrect decisions in comparison with even relatively uninformed electorates.[1]

Methodologically, concentrating on three instances of threat exaggeration opens one up to charges of selecting only on the dependent variable. That is, examining only cases in which threats were exaggerated ignores cases in which threats were presented accurately or were underplayed. This type of analysis brings with it several problems, the most notable of which is the doubt it casts on the power of one's explanatory variables.[2] To overcome this problem, I briefly examine in pre–September 11 anti-terror intelligence and policy an extended episode during which a looming threat was largely ignored.

[1] Irving L. Janis, "Groupthink: The Desperate Drive for Consensus at Any Cost" in Jay M. Shafritz and J. Steven Ott, eds., Classics of Organization Theory. 4th ed. (Fort Worth, TX: Harcourt Brace and Company, 1996), 185–192; Dennis C. Mueller, Public Choice III (Cambridge, MA: Cambridge University Press, 2003), 128–133.

[2] Gary King, Robert Keohane, and Sidney Verba, Designing Social Inquiry: Scientific Inference in Qualitative Research (Princeton, NJ: Princeton University Press, 1994), 130.

THE "RED JUGGERNAUT"

Recent scholarship on the Soviet postwar threat to Western Europe notes that the situation presented to U.S. lawmakers and the public was a grim one.[3] The administration of Harry S Truman argued that a well-equipped, well-trained army of 250 communist divisions could and would easily overrun Western Europe. So pervasive was this perception of Soviet superiority that the U.S. media reported that the overrunning of Europe by the USSR in a conventional war was taken for granted.[4] Indeed, public perception of the Soviets at the time was consistent—nearly all media sources estimated that the Soviets had 2.5 million men and 175 combat-ready divisions, with most slated for an invasion of Western Europe.[5] Furthermore, the threat posed by the Soviets was presented in sinister terms that made Soviet aggression and wider war seen inevitable.

Today, however, we know that this public perception of vastly superior Soviet forces and aggressive, rapacious expansionism was inaccurate. For instance, while the *official* view of the Soviet conventional threat *publicly* crumbled in the mid-60s,[6] earlier intelligence had indicated that the conventional balance in Europe and the larger strategic balance were not so clearly in Moscow's favor. These secret examinations of Soviet strength had cast the USSR as practically incapable of launching a successful offensive into Western Europe *at the same time* the Truman administration was maintaining that Soviet power was overwhelming. Nearly all estimates had concluded that the Soviet threat was political in nature, that the USSR suffered from fundamental weaknesses that could not be easily or quickly overcome, and that the primary risk of war stemmed from miscalculation over U.S. moves on the Eurasian periphery.

Intelligence obtained in 1946, for instance, indicated that the Soviets had retained the majority of their forces from the War, putting Moscow's ground forces at 3.2 million men in 208 divisions, with 66 occupying Eastern Europe. These forces were judged as being "commensurate with immediate occupation and security requirements."[7] Two years after this estimate, however, the U.S. Joint Chiefs of Staff reported that Soviet forces had fallen to the familiar 2.5 million men arranged in 175 divisions, with 31 in Eastern Europe. These new estimates represented a significant reduction in the number of forces

---

[3] Matthew A. Evangelista, "Stalin's Postwar Army Reappraised," *International Security* 7 (Winter 1982–1983): 110–138; John S. Duffield, "The Soviet Military Threat to Western Europe: US Estimates in the 1950s and 1960s," *Journal of Strategic Studies* 15 (June 1992): 208–227.

[4] Evangelista, "Stalin's Postwar Army," 110.

[5] Duffield, "The Soviet Military Threat," 209.

[6] Alain C. Enthoven and K. Wayne Smith, *How Much is Enough? Shaping the Defense Program, 1961-1969* (London: Harper and Row, 1971).

[7] Evangelista, "Stalin's Postwar Army," 114.

officials had earlier thought necessary for occupation duty. Now, they were the "offensively orientated" forces reported in the press.[8]

Thus, within the space of two years, officials went from believing that the Soviets would field an occupation army of 66 divisions capable of doing little more than holding down Eastern Europe to fielding a smaller *blitzkrieg* force with no occupation duties whatsoever. This was a serious contradiction of earlier and then-current estimates of Soviet occupation requirements. U.S. officials, for instance, believed that the political reliability of the satellites in the event of war was questionable and that large numbers of troops would be required to secure Eastern European rear areas.[9] Occupation, reparations, and reconstruction duty, not military training in preparation for an invasion, were also cited as the primary activities of the Soviet postwar army. Yet, the reduction in overall Soviet troop strength was omitted in the story told to the public, as were the occupation and reconstruction duties in which the Soviets were primarily engaged.[10]

Outright subterfuge, however, was the direct comparison of U.S. and Allied ground formations with their Soviet counterparts. Official numbers cited by the press indicated the 175 Soviet divisions were "line" divisions, presumably combat-ready units. CIA reports, however, indicated early on that U.S. officials knew that the manning level of Soviet divisions was not at full strength. In fact, only a third were at 70 percent strength or more, the rest being partial-strength and "cadre" divisions.[11] Western divisions were, in contrast, closer to full strength. The fearsomeness of Soviet conventional forces was also questionable even when fully manned. The CIA, for instance, again *publicly* recognized by 1960 that Soviet divisions were considerably smaller than Western divisions, but Defense Department reports in 1950 estimated the average wartime size of a Soviet division to be 11,000–13,000 men, significantly smaller than a U.S. division. Peacetime manning levels for "combat-ready" divisions were less than wartime levels as well, and the CIA estimated that these divisions had 8,000 men each. In terms of overall manpower, Western and Soviet ground forces were roughly equivalent, with perhaps a slight lead by the USSR.[12]

Soviet forces, moreover, had inferior equipment and organization. Soviet divisions lacked organic logistics elements such as supply, transport, and maintenance units, while support units were smaller and less capable than their Western equivalents. This smaller "tail-to-tooth" ratio meant that Soviet units were relatively fragile and less capable of engaging in sustained combat. Mechanized units also were not fully equipped and were still dependent on

---

[8] Ibid., 115.

[9] Duffield, "The Soviet Military Threat," 212–213, 217; Evangelista, "Stalin's Postwar Army," 116.

[10] Evangelista, "Stalin's Postwar Army," 113, 119, 125–133.

[11] Ibid.," 112.

[12] Duffield, "The Soviet Military Threat," 210–215; Evangelista, "Stalin's Postwar Army," 117–119.

U.S. lend-lease supplies obtained during the War. Reports indicated that Soviet ground forces relied on obsolete, World War II tanks well into the 1950s, while over half the Soviet army, 105 divisions, remained "foot" units or had so few vehicles as to make no difference. Perhaps most telling of how inaccurate public perception of the Soviet ground threat to Western Europe was were estimates by the Joint Chiefs of Staff that half of Soviet military transport was still horse-drawn as late as 1950.[13]

Critics of these revisionist accounts of the Soviet conventional strength in Europe note that U.S. intelligence got many things, such as the actual number of Soviet divisions, correct.[14] Indeed, they note that the careful way in which U.S. intelligence tracked Soviet manpower levels, and then changed their estimates to reflect what they then believed to be true, is evidence that contradicts claims of deliberate exaggeration by U.S. officials. It is clear, however, that the counterclaim of "no exaggeration" by members of the Truman administration cannot be substantiated. Indeed, U.S. military officers intimately involved in estimating Soviet conventional strength at the time admitted as much years afterward. General Lucius Clay, the U.S. military commander of Berlin, for instance, believed that his famous 1948 cable that war could come with "dramatic suddenness" was solicited by his superiors in order to aid them in their congressional budget testimony, and was not, as was then claimed, based on any change in Soviet behavior or strategy.[15] Similarly, a U.S. Air Force general attached to NATO in the early 1950s stated decades later that "there was no question" that the Soviet conventional threat was "intentionally overrated."[16] U.S. intelligence sometimes did offer a picture of Soviet conventional strength in Europe that was inaccurate—such is the nature of intelligence work—but what was then relayed to the public was again greatly exaggerated.[17]

Other facets of the Soviet threat were similarly inflated. Claims that the USSR was capable of striking the United States with nuclear weapons after their first atomic bomb test in 1949, for instance, neglected to mention Moscow's complete lack of delivery systems capable of reaching the United States. To reach U.S. targets, Air Force intelligence admitted, Soviet bombers would have been forced to make one-way suicide missions. In fact, the notion that the Soviet Air Force was capable of hitting the continental United States

---

[13] Duffield, "The Soviet Military Threat," 213–215; Evangelista, "Stalin's Postwar Army," 120–123.

[14] Phillip Karber and Jerald Combs. "The United States, NATO, and the Soviet Threat to Western Europe: Military Estimates and Policy Options, 1945-1963," *Diplomatic History* 22 (Summer 1998): 103–132.

[15] Jean Edward Smith, ed., *The Papers of General Lucius D. Clay* (Bloomington: Indiana University Press, 1974), 568–569.

[16] Matthew Evangelista, "Commentary: The 'Soviet Threat': Intentions, Capabilities, and Context," *Diplomatic History* 22 (Summer 1998): 447.

[17] John S. Duffield, "Commentary: Progress, Problems, and Prospects," *Diplomatic History* 22 (Summer 1998): 431–437; Evangelista, "Commentary: The 'Soviet Threat,'" 439–449.

at all was discounted as "completely unrealistic" by the CIA between 1946 and 1949. The Air Force agreed, noting "subversion" was, at the time, the principle threat to the American homeland.[18]

As with the claims of overwhelming Soviet ground strength, Air Force estimates that the Soviets possessed a comparable aerial juggernaut of 40,000 long-range bombers, transport planes, and "modern" jet fighters as of 1947–1948 went "far beyond" their highest assessments of both Soviet aircraft production and technical capabilities.[19] Public perception that the Soviets had or had nearly "caught up" to the United States in air power and technology was simply at odds with what was known privately. The Air Force, for instance, noted in the late 1940s that the Soviet Air Force remained primarily "tactical" in nature, and suffered acute problems in such areas as base construction, fighter development, military electronics, and engine design—all critical if the Soviets were to fight effectively in the air against a far superior United States.[20]

In fact, nearly all secret estimates of both Soviet strength and intentions in the immediate years after the Second World War indicated that the USSR was neither prepared for war nor seeking a military confrontation. Intelligence noted that the USSR required at least fifteen years to overcome wartime economic losses, ten to build a scientific base, five to ten years to build a strategic air force, between fifteen and twenty-five to build a navy, ten to rebuild its military transport system, fifteen to twenty-five years to fortify the Soviet Far East, ten to pacify Eastern Europe, and three to ten years to develop an atomic bomb.[21] Military analysts knowledgeable about Soviet capabilities after the Second World War believed that U.S. offensive capabilities were so manifestly superior to those of the USSR that war would be far more costly for the Soviets than for the United States. Even the conquest of Europe, noted analysts, would not ensure victory, owing to the manifest inability of the Soviets to strike the United States and to U.S. superior industrial capabilities.

U.S. officials even privately recognized that Soviet statements and moves abroad were less threatening than noted publicly. The Soviets, for instance, willingly withdrew their forces from northern Norway, Manchuria, and, after moderate U.S. pressure, northern Iran. Free elections were allowed in Hungary and Czechoslovakia, while representative governments were established in Finland and Austria. Intelligence also indicated that there was

---

[18] Lawrence Aronsen, "Seeing Red: US Air Force Assessments of the Soviet Union, 1945-1949," *Intelligence and National Security* 16 (Summer 2001): 103–132.

[19] Ibid., 122. See also Frank Kofsky, *Harry S. Truman and the War Scare of 1948: A Successful Campaign to Deceive the Nation* (New York: St. Martin's Press, 1993).

[20] Aronsen, "Seeing Red," 112, 115–116, 124; John Prados, *The Soviet Estimate: US Intelligence Analysis and Russian Military Strength* (New York: The Dial Press, 1982), 38, 41.

[21] Melvyn P. Leffler, "The American Conception of National Security and the Beginnings of the Cold War, 1945-1948," *The American History Review* 89 (April 1984): 361–362; see also Melvyn P. Leffler, *A Preponderance of Power: National Security, the Truman Administration, and the Cold War* (Stanford, CA: Stanford University Press, 1992).

no evidence that the Soviets were lending support to revolutionary movements in Greece, Southeast Asia, and China.[22] Truman's Secretary of State, Dean Acheson, privately admitted that it was difficult to find "direct evidence of literal violations" of U.S.–Soviet agreements by the USSR.[23] U.S. military officials in Germany even acknowledged that the Soviets had largely kept their promises, while other officials indicated that Paris was the main source of U.S. problems in Germany, not Moscow.[24]

This was not, however, the situation publicly presented by the administration. Indeed, regardless of Joseph Stalin's ultimate culpability in starting the Cold War,[25] the fact remains that the Truman administration's portrayal of Soviet military strength was grossly exaggerated and at odds with what administration officials privately read, wrote, and said to each other. Soviet consolidation of Eastern Europe and the attempt to pressure Turkey, for instance, were portrayed by U.S. officials as bolt-from-the-blue attempts by wild-eyed, fanatical ideologues at world conquest, not, as was acknowledged privately, as expected Soviet responses to U.S. moves in Germany.[26] Truman and his officials recognized that the public and their representatives needed to be "shocked" by facts that were "clearer than truth" if they were to support rearmament at home and Cold War abroad.[27]

VIETNAM

The decision to expand the war in Vietnam is a canonical example of administration manipulation. Although dissembling by U.S. policymakers began before the Gulf of Tonkin Affair and continued long after, Tonkin and the subsequent Americanization of the war in 1965 are the crucial episodes. It was Tonkin that allowed Lyndon B. Johnson to argue that war was necessary by giving him the opportunity to cite long-standing U.S. commitments to South Vietnam, belief that the insurgency in the south was aggression directed by Moscow, and understanding that Tonkin was unprovoked aggression on the high seas as precedent for U.S. involvement. The image conveyed by Johnson was one of a North Vietnamese bully attempting to overthrow a regime deserving of U.S. help, while other hawks inside and outside of the government highlighted the struggle against international communism. All played down the roots of the

[22] Leffler, *A Preponderance of Power*, 133.

[23] Ibid., 133.

[24] Ibid., 132–133.

[25] John Lewis Gaddis, *We Now Know: Rethinking Cold War History* (New York: Oxford University Press, 1997); Vojtech Mastny, "Stalin and the Militarization of the Cold War," *International Security* 9 (Winter 1984–1985): 109–129.

[26] Leffler, *A Preponderance of Power*, 123–125; See also Kofsky, *Harry S. Truman*, 92–100.

[27] Leffler, *A Preponderance of Power*, 145; Samuel F. Wells, "Sounding the Tocsin: NSC 68 and the Soviet Threat," *International Security* 4 (Autumn 1979): 116–158; Dean Acheson, *Present at the Creation: My Years in the State Department* (New York: Norton, 1969), 374–375.

insurgency, the illegitimacy of the corrupt Saigon regime, and the nationalist character of Vietnamese communism, and simply lied about the context within which Tonkin took place and the prospects and consequences of intervention.

The Johnson administration, for instance, promoted the fraudulent claim that the Tonkin incident was unprovoked. At the time, U.S. officials maintained that North Vietnamese naval forces attacked U.S. ships while these were on routine patrol in international waters. Indeed, this was the story related to the American people during a televised address by Johnson himself on 4 August 1964.[28] Also stressing the unprovoked nature of the attack was Defense Secretary Robert McNamara, who skillfully avoided questions challenging administration accounts of the attack. Skeptics pointed to "South Vietnamese" raids on the North before the August 4 attack and the possibility that Hanoi believed the United States was involved.[29] McNamara avoided connecting the naval mission and the attack, claiming they were unrelated.

History reports this interpretation as simply untrue. The Tonkin affair was actually two incidents, one public, one secret, and both connected to covert U.S. raids on North Vietnam. In January of 1964, Johnson agreed to plans drawn up by the Defense Department for raids manned by the South Vietnamese but planned, directed, equipped, and supported by the United States. Raids on North Vietnamese targets began in February, concentrating on sabotage, kidnapping, and psychological warfare.[30] Covert attacks escalated to the point where Thailand-based fighter-bombers attacked North Vietnamese villages near the Laotian border on 1 and 2 August, nearly the same time events in the Gulf of Tonkin were unfolding.

Of direct significance was a covert raid by South Vietnamese patrol boats against the North Vietnamese offshore islands of Hon Me and Hon Nieu on the night of 30–31 July 1964.[31] Days later, a U.S. destroyer arrived in the vicinity on an intelligence-gathering mission that, officially, was separate from the earlier raid. Although the North Vietnamese had reinforced the area with naval units in response to the raid, the U.S. mission continued and came under fire from the North's patrol boats on 3 August. Despite later administration claims, radio intercepts cabled to Washington by the patrol commander indicated that the North Vietnamese believed the earlier raids and the U.S. intelligence mission were related.[32] Once the North Vietnamese were repulsed, the U.S. patrol was

[28] Fredrick Logevall, *Choosing War: The Lost Chance for Peace and the Escalation of War in Vietnam* (Berkeley: University of California Press, 1999), 199.

[29] Robert S. McNamara, *In Retrospect: The Tragedy and Lessons of Vietnam* (New York: Times Books, 1995), 136–137.

[30] Neil Sheehan, "The Covert War and Tonkin Gulf: February – August, 1964" in Neil Sheehan, Hedrick Smith, E.W. Kenworthy, and Fox Butterfield, eds., *The Pentagon Papers* (New York: Bantam Books, 1971), 234–242.

[31] Dale Andrade and Kenneth Conboy, "The Secret Side of the Tonkin Gulf Incident," *Naval History Magazine* 13 (August 1999): 27–33.

[32] David Halberstam, *The Best and the Brightest* (New York: Ballentine Books, 1993), 412.

reinforced and ordered to continue. On 4 August, the patrol reported that they were under attack, and aircraft were once again dispatched in support. Confirmation of the attack was slow in coming and details sketchy when Johnson ordered a reprisal strike on North Vietnamese naval facilities later that day. Indeed, eight months later, the President joked about the uncertainty, saying, "For all I know the Navy was shooting at whales out there."[33]

All of this went unreported in the debate over the Gulf of Tonkin Resolution in Congress. McNamara evaded questions attempting to link the "South Vietnamese" raids with the attack on U.S. ships, and Congress remained ignorant of the truth. There is clear evidence, however, that major executive-branch decision makers with knowledge of the raids realized that Hanoi had connected the covert attacks with the Tonkin mission. CIA director John McCone, for instance, advised Johnson that the North was "reacting defensively to our attacks."[34] When Johnson suspended the raids, Maxwell Taylor, U.S. ambassador to South Vietnam, and Secretary of State Dean Rusk dissented. Both believed the raids had put pressure on Hanoi.

The Gulf of Tonkin incident is unfortunately the most poignant example of deception and manipulation in a war where the public and Congress were consistently lied to by those charged with defending them.[35] From the earliest days of U.S. involvement, reports indicating the ineptitude of South Vietnamese units were ignored by the Pentagon, as were State Department analyses reporting that the insurgency was a continuation of the nationalist revolt interrupted by the 1954 Geneva Accords.[36] Indeed, the conclusion reached by the authors of *The Pentagon Papers* was that Hanoi did not come to directly control the insurgency until 1959, suggesting that the inept Saigon regime was responsible for creating the problems, insurgency included, that it faced.[37] Significant analyses by mid-ranking U.S. advisers in South Vietnam and the U.S. Department of State questioning the validity of Pentagon assessments on the progress of the war were buried.[38] Once the

[33] Ibid.

[34] Andrade and Conboy, "The Secret Side," 31.

[35] H.R. McMaster, *Dereliction of Duty: Lyndon Johnson, Robert McNamara, The Joint Chiefs of Staff, and the Lies that Led to Vietnam* (New York: Harper Collins, 1997); David Kaiser, *American Tragedy: Kennedy, Johnson, and the Origins of the Vietnam War* (Cambridge, MA: Belknap/Harvard University Press, 2000); Logevall, *Choosing War*; Daniel Ellsberg, *Secrets: A Memoir of Vietnam and the Pentagon Papers* (New York: Viking Adult, 2002); Stanley Karnow, *Vietnam: A History* (New York: Viking Penguin, 1991).

[36] Neil Sheehan, *A Bright Shining Lie: John Paul Vann and America in Vietnam* (New York: Random House, 1988), 686–690.

[37] Fox Butterfield, "Origins of the Insurgency in South Vietnam" in Sheehan, Smith, Kenworthy, and Butterfield, eds., *The Pentagon Papers*, 67–79.

[38] Sheehan, *A Bright Shining Lie*, 127–200, 267–386; Halberstam, *The Best and the Brightest*, 256–259.

United States had committed combat troops and began to bomb North Vietnamese targets, innumerable analyses predicted and then reported their ineffectiveness.[39] All was kept hidden.

IRAQ

Events leading up to the 2003 U.S. war with Iraq are still fresh, and information concerning it will remain uncertain until scholars examine classified documents decades hence. Evidence, however, suggests that the administration of George W. Bush was not honest about the Iraq threat and about what the United States could expect once it achieved military victory. In one of the best examinations of the march to war with Iraq, one analyst noted that "the administration supplied a steady stream of unreliable statements" that were contradicted by the press.[40] Another states that there is now "broad agreement" that Bush's rationale for war was "exaggerated" and "wholly baseless."[41]

A brief review of the administration's behavior is illustrative. Public statements on Iraqi weapons of mass destruction (WMD) and purported Iraqi links to terror organizations, widely accepted by the public at the time, are now known to be false.[42] Indeed, Bush himself considered intelligence on Iraq weak and unconvincing.[43] The administration claimed, for instance, that Iraq had purchased aluminum tubes and planned to use them to enrich uranium for nuclear weapons. However, UN inspectors and U.S. centrifuge experts had concluded before the war that the tubes were consistent with those used for rockets and could not easily be modified to serve as centrifuges; nor was there evidence that Iraq had purchased other equipment needed for a centrifuge.[44] Bush's claim in his 2003 State of the Union Address that British intelligence had evidence that Iraq had sought to purchase uranium from Niger, which

---

[39] Halberstam, *The Best and the Brightest*, 355–358; George Herring, ed. *The Pentagon Papers*. Abr. ed. (New York: McGraw Hill, 1993), 118–120, 134–137, 148–155, 186, 191, 200.

[40] Louis Fisher, "Deciding on War Against Iraq: Institutional Failures," *Political Science Quarterly* 118 (Fall 2003): 389–410.

[41] Chaim Kaufmann, "Threat Inflation and the Failure of the Marketplace of Ideas: The Selling of the Iraq War," *International Security* 29 (Summer 2004): 5; see also Jon Western, *Selling Intervention and War: The Presidency, the Media, and the American Public* (Baltimore, MD: Johns Hopkins University Press, 2005), 175–219.

[42] Fisher, "Deciding on War," 400–401; Kaufmann, "Threat Inflation," 16–29; John Prados, *Hoodwinked: The Documents that Reveal How Bush Sold Us a War* (New York: The New Press, 2004); James Bamford, *A Pretext for War: 9/11, Iraq, and the Abuse of America's Intelligence Agencies* (New York: Doubleday, 2004).

[43] Bob Woodward, *Plan of Attack* (New York: Simon and Schuster, 2004), 247–249.

[44] Fisher, "Deciding on War," 401; Kaufmann, "Threat Inflation," 19–28; David Barstow, "How White House Embraced Suspect Iraq Arms Intelligence," *The New York Times*, 3 October 2004; Bamford, *A Pretext for War*, 324, 325–336, 333–337, 360–361; Prados, *Hoodwinked*, 28–29; 95, 96–98, 171–170, 190, 193.

suggested that Saddam Hussein was already on his way to building nuclear weapons, was unsubstantiated and based on fabricated documents.[45]

The administration also attempted to draw a direct link between al Qaeda and the terror attacks of 11 September 2001 and Iraq. On 25 September 2002, Bush claimed that Saddam Hussein and al Qaeda worked "in concert," and the following day, he claimed that Iraq had "long-standing and continuing ties to terrorist organizations," and that there were "[al Qaeda] terrorists inside Iraq." Similarly, on 7 October, Bush said that Iraq "trained al Qaeda members in bomb-making and poisons and deadly gasses." Defense Secretary Donald Rumsfeld also announced that the administration had "bulletproof" evidence of Iraqi links to al Qaeda, and indicated that al Qaeda members had recently been in Baghdad. Rumsfeld's claims later turned out to be unsubstantiated. Administration claims about Mohammed Atta, leader of the September 11 attacks, meeting with Iraqi intelligence in Prague in April 2001 were also without foundation. Czech intelligence and the CIA have since said that there was no evidence that the meeting took place. Even the 9/11 Commission Report, the official U.S. investigation into the tragedies of 11 September 2001, has been unable to substantiate claims that al Qaeda and Saddam Hussein's Iraq worked closely together. What links there are point to a series of opaque meetings over the course of the 1990s that, as far as can be currently determined, resulted in no working relationship of the type suggested by the administration.[46]

In addition to exaggerating the threat from Iraq, the administration also downplayed the difficulties and costs that an invasion and occupation would entail. According to the administration, there was no indication of the problems the United States would face after the war. Indeed, after the war, Pentagon hawks claimed there was no memo that "once written, that if we had only listened to that memo, all would be well in Iraq."[47] Numerous reports, studies, and analyses by groups within and outside the government, however, envisioned scenarios remarkably similar to what actually transpired after the war. All were available to Bush administration officials and ignored by them in their public argument for war. The administration, for instance, ignored the State Department's "Future of Iraq" project, a document commissioned a full year before the war and providing an extensive analysis on postwar Iraq.[48] Also ignored were CIA war games and planning exercises on

---

[45] Fisher, "Deciding on War," 402; Bamford, *A Pretext for War*, 298–307; Prados, *Hoodwinked*, 125–127, 155.

[46] Fisher, "Deciding on War," 399–400; Kaufmann, "Threat Inflation," 16–19; Prados, *Hoodwinked*, 113, 118–119, 236–237; National Commission on Terrorist Attacks, *9/11 Commission Report: Final Report of the National Commission on Terrorist Attacks Upon the United States* (New York: W.W. Norton and Company, 2004), 334–336; Bamford, *A Pretext for War*, 285–286.

[47] James Fallows, "Blind Into Baghdad," *The Atlantic Monthly* 01 (January/February 2004): 52–73.

[48] Ibid., 56–58.

postwar Iraq that had begun a year earlier and ran up to the beginning of the U.S. invasion. Indeed, top Pentagon officials had been reprimanded for attending these war games.[49] U.S. government relief agencies responsible for postwar reconstruction, in conjunction with nongovernmental relief agencies, also warned the administration on what might be expected.[50] Military officers responsible for planning for postwar needs and responsibilities were ignored, while the administration downplayed estimates of what war with Iraq would cost, although the Army and others privately estimated its costs would amount to "tens of billions" of dollars.[51]

There is thus substantial evidence that the Bush administration exaggerated the Iraq threat and downplayed the dangers and costs of an occupation in order to manipulate public opinion. Ambiguity or contrasting evidence reported by U.S. intelligence agencies was disregarded. Inconvenient facts were denied. Warnings about the likelihood of an insurgency developing were ignored. Intelligence regarding Iraq was, as is now acknowledged by the then head of Britain's MI6 intelligence service, simply "fixed round the policy" of the Bush administration.[52]

WHY THREAT INFLATION SUCCEEDED

How did these administrations get away with presenting a case that was either blatantly at odds with intelligence held secretly or was otherwise contradicted by the press? While a comprehensive answer is not possible here, I sketch out an explanation below involving four interrelated factors.

Ignorance, Values, and Cueing

Public ignorance and apathy is the first factor likely to have a large impact on an administration's ability to engage in threat inflation. Studies consistently show the public to be ignorant of and apathetic toward foreign affairs, while the sources of what information they do have are generally of low quality.[53] Apathy, ignorance, and the cost of acquiring quality sources of information are disincentives mitigating public willingness to examine an administration's

---

[49] Ibid., 58.

[50] Ibid., 62–63.

[51] Ibid., 62–73.

[52] Nick Fielding, "MI6 Chief Told PM: Americans 'Fixed' Case for War," 20 March 2005, accessed on the website of *The Times Online* at http://www.timesonline.co.uk/, 6 April 2005.

[53] Michael X. Delli Caprini and Scott Keeter, *What Americans Know About Politics and Why It Matters* (New Haven, CT: Yale University Press, 1996); Ole R. Holsti, "Public Opinion and Foreign Policy: Challenges to the Almond-Lippman Consensus, Mershon Series: Research Programs and Debates," *International Studies Quarterly* 36 (November 1992): 439–466; Matthew Baum, "Sex, Lies, and War: How Soft News Brings Foreign Policy to the Inattentive Public," *American Political Science Review* 96 (March 2003): 91–109.

foreign policy in detail. Ignorance, however, does not mean the mass public is a blank slate. The public, for instance, uses "values," or stable, individual-level ideological predispositions as cognitive aids to help bring new information or argumentation into line with what is already known, while research indicates that elites "cue" the public on what opinions they should hold on particular issues.[54] Being more informed than the mass public, elites represent a source that can signal what is or is not true about foreign affairs. Elites, however, often hold differing opinions about what the proper course of action should be or what the true state of affairs really is, and compete with one another to influence the public. Competing elites, therefore, convey information to the mass public that is then filtered through individuals' "value" systems. Threat inflation can succeed if elites conveying the manipulative message are more effective than their opponents, or if popular values are at odds with content conveyed in dove cues, or both.

Bureaucratic Incentives

If an attempt at manipulation is to succeed, then dissent within the bureaucracy must be controlled or eliminated. This is crucial because the security bureaucracies are the primary collectors and analysts of intelligence and are ultimately responsible for national defense. As such, their expertise lends credibility to administration claims and their acquiescence limits information available to opponents. Since perception of threat is correlated with department budgets, prestige, and opportunities in the private sector, many bureaucrats have incentives to cooperate in order to advance either department or personal interests.[55] This is especially true for the Defense Department, as perceived threat is highly correlated with defense outlays. The Department of State and the CIA may be less inclined to present hawkish information, but their institutional relationship with the president and Congress and their small size give them few resources with which to sustain opposition. Bureaucrats thus have incentives to "play ball" in order to maintain their position and prospects when threat inflation is underway.

Trigger Events

Threat inflation cannot rely solely on hot air alone; it must incorporate and use accounts of menacing events abroad that make administration claims plausible. Such triggering events tend to produce a situation in which the public rallies

[54] Holsti, "Public Opinion and Foreign Policy," 445–457; John Zaller, "Information, Values, and Opinion," *American Political Science Review* 85 (December 1991): 1215–1237.

[55] Mueller, *Public Choice*, 359–385; Ronald Wintrobe, "Modern Bureaucratic Theory" in Dennis C. Mueller, *Perspectives on Public Choice: A Handbook* (Cambridge, MA: Cambridge University Press, 1997); Theodore Lowi, *The End of Liberalism: The Second Republic of the United States.*

around whoever is currently president, thus facilitating an attempt at manipulation. Although evidence on what presidents do with this short-term advantage is indeterminate, it is believed that they can use it to push through their preferred agenda.[56] Also critical is the way in which security issues are framed. Prospect theory suggests that individuals will risk and pay much to prevent losses, much more than is rational as predicted by rational choice theory, but will risk or pay little to make gains.[57] Security issues are presented to the public in terms that often promise to prevent damage or loss, suggesting that if hawks can frame policy as loss-preventing, then the public may accept it even if the price is high. The synergy created by the interplay of the rally-'round-the-flag effect and policy framing when a trigger event or events occur may thus make even extreme policy temporarily acceptable.

The Politicization of National Security

Finally, if manipulation is to succeed, political opponents must be neutralized. Despite claims that partisanship stops at the water's edge, national security is a contentious, politically incendiary issue, and ideologues in the United States have not shown great constraint in using it when attacking opponents. The Republican Party, for example, did little to restrain the politically useful demagoguery of Senator Joseph McCarthy in the 1950s. The result is that doves are often painted as being sympathetic toward U.S. enemies or ignorant of world affairs, and when the public feels threatened, doves must combat these claims in a charged political environment. It is also difficult for legislators concerned with securing reelection to hold dove positions, because these are difficult to quantify, and the results are hard to identify and impossible to claim credit for. Negotiations, for instance, are risky, time-consuming exercises conducted by bureaucratic experts over whom Congress has little direct influence. The gains from these policies are not easily quantifiable or even readily tangible, and doves cannot point out "X-amount of peace produced" as evidence that dove policies are working. Hawkish policies are tangible, quan-

2nd ed. (New York: W.W. Norton & Company, 1979), 139–144; C. Wright Mills, *The Power Elite* (London: Oxford University Press, 2000).

[56] Bradley Lian and John Oneal, "Presidents, the Use of Military Force, and Public Opinion," *Journal of Conflict Resolution* 19 (June 1993): 277–300; John R. Oneal and Annal Lillian Bryan, "The Rally Round the Flag Effect in US Foreign Policy Crises, 1950-1985," *Political Behavior* 17 (December 1995): 379–401; Patrick James and James Rioux, "International Crises and Linkage Politics: The Experience of the United States, 1953–1994," *Political Research Quarterly* 51 (September 1998): 781–812; David H. Clark, "Agreeing to Disagree: Domestic Institutional Congruence and US Dispute Behavior," *Political Research Quarterly* 53 (June 2000): 375–400.

[57] Daniel Kahneman and Amos Tversky, "Prospect Theory: An Analysis of Decision Under Risk," *Econometrica* 47 (1979): 263–291; Miroslav Nincic, "Loss Aversion and the Domestic Context of Military Intervention," *Political Research Quarterly* 50 (March 1997): 97–120.

tifiable, and distributable, and therefore serve as convincing props and lucrative pork for reelection purposes.

EXPLAINING INSTITUTIONAL FAILURE

To what extent were these factors present in these cases? Were advocates of hawkish policies in the media more capable of spreading their message, and was the audience receptive to that message? Was dissent in the bureaucracy stifled? What role did the framing of issues by the administration and rally-'round-the-flag effects play? Were doves in Congress pressured to accept hawkish policies for political reasons?

Ignorance, Values, and Cueing

The Red Juggernaut. Public knowledge regarding the USSR was extremely limited during the early years of the Cold War. Information outlets taken for granted today simply did not exist, and expertise was confined to Ivy League universities, elite think tanks, and, of course, government. Objective information on the USSR was only available in classified reports produced by and for the government. If quality information was scarce and the public ignorant, available sources were monolithic in their presentation. The press viewed the USSR as a danger, and major media outlets, including newspapers, radio and television networks, and movie studios, cooperated with the federal government to produce what was, in essence, propaganda that portrayed the Soviet Union as an imminent, mortal threat.[58] Media dissent was extremely limited and became even more so as the Cold War deepened after 1950. Whether it was the elite media, small-town newspapers, or leftist publications, the range and scope of media debate over the Cold War narrowed to the point where questioning the assumption that the USSR was a military threat was unacceptable.[59]

The distribution of values among the members of the mass public also aided elite attempts to paint the Soviets as a threat. Contemporary polls that indicated the public's willingness to cooperate with Moscow masked an underlying historical mistrust and loathing of communism and the USSR.[60]

---

[58] Nancy Bernhard, *US Television News and Cold War Propaganda, 1947-1960* (Cambridge MA: Cambridge University Press, 1999), 69–93.

[59] Ibid., 155–177; John Fousek, *To Lead the Free World: American Nationalism & the Culture of the Cold War* (University of North Carolina Press, 2000); Michael J. Hogan, *A Cross of Iron: Harry S. Truman and the Origins of the National Security State, 1945–1954* (Cambridge, MA: Cambridge University Press, 1998), 419–462.

[60] Ted Morgan, *Reds: McCarthyism in Twentieth-Century America* (New York: Random House, 2002); Lisle Rose, *The Cold War Comes to Main Street: America in 1950* (Lawrence: University Press of Kansas, 1999).

These feelings, in turn, could be exploited to the full in a media environment that relegated dovish opinion to the fringes of acceptable political debate. Furthermore, the postwar demobilization of veterans also released into the general population large numbers of young men socialized to military life, trust in the state, and the necessity of using force, all attributes making them susceptible to the new ideology of national security being promulgated by anti-communist elites.[61] The pump was primed, in other words, for the public to accept hawkish views of the USSR in a way that quickly transformed the public's perception of a recent ally into that of a recently defeated enemy.[62]

Vietnam. The early years of U.S. involvement in Vietnam went surprisingly unnoticed by most of the major media outlets in the United States.[63] A few of the larger outlets had offices in-country, and, as admitted in *The Pentagon Papers*, produced objective pieces on U.S. involvement in South Vietnam.[64] Unfortunately, media presence in pre-Tonkin Vietnam was such that it was difficult to cover every aspect of the war in detail. Media reports on particular engagements, guerilla activity, and Saigon's corruption could only capture small slices of the war at any given time. Pre-Tonkin reporting failed to ask "big questions," such as the end goal of the U.S. commitment, whether the United States should have been in Vietnam at all, or whether Hanoi represented a legitimate form of Vietnamese nationalism.[65]

After Tonkin and U.S. troop commitments in 1965, U.S. media presence in the country increased. Print outlets already in Vietnam expanded their bureaus to increase coverage, while newspapers previously content to use wire feed opened their own bureaus in Saigon. The introduction of widespread television news coverage also brought home the immediacy of the war to the American public in a way print and radio outlets had not been able to accomplish. The expansion of higher education brought on by the baby boom also opened up a source of information and expertise, the academy, to a larger, more diverse audience than had previously been the case. As the war went on and costs began to mount, an increasingly interested public was able to keep abreast of events in a way it had not been able to a decade earlier.

In 1964, however, the established print media still controlled public discourse on foreign policy, while television was restricted by technology in what

---

[61] Hogan, *A Cross of Iron*, 1–22; Michael Mann, *Fascists* (Cambridge, MA: Cambridge University Press, 2004), 1–30, 353, 376.

[62] Les K. Adler and Thomas Paterson, "Red Fascism: The Merger of Nazi Germany and Soviet Russia in the American Image of Totalitarianism, 1930s-1950s," *American Historical Review* 75 (April 1970): 1046–1064.

[63] William Prochnau, *Once Upon a Distant War* (New York: Times Books, 1995); McMaster, *Dereliction of Duty*, 37.

[64] Sheehan, *A Bright Shining Lie*, 686–690.

[65] Halberstam, *The Best and the Brightest*, 670; Sheehan, *A Bright Shining Lie*, 685–686.

it could report. This meant that the voices of dissent coming from Southeast Asia did little to overturn entrenched hawkish views. Indeed, the major U.S. print and broadcast outlets uncritically parroted the administration's line that the Tonkin incident was the result of an unprovoked attack by the North Vietnamese, showing that the established media's dependence on official sources inside Washington and in South Vietnam, as in the Iraq case, meant it could not stray far from the official line when confronted by a seemingly united administration.[66] In terms of the public's values, the generation that fought and came of age during the Second World War had now attained positions of influence within American society. The "silent majority" Nixon later appealed to represented not so much any one political party so much as the members of this generation who had committed to avoiding a repetition of the perceived mistakes of the 1930s.[67]

Iraq. If information with which to judge the merits of policy was scarce in the previous cases, the same cannot be said about Iraq. Media coverage included 24-hour television news, widespread print coverage, and Internet-based reporting. Media sources were diverse, and the Internet provided a platform for the presentation and dissemination of views that might not have otherwise made it into the public domain. Experts were called upon to debate Iraq policy, and nongovernmental sources of information on the pros and cons of war with Iraq were widely available. The U.S.–Iraq war in 1991 and U.S. involvement there since also gave the public a sense of familiarity with Iraq.

Cracks in the established U.S. media first seen in Vietnam had by now, however, widened into a divide separated not so much by technology as by ideology. The reemergence of a political press in the United States provided more platforms for dissent, but also segmented recipients of news by political ideology. Individuals discount news and information coming from outside their ideological milieu, making it no surprise that press reports from "liberal" outlets that questioned administration evidence on Iraq had little impact on public opinion. Conservative media, in fact, insulated war supporters from these reports. One study, for instance, reported that viewers of conservative FOX News would not only be more likely to hold factually incorrect beliefs about the Iraq war after the war's conclusion, but actually had become less informed the more they watched.[68] Finally, as in Vietnam, the U.S. media's overreliance on government sources and relative lack of access to and expertise on Iraq meant that the media in general and conservative media in particular served as an echo chamber that reverberated "myths of empire" to a public

---

[66] Daniel C. Hallin, *The Uncensored War: The Media and Vietnam* (Berkeley: University of California Press, 1989).

[67] Kaiser, *American Tragedy*, 7–9, 485–487.

[68] Steven Kull, Clay Ramsay, and Evan Lewis, "Misperceptions, the Media, and the Iraq War," *Political Science Quarterly* 118 (Winter 2003–04): 569–598.

long comfortable with viewing U.S. power as a unique, righteous force for good in world affairs.[69]

Bureaucratic Incentives

The Red Juggernaut. The Soviet threat created the modern U.S. national security bureaucracy. Previous U.S. wars had been followed by periods of foreign retrenchment; thus, those wishing to prevent this needed to highlight potential postwar threats to national security.[70] The effort to identify the USSR as the nation's primary enemy coincided with the passage of the National Security Act of 1947 and the creation of new institutional arrangements for the nation's military services. Defense unification under a weak defense secretary and the emergence of an independent Air Force resulted in acute interservice rivalry, leading to services that could neither agree on basic strategy nor coordinate their budget requests to Congress. When rearmament was authorized in the crisis atmosphere of the Korean War, these interservice disputes were transferred from an environment of financial scarcity to one of financial plenty, with funds lavished on services that still had not reconciled their policy differences. What resulted was a process of capabilities–resources ratcheting, a situation wherein an expansion of capabilities brought with it an expansion of responsibilities that due to service-defined military necessity, required the acquisition of new resources. This, along with secrecy that prevented outsiders from reviewing military planning, and the sidelining of bureaucratic economizers opposed to massive rearmament, produced the atomic Air Force, overkill, and a tripling of the annual military budget from $13.5 billion to $45 billion between 1949 and 1951, of which only a portion went to support the war in Korea.[71]

Vietnam. The acute interservice rivalry that facilitated the massive expansion of the U.S. armed forces in the late '40s and early '50s similarly prevented the military chiefs from effectively opposing Johnson's policy in Vietnam. Instead, the chiefs accepted Johnson and McNamara's policy of "gradual escalation" despite their misgivings about its ultimate efficacy, and

---

[69] Michael Massing, *Now They Tell Us: The American Press and Iraq* (New York: New York Review of Books, 2004); Paul T. McCartney, "American Nationalism and US Foreign Policy: From September 11th to the Iraq War," *Political Science Quarterly* 119 (Fall 2004): 399–423; Jack Snyder, *Myths of Empire: Domestic Politics and International Ambition* (Ithaca, NY: Cornell University Press, 1993).

[70] Leffler, "The American Conception," 348–349.

[71] David Rosenberg, "The Origins of Overkill: Nuclear Weapons and American Strategy, 1945-1960," *International Security* 7 (Spring 1983): 3–71; Benjamin O. Fordham, *Building the Cold War Consensus: The Political Economy of US National Security Policy, 1949-1951* (Ann Arbor: University of Michigan Press, 1998), 25–74; Hogan, *A Cross of Iron*, 23–68, 159–208, 264–366.

instead fought to increase their respective shares of the Vietnam "pie."[72] The bureaucracy, furthermore, buried those who disagreed with or documented the failure of U.S. policy in Vietnam. Indeed, military officers and administration officials expressing doubt were often ignored and punished, as were Vice President Hubert Humphrey, CIA director McCone, and even Defense Secretary McNamara.

Iraq. The end of the Cold War brought significant budget cuts in national security spending, while bureaucratic inertia and the lack of a clear threat prevented resources from being reallocated quickly or efficiently.[73] This general malaise in the intelligence community, especially the perception that the CIA was mired in decline, provided hawkish policy entrepreneurs newly ensconced within the bureaucracy the unique opportunity to influence policy on Iraq. These individuals and their associates outside government were able to collectively direct attention toward Iraq after the attacks of September 11 and then use their influence and the low reputation of U.S. intelligence agencies to suppress doubts about the veracity of administration statements on Iraq. Once it became apparent that war was inevitable, there were few incentives, despite uneasiness among many military and civilian officials, for bureaucrats to voice dissent. Those expressing doubt as to the viability of the postwar occupation plan or the cost of the invasion were, like in the Vietnam case, fired or reprimanded.

Trigger Events

The Red Juggernaut. Soviet expansion into Eastern Europe, the loss of China to Mao Zedong in 1949, and the outbreak of the Korean War in 1950 contributed to a hardening of public opinion toward communism in general and the USSR in particular. These events confirmed in the minds of the U.S. public that the communist threat was real and gaining strength, framing future policy toward the Soviet Union in terms of loss prevention. The "Long Telegram" and "X" article in *Foreign Affairs* articulated containment's loss-prevention strategy,[74] while U.S. policymakers focused on denying communism further strategic gains regardless of whether local circumstances, such as in Indochina, suggested that a looser interpretation of containment might be more appropriate. Indeed, the Korean War allowed the conflict in Indochina

---

[72] McMaster, *Dereliction of Duty*, 327–328.

[73] *9/11 Commission Report*, 71–134; Bamford, *A Pretext for War*, 129, 157–161.

[74] George Kennan as "X", "The Sources of Soviet Conduct," *Foreign Affairs* XXV (July 1947): 575–576; U.S. embassy (Moscow) cable, "Answer to Department's 284, Feb 3 [13]" (Sources of Conduct), 22 February 1946, Secret, accessed at http://www.gwu.edu/~nsarchiv/coldwar/documents/episode-1/kennan.htm, 4 October 2005.

to be reinterpreted as a free-world struggle against worldwide communism relatively quickly. Less than a month after the outbreak of hostilities on the Korean peninsula, the Truman administration authorized the dispatch of military aid and advisers to aid the French in Vietnam. By 1954, what effectively had been a colonial war between aspiring Vietnamese, albeit communist, nationalists and French colonialism had been transformed into a front in the U.S. "global war" on communism, resulting in the eventual deployment of over 4,600 troops to French Indochina and the supplying of 80 percent of French war materiel at a total cost of over $3 billion.[75] Finally, the bunker mentality permeating containment, moreover, necessitated tracking U.S.–Soviet relations as a win/lose situation in which the slightest loss might lead to catastrophe. Direct involvement in Korea also facilitated this change in framing, and dramatically recast public perception of the Cold War. Indeed, the dispatch of troops to the peninsula made questioning U.S. Cold War policy unpatriotic and dangerous because it signaled weak resolve.

Vietnam. The Tonkin incident similarly refashioned public perception of the conflict in Vietnam. Whereas before Tonkin, U.S. commitments to Saigon were seen in terms of efficacy of policy, the attacks recast the conflict as a direct challenge to the United States. U.S. forces had been attacked, and honor dictated a response behind which a patriotic public rallied. Questioning the wisdom of bombing or troop deployments manifested itself in public only well after U.S. actions had proven both ineffective and costly.[76] Avoiding defeat in Vietnam in order to avoid an even larger loss through the fall of the whole of Southeast Asia was also an important factor in galvanizing support.

Escalation, however, was painstaking and slow, and the invasion and occupation of the North was never considered for fear of widening the conflict. Intervention on the ground in South Vietnam thus represented a risky, costly gamble that was undertaken to avoid a loss.

Iraq. Consideration of the 2003 U.S. invasion of Iraq cannot be made without reference to the terrorist attacks of 11 September 2001. The public rallied behind the President, and opposition to the campaign to topple the Taliban was nonexistent. Measures taken to combat terrorism at home, such as creation of the Department of Homeland Security and passage of the Patriot Act, were widely supported. Crucially, consensus that the root cause of Islamic terror threatening the United States could be found in the oppressive regimes

[75] Robert Mann, *A Grand Delusion: America's Descent into Vietnam* (New York: Basic Books, 2001), 87–92; Tim Kane, *Global US Troop Deployment: 1950-2003. Center for Data Analysis Report #04-11* (Washington DC: Heritage Foundation, 2004).

[76] Frank Newport and Joseph Carroll, "Iraq versus Vietnam: A Comparison of Public Opinion," *The Gallup Poll*, 24 August 2005, accessed on the website of The Gallup Poll at http://galluppole.com/content//?ci=18097, 5 September 2005.

of the Middle East laid the foundation for war against Iraq. The "enemy" was not merely al Qaeda, but had expanded to include most of the regimes in the region. Arguments for the invasion were also cast in "loss-prevention" frames during public debate, that is, Saddam Hussein posed a threat that in the future the United States *might* suffer devastating losses. Implicit in this assertion was a link between Iraq's alleged WMD possession and the Iraqi state to al Qaeda. The administration carefully crafted its war message to argue that war would remove an imminent danger. An argument not emphasized in the public debate before the war, however, was the notion that installing democracy and freeing the Iraqi people from Saddam's rule was a legitimate justification for war—which the consensus over the root cause of the September 11 terror attacks would have suggested. Instead, officials apparently decided that the public reason for war would be the potential WMD threat and the future losses that it could entail, rather than the gains from removing Saddam and installing a democratic regime.[77]

The Politicization of National Security

The Red Juggernaut. The early Cold War saw the heavy politicization of national security in a manner that still affected U.S. politics decades later. Politicians advocating dovish positions on foreign policy and a lessening of Cold War tensions were targets for slanderous attacks by both the right and the political center. The atmosphere of paranoia and cheap political demagoguery permeating the late '40s and '50s made it difficult for politicians and others to openly question the nature of the Soviet threat.[78] Policies adopted to mitigate the threat—political and security ties abroad and rearmament at home—were also more lucrative and substantive than negotiations and peaceful coexistence. Military spending brought jobs and income to districts and states containing defense industries and bases, while Marshall Plan aid to Europe invigorated U.S. industry.[79] The benefits of lessened tensions with the USSR, in theory no less substantial, were diffuse and hard to measure or verify, while the costs were concentrated on groups benefiting most from competition with Moscow.

Vietnam. Johnson was keen on avoiding a defeat in Vietnam for fear of what defeat abroad would do to his prospects for reelection and, after re-

---

[77] Rodger D. Hodge, "Weekly Review," 28 May 2003, accessed on the website of *Harpers Magazine* at http://harpers.org/WeeklyReview2003-06-03.html, 15 April 2004.

[78] Morgan, *Reds*; David Caute, *The Great Fear: The Anti-Communist Purge under Truman and Eisenhower* (New York: Simon and Schuster, 1978).

[79] Fordham, *Building the Cold War Consensus*; Kofsky, *Harry S. Truman*; Ann Markusen, Scott Campbell, Peter Hall, and Sabrina Dietrick, *The Rise of the Gunbelt: The Military Remapping of Industrial America* (New York: Oxford University Press, 1991).

election, his chances to pass his Great Society legislation. While Johnson's *machismo*, strident anti-communism, his and his advisers' misguided desire to project credibility, bureaucratic lethargy and policy inertia, and global power imbalances in favor of the United States may all have ultimately been responsible for his decision for war, domestic political considerations played a crucial role in the way he went about committing the United States in Southeast Asia.[80] Johnson, for instance, had little foreign policy experience upon taking office after the assassination of John F. Kennedy in 1963, and he banked upon the credibility of Kennedy advisers like McNamara, Maxwell Taylor, and McGeorge Bundy in order to lend himself legitimacy on national security. Indeed, Johnson was well aware of the perils that awaited a president when confronted with a seemingly unsuccessful foreign policy, having witnessed the diminishment of Truman's political capital after the loss of China in 1949 and the stalemate in Korea.

As the front-runner in the 1964 election, Johnson desired to keep Vietnam on the back burner, avoiding decisions that might force him into a position of either losing Vietnam or stumbling into war. To do this, Johnson adopted a "holding" strategy that kept pressure on the North through covert action in order to hide the growing scale and depth of the U.S. commitment. When Barry Goldwater, his Republican challenger, attacked Johnson for being "soft" and "irresolute" in dealing with the communist North, the President deftly used the opportunity presented by Tonkin to rebut those charges. Indeed, it is clear that domestic political considerations topped Johnson's list of concerns when he ordered the strike. Retaliatory options, for instance, were judged according to how the Republicans, the Congress, and the press would react, and the President's announcement of U.S. retaliation was timed so as to not miss the deadlines of the Eastern papers, not for reasons of operational security; the announcement came well before U.S. planes hit their targets.[81] The political motivation for the Tonkin air strikes is highlighted by the fact that a month later, a similarly ambiguous naval action in the Gulf of Tonkin failed to elicit a military response from Johnson. Having already proven his credibility, Johnson had no desire to spook voters so close to the November elections when, in his opinion, "those dumb, stupid sailors were probably just shooting at flying fish."[82]

This concern with credibility and the calculus of domestic politics laced Johnson's decision making throughout the period of deepening U.S. involvement after the election. Throughout 1965, Johnson kept the growing commitment in Vietnam hidden, skillfully using the credibility of McNamara, the

---

[80] Kaiser, *American Tragedy*, 485–493; Logevall, *Choosing War*, 375–413; McMaster, *Dereliction of Duty*, 300–322; Gareth Porter, *Perils of Dominance: Imbalance of Power and the Road to War in Vietnam* (Berkeley: University of California Press, 2005).

[81] McMaster, *Dereliction of Duty*, 128, 132–133.

[82] Ibid., 161.

Joint Chiefs, and even former Presidents Truman and Dwight D. Eisenhower to deflect criticism. The Viet Cong attack on the U.S. installation at Pleiku was used to justify troop deployments and an aerial bombardment of the North that had been planned but was delayed because of the election.[83] Johnson always sent enough troops and materiel to Vietnam to meet immediate needs—but only enough—to avoid a real debate on Vietnam that might have undermined support for his expensive Great Society reforms and threatened the political coalition he and his party had built.[84]

Iraq. Despite the end of the Cold War, national security remained a topic for vitriolic debate. Conservatives claimed that the Ronald Reagan-era military buildup had "defeated" the Soviets, thus giving them credibility with the public when advocating *realpolitik*. Those advocating dovish policies were discredited by the seeming success of the administrations of Ronald Reagan and George H.W. Bush in dealing with the Soviets. In this environment, doves advocating multilateralism and international institution building were cast as being "soft" on defense, and willing to expend American lives in unfruitful nation-building exercises abroad.

Critics described liberal policies as "weakening" the military, and painted doves as unwilling to use force to protect American interests abroad. The Bill Clinton administration's response to terror attacks against U.S. targets were, in particular, painted as being "soft" despite the lack of realistic alternatives then acceptable to the U.S. electorate. The attacks of September 11, therefore, did not occur in a political vacuum. Rather, they occurred at a time when dovish positions were castigated by hawks as being ineffective and dangerous. Since the fruits of multilateral diplomacy and global institution building were not readily measurable or easily discernible to an ignorant and skeptical public, doves could not point to an "X-amount of peace and security" produced. Hawks, on the other hand, used this inability to measure the product of dovish policy as being an indicator of failure, and were able to cite terrorist attacks as evidence of that failure. The attacks of September 11 made this standing critique more poignant and difficult to deflect.

NEGATIVE CASE: PRE–SEPTEMBER 11 ANTI-TERROR POLICY

The terrorist attacks of 11 September 2001 were the largest mass-casualty attacks in U.S. history, and warnings collected by the bureaucracy in the years, months, and weeks preceding them indicated that the al Qaeda threat was real, growing, and likely to strike U.S. soil. Why was so little done to prevent these attacks? It is surprising that the threat from al Qaeda and the specter of mass-

---

[83] Ibid., 174, 240–241.
[84] Ibid., 312, 316–317, 320.

casualty terrorism didn't move officials to do anything, let alone use it as the leading prop in an attempt at threat inflation and policy manipulation. Why was inaction, possibly even threat deflation, the result?

First, terrorism, unlike the threats in the previous cases, was something of which even U.S. elites, let alone the public, were only dimly aware. The nature of terrorism and the lack of a clear enemy presented the public and cueing elites alike with a subject that could not be easily incorporated into the old state-centered threat matrix of the Cold War. Terrorism's amorphous nature, multiple players, and differing goals presented no consistent theme that could be used to justify rearmament, bureaucratic reorganization, or an aggressive foreign policy. If terrorism was a threat far distant from the everyday experience of the U.S. public and elite to begin with, then Islamic fundamentalism and groups like al Qaeda were almost exclusively the preserve of dedicated government and academic experts and policy entrepreneurs. Terrorism prior to September 11 and, specifically, al Qaeda's distant exoticness made them too implausible an enemy with which to either galvanize support for an anti-terrorism campaign abroad or as the central character in any scare story peddled by a manipulative administration.

Second, the bureaucratic agents responsible for tracking and defending against the terrorist threat were ill-prepared to handle a transnational organization like al Qaeda, while rivalry over jurisdiction, assets, and information prevented bureaucratic coordination. The CIA and State Department, for instance, suffered from budget cutbacks, morale problems, and a critical lack of assets and expertise in transnational terrorism, while the Department of Defense was institutionally averse to taking on counter-terrorism missions that held potential for significant mission creep. The FBI, although skilled in investigation of terrorist incidents, remained focused on law enforcement activities that could lead to legal prosecution, not on threat detection and prevention. With no agency or department having much to gain from focusing national attention on terrorism, it is not surprising that the pre–September 11 national security bureaucracies did not focus on the threat, absent White House direction.

Third, although there were a series of terrorist attacks against U.S. targets by Islamic fundamentalist groups in the 1990s, there was no dramatic attack on the scale of September 11 that could galvanize a rally-'round-the-flag effect or push the population into the domain of losses. Without either, risky and expensive loss-avoiding policies that could have been sold to the public as effective in either containing or eliminating al Qaeda before September 11 were never floated, for lack of obvious public support. This was, again, probably owing to the fact that the most dramatic al Qaeda attacks, such as the attempted sinking of the USS Cole in October 2000 and the U.S. embassy bombings in Kenya and Tanzania in 1998, were far away and failed to kill more Americans than the bombing by domestic terrorists of the Oklahoma City federal building. There were no terror attacks prior to September 11 powerful enough to make threat inflation centered on terrorism credible.

Fourth, the relaxation of international tensions brought about by the end of the Cold War and the collapse of the Soviet Union made political attacks on liberal-leaning foreign policy far less acute. Without an enemy, charges that doves were weak or soft on national security simply had far less traction with the public. Indeed, with no clear enemy, foreign affairs was even more absent than usual during the 2000 election. Furthermore, the only significant use of U.S. military force abroad at the time was in the Balkans, a situation that led traditional defense hawks to criticize a military intervention led by a liberal internationalist on the grounds that the conflict posed no threat to U.S. security and might develop into an open-ended nation-building exercise.

ANALYSIS

Table 1 summarizes the cases and factors discussed above. The limited number of cases, of course, necessarily requires a significant degree of caution when interpreting and drawing inferences from them, but analysis suggests that the conditions under which threat inflation occurs are varied and the results of inflation dependent upon the context in which it takes place. So how and why does threat inflation succeed?

First, the public's lack of knowledge is, surprisingly, relatively unimportant. The public was arguably best informed on Vietnam and Iraq, but threat inflation still took place and succeeded, whereas the public was arguably least informed about the Red Juggernaut and pre–September 11 terrorism, yet threat inflation occurred in the former case but not the latter. Clearly, public knowledge is only relevant within the context of elite cueing and existing public values. Here, we see the polar cases of monolithic cueing and monolithic values in favor of opposing communism crystallizing into the Cold War consensus and the domestic "Red Scare," while divided elites and divided values prior to September 11 are associated with policy inaction and apathy. Iraq and Vietnam were middling cases. Vietnam can best be characterized as a time when both elites and the mass public were weakly monolithic as to the need to confront and contain communism in Southeast Asia, with division occurring over the proper policy to adopt and whether military intervention by U.S. forces was practical. Iraq, on the other hand, was a case in which both elites and the public could be characterized as weakly divided over the need, practicality, and appropriateness of a U.S. invasion of Iraq in the wider campaign against terrorism.

Second, executive branch capture of the bureaucracy occurred in all three cases of threat inflation, although the extent to which and the method of how control was established differed. The case of the early Cold War saw the complete capture of the bureaucracy by hawks, which was facilitated by the congruence of agency incentives with administration policy and coupled to heavy policing of dissent. Vietnam saw strong but not complete capture of the bureaucracy, largely because, despite heavy policing, not all bureaucratic agents or agencies were in agreement on the efficacy of U.S. intervention. The

TABLE 1

Threat Inflation in Four Cases

	Red Juggernaut	Vietnam	Iraq	Pre–September 11
Information Availability	1	2	3	1
Elite cueing	Monolithic	Weakly monolithic	Weakly divided	Divided
Public values	Monolithic	Weakly monolithic	Weakly divided	Divided
Bureaucracy	Total capture	Strong capture	Modest capture	No capture
Trigger event	2–3	1–2	3	1
National security politicization	3	2	2	1
Threat inflation	Yes	Yes	Yes	No
Result	Cold War consensus	Gradual escalation	Iraq invasion	September 11

1, weak/little; 2, medium/some; 3, strong/a great deal.

Iraq case, on the other hand, saw only moderate capture of the bureaucracy, largely owing to the inability of the administration to adequately police those unhappy with either the invasion itself or the manner of its implementation. In the pre–September 11 case, on the other hand, not only was there wide bureaucratic disagreement over the proper U.S. response to terrorism, there were few attempts to police the bureaucracy through either coercion or cooptation. Weak coordination at the top failed to bring either order or consistency to U.S. anti-terror policy.

Third, the occurrence of a precipitating trigger event or events that sets the stage for a later attempt at threat inflation is, unsurprisingly, a critical precondition. Iraq arguably had the strongest precipitating event, September 11, while the Red Juggernaut case saw a string of menacing events abroad culminate in the invasion of South Korea. Vietnam and the pre–September 11 era had the weakest precipitating events, but these differed in context. Tonkin and subsequent guerrilla attacks against U.S. advisory forces in South Vietnam occurred during the Cold War and could plausibly be linked to U.S. rivals. Terrorism prior to September 11, on the other hand, did not occur during a period of geopolitical rivalry and could not be linked to a plausible enemy.

Finally, the politicization of national security was a significant factor in all three cases of threat inflation. Opposition to hawkish policy was the most politically dangerous in the early Cold War era for several reasons. The USSR appeared menacing, elite cueing and public opinion indicated anti-communism abroad was both popular and legitimate, bureaucratic allies were few, and, finally, massive military spending was useful for reelection purposes. Vietnam and Iraq likewise saw the politicization of national security, but politicization was less heavy than during the initial years of the Cold War for different reasons. Vietnam had significant elite and popular support, as evidenced by the weakly monolithic consensus over Vietnamese policy, and there were initially few bureaucratic agents that dovish lawmakers could use as allies, but the weakness of the precipitating events that contextualized U.S. involvement and the paucity of electoral pork that came with Vietnam did not turn opposition into a political dead end. The precipitating event in the Iraq case, on the other hand, was such a shock that even a weakly divided elite and mass public, a fair degree of bureaucratic opposition, and next to no political pork were unable to overcome the political disadvantages of opposition. The pre–September 11 era, in contrast to all three positive cases, saw relatively little politicization of anti-terrorism policy because widespread disagreement among elites, the bureaucracy, and the mass public provided ample space for political opposition.

These differences, in turn, explain the relative success of threat inflation in each case, and answer the question of how these administrations "got away with it." Truman's threat inflation was an overwhelming success; it literally brought into existence the modern U.S. national security state and legitimized a half-century of Cold War. It succeeded because of a unique set of circumstances: monolithic elite and popular opinion that was mutually agreeable on foreign policy, an almost complete absence of bureaucratic dissent, and a series of menacing events abroad that first pushed the public into the domain of losses and then created a rally-'round-the-flag effect during the Korean War. The Truman administration may have produced the play, but events abroad provided the stage, bureaucrats the script, and elites the direction, while the public largely applauded. Political opposition was simply impossible in such a situation.

Vietnam and Iraq, in contrast, were far less successful instances of threat inflation. In Vietnam, moderate consensus over the legitimacy of U.S. actions in Southeast Asia allowed Johnson to use Tonkin as a pretext for further U.S. intervention, but the weakness of Tonkin as a precipitating event did not allow him to send hundreds of thousands of troops immediately nor, in the end, invade and occupy North Vietnam. Capturing the bureaucracy, in turn, merely allowed administration policy to go farther and lies to be hidden for longer than might have otherwise been the case. Vietnam was a case in which commitment increased secretly and slowly, while initial support dwindled over time.

Threat inflation in Iraq was, in the end, even less successful than in Vietnam. True, the Bush administration was able to spin lurid tales of Iraqi WMD in the hands of terrorists into a successful invasion, but it has not been able to sustain support in the face of significant opposition from large segments of the elite, the public, and the national security bureaucracy itself. Indeed, support has dwindled far more quickly for the Iraq intervention than it did for Vietnam. Thus, Iraq is something of a fluke, largely caused by the shock of September 11. Without September 11, it is doubtful whether threat inflation and invasion would have been remotely feasible. Finally, the lack of all these factors contributed to the absence of threat inflation, possibly even contributed to threat *deflation*, in the years prior to September 11. Elite and public values were divided, the threat indistinct and shadowy, and the bureaucracy un-interested and weakly policed. In such an environment, political opposition could thrive and thwart any attempt to use terrorism as the central prop in threat inflation.

CONCLUSION: TRUST ... BUT VERIFY

The picture presented here as to the efficacy of U.S. institutions in preventing threat inflation or rationally confronting threats to U.S. security is not a pretty one. Given strong enough trigger events and the presence of some degree of elite and popular consensus, secrecy, and the president's commanding position over the security bureaucracies provide significant opportunities to engage in threat inflation. More disturbing still is that threat inflation has succeeded not just once, but at least three times in the past half century and has resulted in the unneeded expenditure of vast amounts of blood and treasure. A communist Vietnam proved inconsequential to U.S. security, while Iraq, as of yet, has increased antipathy toward U.S. policy abroad, failed to resolve the Israeli–Palestinian conflict, has not brought significant political liberalization to the Middle East, and has, moreover, increased terrorism and unleashed chaos in the heart of the world's most important oil-producing region. The Cold War, although probably inevitable, was made more dangerous and more expensive by fear mongering that demonized the Soviet Union. All this suggests that the way in which the United States formulates its foreign policy is deeply flawed. Current emphasis on intelligence reorganization will probably solve little, because the ultimate sources of threat inflation or deflation lie outside the purview of intelligence collection and analysis. Threat inflation or deflation occurs and succeeds because it is politically feasible, even beneficial, to instigate or go along with it. It is at heart a political act, and only political reform will make engaging in it more difficult.

First and fundamentally, Congress's devolution of power and deference to the executive branch in the area of national security is unconscionable, yet its subservience continues because it is politically expedient. Its committee system has produced a large number of oversight committees on national security and foreign affairs that do little other than promote legislative baronies that create inefficiency, produce pork, contribute to legislative shirking, and provide bureaucratic agents numberless opportunities to play congressional actors against one another. It makes little sense to have separate committees and subcommittees for intelligence, foreign affairs, and the armed services when, in the real world, a substantive grasp of foreign policy requires expertise in all three areas. Consolidating these into one expanded, strictly bipartisan committee with significant oversight and funding authority for all the national security bureaucracies is a first step that would simultaneously expand and make accountable congressional power. The adoption of a rotating chairmanship, in addition to strict bipartisanship, would also help promote partisan comity and cooperation in an area that has far too often been politicized at the nation's expense.

These particular reforms would no doubt be difficult to enact, as they would ruffle the feathers of the many vested interests that would lose influence if the current system of congressional oversight were to be significantly changed. However, expecting congressional members to suddenly find under the current system the political will to overcome the entrenched disincentives to overseeing executive branch stewardship of national security is simply putting hope before experience. A good deal of the president's legitimacy, for instance, is derived from the fact that he or she is clearly the head of the executive branch. If something goes wrong, he or she can be held accountable. Who is responsible for congressional oversight, on the other hand, is not evident at all. Congressional oversight, as a collective endeavor, is susceptible to collective-action problems and, obviously, has failed quite often. Committee consolidation would clearly delineate who is responsible and, indeed, increase overall expertise. The same committee determining whether the army should be increased will also hear testimony from intelligence officials as to what threats that army will have to face. Furthermore, institutionalized bipartisanship will make substantive congressional oversight more credible and, therefore, a greater deterrent to administration malfeasance. No one, for instance, expects a congressional inquiry into executive branch activities to amount to more than a televised whitewash when the same party controls both branches.

Expansion of congressional power and the institution of practices that are designed to increase bipartisanship, however, will only help constrain the executive if lawmakers are more informed. Congress, at present, receives a hodge-podge of information through its oversight committees that presents lawmakers with, at best, a highly biased overview of U.S. intelligence assessments. Indeed, it is apparent that the oversight hearings in the above cases rather quickly devolved into meaningless dog-and-pony shows wherein bureaucratic and administration officials easily evaded answering tough questions by a Congress either too uninformed, too cowed, or too lazy to press further. Clearly, Congress needs better access to timely, high-quality information.

One way this might be achieved is to distribute to members of the relevant committee or committees congressional versions of the President's Daily Brief, thereby giving legislative overseers as much information as is available to the president. Other remedies, however, should focus on weakening presidential control of bureaucratic agents in order to prevent retribution for informing Congress of malfeasance. Whistle-blower protection, for instance, should be strengthened even further, while bureaucratic agents should be given the right to anonymously give testimony to or otherwise secretly inform Congress of administration wrongdoing through a congressional–executive ombudsman. The extension of the length of service of the directors of central and, now, national intelligence beyond one presidential term, as well as the establishment of supermajority requirements for Senate approval of major appointments to the national security bureaucracy, would make these bureaucrats less creatures of the administration and more public servants accountable to both the president and Congress. Finally, a series of sunshine laws should be adopted that place limits on what documents can be classified, require that public and private papers of all high administration officials be made public, and make more-efficient Freedom of Information Act requests in the area of national security.

These reforms will not end the problem of threat inflation, but strengthening and depoliticizing congressional power and weakening the president's hold over the bureaucracy may free up information held in the deep recesses of these agencies that could make political opposition to threat inflation more feasible. Executive power would thus be curtailed, but the possibility that the president would be unduly subject to the will of the legislature is small. The president would retain the ability to command troops, would still set the national security agenda, and would still be responsible for the overall thrust of foreign policy. All that these initial reforms would do is ensure that the person hired to do the job is honest about the job needing to be done.

The Rise of a European Defense

SETH G. JONES

Over the last decade, the European Union's major powers have collaborated to build an increasingly integrated and technologically advanced defense industry. In Britain, for example, key weapons programs include the Storm Shadow long-range cruise missile, the Brimstone anti-tank missile, and the Eurofighter combat aircraft. In Germany, key programs include the A400M tactical and strategic airlift and the Taurus air-to-surface guided missile. In France, programs include the Galileo global navigation satellite system, the European medium-altitude long-endurance unmanned aerial vehicle, and the Scalp cruise missile. All of these weapons and platforms have something significant in common: they are being developed and produced in collaboration with other European states and firms. In some areas, such as missiles, research and development occur almost exclusively at the European level through the transnational European firm MBDA. The European Union's establishment of a European Defense Agency in 2004 in Brussels has further increased the prospect of an integrated European defense market. As Henry Kissinger argues: "The emergence of a unified Europe is one of the most revolutionary events of our time."[1]

These developments are striking. Most Americans consider European defense cooperation more fiction than fact.[2] However, a significant amount of quantitative and qualitative evidence strongly suggests that EU states are gradually building a strong and integrated defense industrial base. This will likely have important implications for the future of the transatlantic relationship. It will also

---

[1] Henry Kissinger, *Does America Need a Foreign Policy? Toward a Diplomacy for the 21st Century* (New York: Simon & Schuster, 2001), 47.

[2] See, for example, John J. Mearsheimer, *The Tragedy of Great Power Politics* (New York: W.W. Norton, 2001), 360–402; Philip Gordon, "Europe's Uncommon Foreign Policy," *International Security* 22 (Winter 1997/98): 74–100; Robert J. Art, "Why Western Europe Needs the United States and NATO," *Political Science Quarterly* 111 (Spring 1996): 1–39; Robert Kagan, *Of Paradise and Power: America and Europe in the New World Order* (New York: Alfred A. Knopf, 2003).

SETH G. JONES is an adjunct professor in the Security Studies Program at Georgetown University and a political scientist at the RAND Corporation. He is the author most recently of *The Rise of European Security Cooperation* (Cambridge University Press).

have significant ramifications on the structure of the international system if Europe continues to become an integrated political, economic, and defense actor.

Why are European states increasingly collaborating in the defense industry? To answer the question, this article has two objectives. First, it argues that the changing structure of the international system explains the shift to intra-European collaboration in the post-Cold War era. During the Cold War, European states were primarily concerned about balancing the Soviet Union. They were more likely to collaborate on advanced weapons with the United States and U.S. firms than with each other. However, this changed at the end of the Cold War. In a unipolar international system, EU states led by Germany, France, and Britain have collaborated in the defense industry to increase their economic and defense power and decrease reliance on the United States. To be clear, the United States does not pose a military threat to Europe. Rather, European defense firms are motivated to collaborate in order to globally compete with the U.S. defense industry in terms of arms sales and spin-offs, as well as to lessen reliance on the United States for weapons. The 2003 U.S.-led war in Iraq only increased these trends.

Second, in order to test the argument, this article adopts two methodological approaches: it compiles a data set of defense mergers and acquisitions, coproduction projects, and codevelopment projects; and it uses a case study approach. It compiles and examines a data set of 478 cases of interstate collaboration involving European defense firms between 1961 and 2000. Of particular interest is identifying trends in the data over time. It also adopts a case study approach to understand the motivation of French, German, and British leaders. It examines primary and secondary sources, such as documents from the French procurement agency Délégation Ministérielle de l'Armement (DGA), German defense *White Papers*, British Ministry of Defence documents, and EU defense documents such as the *Strategic Aerospace Review for the 21st Century*.

The article is divided into five sections. First, it lays out states' procurement options and sketches the argument. Second, it briefly examines the defense production data. Third, it explores coproduction, codevelopment, and mergers and acquisitions (M&As) developments during the Cold War. Fourth, it analyzes changes in the European defense industry since the end of the Cold War. Fifth, it concludes by examining the future of the transatlantic relationship.

DEFENSE PROCUREMENT OPTIONS

National governments play the most important role in determining the shape of defense industries. Ministries of Defense are the only—or at least the major—buyers of weapons, and consequently are able to wield substantial power on the demand side of the market. This marks a strong contrast with most non-defense markets. Defense firms generally do not develop equipment and then attempt to sell it to their governments. Rather, governments and defense departments collect classified information about foreign capabilities and threats, devise a grand strategy to curb those threats, and then equip themselves accordingly. The influence of governments is particularly significant regarding transnational activity. For example, M&As involving foreign firms require the consent of the government to prevent the export of critical technologies or jobs. Arms exports require special permission to protect national security and ensure that they are consistent with foreign policy objectives. Governments may even wish to prevent the export of weapons or technology to allied countries because of concern that they will find their way to adversaries. In short, governments play the central role vis-a-vis transnational activity because of security concerns. These attributes make the defense market very different from conventional markets.[3]

State Options

States have three general options when procuring weapons and systems. They can develop and produce weapons domestically (autarky), purchase from abroad (foreign dependence), or cooperate in the development and production of weapons (collaboration) (Table 1).

First, states may choose *autarky*. They can design and produce weapons domestically, either through a nationalized defense industry or through private firms that are domestically owned. Realists have long noted that in an anarchic international system, states will prefer autarky and self-sufficiency to cooperation. "In a self-help system, considerations of security subordinate economic gain to political interest," Kenneth Waltz argues. "Defense spending, moreover, is unproductive for all and unavoidable for most. Rather than increased well-being, their reward is in the maintenance of their autonomy. States compete, but not by contributing their individual efforts to the joint production of goods for their mutual benefit."[4] Great powers have historically preferred autarky when procuring weapons because it ensures security of supply, sustains a strong defense industrial base, and maintains national technological capabilities.[5] Chinese leaders learned this when the USSR abruptly

---

[3] On defense economics, see Keith Hartley, *NATO Arms Co-operation: A Study in Economics and Politics* (London: Allen & Unwin, 1983); Todd Sandler and Keith Hartley, *The Political Economy of NATO: Past, Present, and Into the 21st Century* (New York: Cambridge University Press, 1999); Todd Sandler and Keith Hartley, *The Economics of Defense* (New York: Cambridge University Press, 1995); Gavin Kennedy, *The Economics of Defence* (London: Faber and Faber, 1975); Gavin Kennedy, *Defense Economics* (New York: St. Martin's Press, 1983); Frederic M. Scherer, *The Weapons Acquisition Process: Economic Incentives* (Boston, MA: Division of Research, Graduate School of Business at Harvard University, 1964).

[4] Kenneth Waltz, *Theory of International Politics* (New York: McGraw-Hill, 1979), 107.

[5] Trevor Taylor and Keith Hayward, *The UK Defence Industrial Base: Development and Future Policy Options* (Washington DC: Brassey's Defence Publishers, 1989), 67; Aaron L. Friedberg, *In the Shadow of the Garrison State: America's Anti-Statism and Its Cold War Grand Strategy* (Princeton, NJ: Princeton University Press, 2000), 245–295; E.H. Carr, *The Twenty Years' Crisis: 1919–1939* (New York: Harper & Row, 1964), 120–121.

TABLE 1

Summary of Procurement Options

Options	Characteristics
Autarky	Weapons are developed and produced domestically
Foreign Dependence	All or most weapons and technology imported
Collaboration	Weapons are developed and produced with foreign nations and defense firms. Can include M&As, coproduction, and codevelopment projects

cut off military aid in the early 1960s and Western countries imposed an arms embargo after the 1989 Tiananmen Square incident.

Second, at the other end of the spectrum, states may pursue a procurement policy of *foreign dependence*. Weaker states are generally forced to adopt a policy of foreign dependence because they lack the power to be autarkic. States need a substantial amount of resources, technology, and personnel to build weapons. This is particularly true in the modern era because the high cost of advanced weapons makes them either difficult or impossible for small powers to develop and produce on their own.[6] For example, research, development, and production costs of modern fighter aircraft can be exorbitant. Consider the Lockheed Martin Joint Strike Fighter, whose development and production costs are estimated to exceed $300 billion over twenty-five years.[7] Manufacturing complex modern weapon systems, such as combat aircraft and submarines, requires skill levels that only the most industrialized countries possess.[8] Third-world and many industrializing states simply do not have the money and resources necessary to build technologically advanced militaries, and consequently, they are dependent on foreign weapons and technology. For these states, foreign dependence may be most efficient because it allows them to devote scarce resources to commercial rather than defense industries.

---

[6] Edward A. Kolodziej, *Making and Marketing Arms: The French Experience and Its Implications for the International System* (Princeton, NJ: Princeton University Press, 1987), 141. On rising costs, see Hartley, *NATO Arms Co-operation*, 30; Michael Brzoska and Peter Lock, eds., "Restructuring of Arms Production in Western Europe: Introduction" in Michael Brzoska and Peter Lock, eds., *Restructuring of Arms Production in Western Europe* (New York: Oxford University Press, 1992), 4–5; Jacques Gansler, "Needed: A U.S. Defense Industrial Strategy," *International Security* 12 (Autumn 1987): 45–62.

[7] The Joint Strike Fighter estimates are based on 3,000 aircraft configured in conventional takeoff and landing (CTOL) variant, short takeoff and vertical landing (STOVL) variant, and carrier variant (CV). Target flyaway costs for each variant are approximately $28 million for the CTOL, $30–$35 million for the STOVL, and $31–$38 million for the CV in 1994 dollars. See John Birkler, et al., *Assessing Competitive Strategies for the Joint Strike Fighter: Opportunities and Options* (Santa Monica, CA: RAND, 2001), 2.

[8] Klauss Knorr, "Military Strength: Economic and Non-Economic Bases" in Klauss Knorr and Frank N. Trager, eds., *Economic Issues and National Security* (Lawrence: University Press of Kansas, 1982), 185.

Third, states may pursue a policy of transnational *collaboration*. This entails the design and production of weapons in cooperation with foreign nations and defense firms. There are at least three types of transnational collaboration:

- M&As—The merger with or outright purchase of a foreign defense firm. M&As generally include the purchase of company shares up to gaining majority control.
- Coproduction—Shared production and assembly of a weapon, class of weapons, or weapon part. Defense contractors from participant countries purchase the same equipment and jointly produce the weapon.
- Codevelopment—The joint design, engineering, and development of a weapon, class of weapons, or weapons part. Codevelopment involves two or more firms agreeing to a common requirement, sharing research and development costs, and combining national orders.

Why Defense Industry Collaboration?

Under what conditions will states pursue a strategy of multilateral defense collaboration? Significant interstate collaboration has been rare among great powers. However, the existence of a preponderant power such as the United States can create a strong impetus for weaker states to collaborate on defense production to increase power and decrease reliance.

I begin with the same assumptions as most realists. First, the international system is anarchic. This is an ordering principle; it does not mean that the international system is chaotic or disorderly. Rather, it means that there is no world government or authority above states to enforce agreements or guarantee security. Second, states can never know with 100 percent certainty the current and future intentions of others. There are limits to transparency and information sharing. States may have an incentive to misrepresent such information, and intentions can change. Third, states are rational actors. Policymakers are aware of their external environment, and they think strategically about how to survive in it. They are forward-looking and calculate the best means to ensure their own survival, given the actions and reactions of other states.[9]

Taken together, these assumptions mean that states care a great deal about power, especially the distribution of power. Power in this context refers to material capabilities, and particularly to military and economic assets. Power is important because it can make states more secure, and it can increase their

---

[9] Waltz, *Theory of International Politics*, 102–128; Hans J. Morgenthau, *Politics Among Nations: The Struggle for Power and Peace* (New York: Alfred A. Knopf, 1963), 3–15; Mearsheimer, *The Tragedy of Great Power Politics*, 31; Stephen M. Walt, *The Origins of Alliances* (Ithaca, NY: Cornell University Press, 1987), 17–49.

ability to influence, deter, and coerce others. Conversely, the absence of power decreases the ability of states to do these things, and makes them more reliant on those with greater power. Power is thus relative.[10] Weaker states have a strong incentive to increase their power and decrease reliance on more powerful states. Because power is the key means and end of states, the distribution of power in international and regional systems is an important causal variable. Historically, two distributions of power have existed: multipolarity and bipolarity. In the aftermath of the Cold War, the international system moved to yet another distribution of power: unipolarity. With the demise of the Soviet Union, the United States became the most powerful state in the international system. As Samuel Huntington argues, the shift to a unipolar international system has had a profound impact on international politics by triggering efforts to challenge America's economic and defense primacy.[11] Collaboration increases power by aggregating economic and defense resources, and decreases reliance on the preponderant state.

First, aggregating defense resources increases the military and economic power of weaker states. Because of their unrivaled position in the international system, preponderant states tend to feel few restraints. This increases their incentive to assert power around the globe.[12] Hans Morgenthau argued that "without a state of equilibrium among them, one element will gain ascendancy over the others" and "encroach upon their interests and rights."[13] In the defense industry, a preponderant state's defense firms are likely to have global power and reach in an open international trading system. It will try to expand its arms sales to foreign markets, pursue an arms monopoly, and thereby increase influence over others. These actions create a strong impetus for other states to combine power. By collaborating and pooling resources, weaker states can build more technologically advanced weapons and sell them abroad. Collaboration allows them to increase their competitiveness on the global arms market, especially relative to the dominant power. The cost can be high of failing to collaborate or build sufficient power through an autarkic strategy: weaker states and firms will lose market share and weaken their defense industrial base.

In a unipolar international system, U.S. economic and defense dominance has created a strong impetus for European states to collaborate to increase European economic and defense power. Collaboration increases the global power of European defense firms and allows them to compete more effectively with the United States in terms of arms sales and the spin-offs that defense

---

[10] Joseph M. Grieco, "Anarchy and the Limits of Cooperation: A Realist Critique of the Newest Liberal Institutionalism," *International Organization* 42 (Summer 1988): 485–507.

[11] Samuel P. Huntington, "Why Primacy Matters," *International Security* 17 (Spring 1993): 68–83.

[12] Robert Jervis, "The Compulsive Empire," *Foreign Policy* 137 (July/August 2003): 83–87.

[13] Morgenthau, *Politics Among Nations*, 169. Also see Hans Morgenthau and Kenneth Thompson, eds., *Principles and Problems of International Politics* (New York: Knopf, 1950), 104; Inis L. Claude, *Power and International Relations* (New York: Random House, 1962), 11–39.

industries can produce. To be clear, the United States does not pose a military threat to Europe. European states are not motivated to aggregate resources to contain an America that threatens their security through military conquest. Rather, as noted by John Rose, former chief executive of Rolls-Royce, European states and defense firms are collaborating in order to globally compete with the U.S. defense industry in terms of arms sales and spin-offs. "Competition for Europe's aerospace industry comes primarily from the US. The US industry is roughly twice the size in terms of employment and turnover. ... The need to strengthen R&D efforts at a European level and to coordinate with national programs is quite simply, essential."[14] Former General Electric Company director Arnold Weinstock similarly noted that European companies "have to respond to the changes in America. They are producing giant companies through these mergers. ... We have to form companies of sufficient size to compete effectively with them."[15] The cost of not collaborating is straightforward: European states could not compete with the United States on the global arms market. European defense companies might be reduced to second- or third-tier companies, or possibly face extinction.

Second, weaker states may aggregate power to decrease reliance on a preponderant state. The risk for weaker states is that a failure to aggregate power may create a reliance on the preponderant state for defense resources and lead to foreign dependence. Dependence decreases security of supply and compromises the viability of a state's defense industrial base. In general, reliance on a preponderant power for weapons and military resources decreases a state's security by placing its supply in the hands of someone else. This may be fine under most conditions. But can dependent states always rely on the preponderant power for spare parts and regular access? If weaker states do not collaborate and are unable to compete with the preponderant power by adopting an autarkic strategy, they will be forced into dependence. They will increasingly rely on the preponderant power for advanced weapons and systems, lose security of supply, and fail to maintain their technological capabilities. In short, the cost of not collaborating is greater dependence.

In Europe, collaboration decreases reliance on the United States and its defense industry. The concern among European states is that a failure to collaborate would raise Europe's reliance on the United States, which would have several implications. It would decrease the security of supply, especially for Europe's largest defense spenders—Germany, France, and Britain; weaken their industrial bases; and decrease their ability to develop cutting-edge technology. It might also increase the ability of the United States to cut off weapons

[14] John Rose, "New Structure, New Programmes, Bright Future," 4 July 1999, comment on the situation of the aerospace industry at the annual AECMA press conference, accessed at www.aecma.org/stats/speech, 21 April 2006.

[15] Bernard Gray, "Financial Strength Is the Issue Not Competition," *Financial Times*, 4 November 1991, 18.

or supplies in an emergency. This is particularly acute in some areas, such as global satellite navigation systems, in which the United States controls supply. As a European Commission report concluded: "There is a danger that European industry could be reduced to the status of sub-supplier to prime US contractors, while the key know-how is reserved for US firms."[16] If Europe does not aggregate defense resources, President Jacques Chirac warned, it risks "vassal status" to a preponderant United States.[17] As another European Commission document noted: "If the EU finds it necessary to undertake a security mission that the US does not consider to be in its interest, [the EU] will be impotent unless it has the satellite navigation technology that is now indispensable."[18]

The 1991 Persian Gulf War, 1995 war in Bosnia, and 1999 war in Kosovo were stark reminders that European countries were largely dependent on U.S. power to conduct even modest military operations. For example, the British House of Commons Defence Committee concluded in its report on the lessons of Kosovo that the operation demonstrated how reliant Europe was on U.S. power.[19] The British Ministry of Defence's document *European Defence* argued that Europe should develop its own regional defense capabilities: "As the lessons of Kosovo showed ... European nations need significantly to improve their military capabilities. They should not continue to depend so heavily on the United States in dealing with crises in and around Europe. Europe needs to improve its ability to act in circumstances where NATO is not engaged."[20]

[16] *Towards an EU Defence Equipment Policy*, COM (2003) 113 Final (Brussels: Commission of the European Communities, 2003), 11.

[17] Martin Fletcher, "Europe's Galileo Navigation System Puts US on the Spot," *Times,* 26 March 2002. On the U.S. and the European defense industries, also see Alain Richard, "European Defense" (speech at the Symposium of the Association Diplomatie et Defense, Washington DC, Embassy of France in the United States, 18 April 2001).

[18] Dee Ann Divis, "Military Role for Galileo Emerges," *GPS World* 13 (May 2002): 10. On the military uses of Galileo also see *Space: A New European Frontier for an Expanding Union* (Brussels: Commission of the European Communities, 2003); Michael A. Taverna, "European Union's New Space Role Could Help Meet Military Goals," *Aviation Week & Space Technology* 27 (November 2000): 29; "Military Pushes for Galileo," *Aviation Week & Space Technology*, 18 (February 2002): 28.

[19] *Lessons of Kosovo*, Fourteenth Report (London: Her Majesty's Stationery Office, 2000), para. 313. Also see Elizabeth Pond, "Kosovo: Catalyst for Europe," *Washington Quarterly* 22 (Autumn 1999): 77–92; Christopher Layne, "Death Knell for NATO? The Bush Administration Confronts the European Security and Defense Policy," *Policy Analysis* 4 (April 2001): 1–15; Mary Elise Sarotte, *German Military Reform and European Security*, Adelphi Paper 340 (London: International Institute for Strategic Studies, 2001), 54.

[20] *European Defence*, Paper No. 3 (London: Ministry of Defence, 2001). On British policymakers and the U.S./NATO commitment, also see Gilles Andreani, Christoph Bertram, and Charles Grant, *Europe's Military Revolution* (London: Centre for European Reform, 2001), 11; *Defense Policy 2001* (London: Her Majesty's Stationery Office, 2001), para. 19; Alister John Miskimmon, "Recasting the Security Bargains: Germany, European Security Policy and the Transatlantic Partnership," *German Politics* 10 (April 2001): 90.

If EU states and defense firms have aggregated resources in response to structural conditions, we should expect to see at least two things. First, we should see an increase in intra-European defense collaboration in the post-Cold War era. This should contrast with European collaboration during the Cold War, which should be transatlantic because balancing the Soviet Union was their primary focus. Second, intra-European collaboration should be causally linked with a desire to decrease reliance on the United States and increase their relative power and competitiveness. That is, European states would not take these actions if the United States—and U.S. defense firms—were not so powerful. To sum up, we should expect the following:

- During the Cold War, transnational weapons collaboration should largely be transatlantic rather than intra-European. Because the international system was bipolar, European states and defense firms should be primarily concerned about balancing the USSR and collaborating with the United States.
- During the post-Cold War era, transnational collaboration should largely be intra-European. Because the international system is unipolar, European states should be concerned about U.S. power and collaborate with each other.

THE DEFENSE PRODUCTION DATA

The next step is to examine the data on European weapons production. The Defense Budget Project's Globalization Database includes data on all cases ($N = 478$) of collaboration involving European defense firms between 1961 and 2000 in the following areas: M&As, coproduction projects, and codevelopment projects. Because we are particularly interested in examining trends in transnational weapons collaboration, the cases are divided into three categories: intra-European, European–U.S., and European–other. This allows us to see which firms European defense companies collaborated with.

First, *intra-European* includes transnational collaboration among defense firms from European Community (EC) and EU countries. Collaboration involving defense firms from such European countries as Switzerland were excluded if they were not members of the EC or EU, and were coded as "European–other." Examples of intra-European collaboration include cases of bilateral cooperation such as Thomson-CSF's (France) acquisition of Link-Miles (Britain) in the 1980s, as well as multilateral cooperation, such as German, Italian, and British cooperation in developing and producing the Tornado multi-role fighter aircraft in the 1970s. Second, *European–U.S.* involves collaboration between defense firms from the United States and EU countries. Examples include Raytheon's (U.S.) acquisition of Anschuetz (Germany) in the 1990s, as well as NATO collaboration on Seasparrow surface-to-air missiles in the 1960s. Third, *European–other* refers to bilateral and multilateral collaboration between defense firms from EU countries and other regions—Asia, Latin America, Africa, the Middle East, and Eastern Europe.

There are at least two limitations with the data. First, it does not include domestic M&As and coproduction and codevelopment projects. It might be interesting to know, for example, the total number of defense M&As within Germany between 1961 and 2000. This would allow us to examine how often German firms merged with or acquired other German firms, and to compare these figures with transnational M&As. Because the data does not include information on domestic activity, it has little to say about whether European states are becoming more or less interdependent. However, this is not a major problem; the primary focus of this article is on transnational defense cooperation. When European states and defense firms choose to collaborate abroad, with whom are they collaborating?

Second, the data does not include the monetary value of M&As and coproduction and codevelopment projects. Although it would be useful to have this information, much of it does not exist. For M&As in which both companies are private firms, there are no requirements to report specific information about the deal—including financial data. For M&As involving a combination of public and private firms, the likelihood that financial data will be publicly available varies, depending on the size of the M&A and company reporting practices. The data also does not include the value of coproduction and codevelopment projects. These values are not included, because they present enormous measurement problems. The total cost of transnational weapons and systems incorporates an amalgam of research, development, and production costs from multiple countries that span the life of the project. The data is often classified and unavailable. While it would be helpful to have the value of collaboration cases, it is not an insurmountable problem. Examining the number of cases and the motivations of European leaders should provide a fairly reliable picture of the European defense industry.

COLD WAR COOPERATION

As Figure 1 illustrates, European defense firms were more likely to collaborate with American defense firms on coproduction and codevelopment projects than with other European firms during the Cold War. In addition, European defense firms were more likely to consolidate with American than European firms through M&As. The reason is largely tied to the structure of the international system.

During the bipolar Cold War, European states were concerned about balancing the Soviet Union. They were more likely to cooperate with the United States to improve NATO interoperability and standardization in case of a war with the Soviet Union. The emerging parity in strategic forces between the United States and the USSR meant that NATO countries needed to rely on a coordinated military capability to meet a surprise Soviet attack. "West Berlin,

FIGURE 1
Cold War Defense Cooperation

Coproduction and Codevelopment Projects

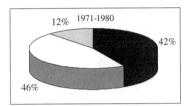
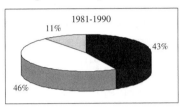

Mergers and Acquisitions

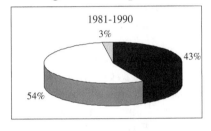

EU
EU–US
EU–Other

Source: Defense Budget Project's Globalization Database; thanks to Richard Bitzinger for providing access to the database.

which has frequently enough been subject to political pressure by the Soviet Union and her allies, is particularly vulnerable. It is under a permanent threat," argued Germany's 1970 *White Paper.* "The effectiveness of the Alliance is contingent upon the harmonization of military resources which, in turn, permits their coordinated employment in case of an emergency; national elements alone will not do."[21] In addition, transatlantic defense collaboration helped tie the United States to Europe. British leaders, for example, preferred a long-term U.S. commitment to Europe to balance Soviet power; European states were too weak to do it by themselves. The importance of collaboration with the United States was seconded by German, Dutch, Belgian, and a number of other European leaders.[22] To make U.S. promises more credible, this meant U.S. participation in collaborative defense projects, M&As, as well as the presence of U.S. military forces.

[21] *White Paper 1970: The Security of the Federal Republic of Germany and the Development of the Federal Armed Forces* (Bonn: Federal Minister of Defence, 1970), 20–21, 25.

[22] "Jebb to Younger, September 12, 1950," in Roger Bullen and M.E. Pelly, eds., *Documents on British Policy Overseas, 1950* Series II, Vol. III (London: Her Majesty's Stationery Office, 1986), 28–31; "Cabinet meeting held at 10 Downing Street, November 16, 1950" in Bullen and Pelly, eds., *Documents on British Policy Overseas,* 263–266. Also see, for example, Dirk U. Stikker, *Men of Responsibility: A Memoir* (New York: Harper & Row, 1965), 303–304; Paul-Henri Spaak, *The Continuing Battle: Memoirs of a European, 1936-1966* (London: Weidenfeld and Nicolson, 1971), 150; Konrad Adenauer, *Memoirs, 1945-53* (Chicago, IL: Henry Regnery, 1966), 320.

NATO Collaborative Projects

In 1949, NATO established a Military Production and Supply Board to co-ordinate production, standardization, and technical research in the weapons industry. After a number of modifications, this body became the Defense Production Committee in 1954 to supervise joint production programs and promote the standardization of weapons. In the late 1960s, NATO established the Conference of National Armaments Directors to promote trans-atlantic projects and exchange information on operational requirements and national equipment plans. The result of this collaboration included at least fourteen NATO projects by 1976, such as the Jaguar and Tornado air-craft, the Milan missile, and the rolling airframe missile (RAM) air defense system. Other examples included German-American codevelopment of the RAM air defense system and British–American codevelopment of the Harrier fighter aircraft.

In France, limited NATO codevelopment and coproduction projects were supported by the French government to counter Soviet military power.[23] The government's *Délégation Ministérielle de l'Armement* (DGA) was responsible for defense procurement, industrial liaison, and equipment collaboration, and largely determined the shape of the French defense industry. As Army General Guy Méry argued, NATO cooperation in a war with the Soviet Union "would pose a certain number of problems which we are trying to solve gradually." One of the most significant was the "problem of differences in procedures, equipment and tactical methods, which leads us to seek a certain interoper-ability of forces and to carry out exercises with Allied forces which are also extremely beneficial for training our own units."[24] Examples of French involve-ment in transatlantic cooperation included the Multiple Launch Rocket Sys-tem, a mobile automatic all-weather system used as NATO's standard rocket; the NH-90, a multi-role medium helicopter designed as NATO's he-licopter for the 1990s; and the CFM turbofan engine, produced jointly by France's Société Nationale d'Etude et de Construction de Moteurs d'Aviation (SNECMA) and the U.S.'s General Electric and used to power the KC-135 refueling tanker.[25]

---

[23] On French armaments policy, see Marc Cauchie, "Coopération internationale dans le domaine des armements," *Défense Nationale* 36 (June 1980): 25–42; Marc Defourneaux, "France and a Euro-pean Armament Policy," *NATO Review* 5 (September–October 1979): 19–25; Marc Defourneaux, "Indépendence nationale et coopération internationale en matière d'armements," *Défense Nationale* 35 (February 1979): 35–48; Marc Defourneaux, "Coopération et indépendance technologique," *Dé-fense Nationale* 39 (March 1983): 105–118.

[24] General Guy Méry, "Une armée pour quoi faire et comment?" *Défense Nationale* 32 (June 1976): 17. Also see General Guy Méry, "French Defence Policy," *Survival* 18 (September/October 1976): 227.

[25] For the MLRS, see *Jane's Weapons Systems, 1987-88* (London: Jane's Information Group, 1988), 128–129. For the NH-90, see *Jane's All the World's Aircraft, 2002-2003* (London: Jane's Information Group, 2003), 255–258. For the CFM turbofan engine, see *Jane's Aero-Engines* (London: Jane's Information Group, 2002).

British leaders were also willing to pursue limited transatlantic collaboration in weapons procurement to improve NATO power and efficiency. British Secretary of State for Defence Roy Mason argued that the advantage of weapons collaboration was substantial.[26] This view dovetailed with Britain's grand strategy during the Cold War, which supported NATO cooperation as one of the country's fundamental security tenets. As the 1970 *Supplementary Statement on Defence Policy* argued: "The security of Britain rests on the strength of the North Atlantic Alliance. The maintenance and improvement of our military contribution to NATO remains the first priority of our defence policy."[27] Britain's involvement in transatlantic collaboration during the Cold War included a number of projects, such as joint production of the Sky Flash/AIM-7 medium-range air-to-air missile; the advanced short-range air-to-air missile (ASRAAM); and the AV-8B Harrier attack and reconnaissance aircraft. All three involved close cooperation with American defense firms: Raytheon with the Sky Flash, Hughes with the ASRAAM, and McDonnell Douglas with the Harrier. British defense officials argued that procurement collaboration along transatlantic lines was important to increasing economic and military efficiency, and they were primarily responsible for pushing transatlantic cooperation.

In West Germany, NATO cooperation was particularly important because West Berlin was a major point of contention between the United States and the USSR. West Germany's geographic location meant that a conventional war between NATO and Warsaw Pact countries would likely be fought on its soil.[28] "The armament of the Bundeswehr is determined by its mission within the Alliance," noted the 1971/1972 *White Paper*.[29] German defense officials pursued coproduction and codevelopment projects within the context of NATO to increase the alliance's military power and fighting effectiveness.[30] Consequently, West Germany was involved in transatlantic coproduction and codevelopment projects during the Cold War. Germany's Ministry of Defense and its procurement agency, the Bundesamt für Wehrtechnik und Beschaffung, were largely responsible for selecting, approving, and overseeing transnational collaboration projects—not German defense firms.[31] Notable examples in-

[26] Roy Mason, "Setting British Defence Priorities," *Survival* 17 (September/October 1975): 221–222.

[27] *Supplementary Statement on Defence Policy*, Cmnd. 4521 (London: Her Majesty's Stationery Office, 1970).

[28] Marc Trachtenberg, *A Constructed Peace: The Making of the European Settlement, 1945-1963* (Princeton, NJ: Princeton University Press, 1999).

[29] *White Paper 1971/1972: The Security of the Federal Republic of Germany and the Development of the Federal Armed Forces* (Bonn: Federal Minister of Defence, 1971/1972), 149–150. Also see the *White Paper 1973/1974: The Security of the Federal Republic of Germany and the Development of the Federal Armed Forces* (Bonn: Federal Minister of Defence, 1973/1974), 179.

[30] *White Paper 1985: The Situation and Development of the Federal Armed Forces* (Bonn: Federal Minister of Defence, 1985), 367.

[31] Regina H.E. Cowen, *Defense Procurement in the Federal Republic of Germany: Politics and Organization* (Boulder, CO: Westview Press, 1986).

cluded development of the Seasparrow surface-to-air missile, a joint NATO project to provide ships with an effective surface-to-air anti-missile defense. It also included the RAM air defense system, designed by the United States and Germany to enable surface ships to engage incoming anti-ship cruise missiles.

Transatlantic Mergers and Acquisitions

Transnational M&As also tended to be transatlantic rather than intra-European during the Cold War. Despite Charles de Gaulle's establishment of a nuclear *force de frappe* and partial withdrawal from NATO, French leaders believed that cooperation with NATO was important to balance against the Soviet Union. General Michel Fourquet, chief of staff of the armed forces, noted in March 1969 that a Soviet conventional attack from the east would require a coordinated response from NATO countries: "Engaged along the northern and eastern borders against an enemy coming from the East, the [French] force will normally act in close coordination with the forces of our allies."[32] One aspect of NATO cooperation involved transatlantic M&As. For example, Thomson-CSF acquired such U.S. defense firms in the 1980s as Ocean Defense Corporation, which manufactured helicopter sonar and equipment for antisubmarine warfare, and Wilcox Electric, which produced microwave landing systems. In the aerospace industry, a series of domestic and transatlantic mergers established Dassault-Breguet as one of NATO's primary producers of military aircraft, including the Mirage series of fighter aircraft and the Atlantique reconnaissance aircraft.

In Britain, there were a limited number of transnational M&As during the Cold War, and most were transatlantic. Examples of transatlantic M&As involving British firms included British Aerospace's acquisition of such U.S. firms as Nanoquest, Sperry Gyroscope, Reflectone, and Steinheil Optronics. Furthermore, Plessey acquired several U.S. firms, such as Electronic Systems Division, Leigh Instruments, Nash Engineering, Sippican, and Singer Electronics. In the wake of British Prime Minister Margaret Thatcher's decision to privatize the British defense industry in the 1980s, firms such as British Aerospace "were encouraged to adopt an international orientation," especially among NATO countries.[33] Transatlantic M&As were acceptable because they facilitated NATO's fighting effectiveness.

In West Germany, transatlantic defense consolidation through M&As was important because of the Soviet threat. "The military aim is the [NATO]

---

[32] See General Michel Fourquet, "Emploi des différents systèmes de forces dans le cadre de la stratégie de dissuasion," *Revue de défense nationale*, 25 (May 1969): 757–767. On French military independence, also see the "Loi de Programme 1971-1975" in Dominique David, ed., *La politique de défense de la france: Textes et documents* (Paris: Fondation Pour les Etudes de Défense Nationale, 1989).

[33] Trevor Taylor, "The British Restructuring Experience" in Brzoska and Lock, eds., *Restructuring of Arms Production*, 87.

standardization of military equipment and procedures," argued the 1984 German *White Paper*.[34] Consequently, the German government encouraged some transatlantic M&A activity during the Cold War. For instance, Daimler-Benz acquired the industrial automation systems division of the U.S. firm Gould, and Siemens acquired U.S. defense firms Bendix and Cardion.[35]

In sum, European codevelopment, coproduction, and M&A behavior during the Cold War is explained by the structure of the international system. There was less intra-European collaboration during the Cold War, because European states were primarily concerned about balancing the USSR through NATO. As one study in 1977 rather bluntly concluded: "Despite a number of successful joint projects involving two or sometimes three countries, all attempts so far to produce a sustained and collective European effort have failed."[36]

THE RISE OF EUROPE

The structural shift from bipolarity to unipolarity caused a notable shift in the European defense industry. As Figure 2 illustrates, there has been a substantial increase in intra-European codevelopment and coproduction weapons projects in the post-Cold War era. This marks a stark contrast from the Cold War. The percentage of intra-European projects increased from 42 percent and 43 percent in the 1970s and 1980s, respectively, to 57 percent in the 1990s. European defense firms have been almost twice as likely to pursue coproduction and codevelopment projects with each other than with U.S. firms, and over three times more likely than with defense firms from other regions. In addition, there has been a substantial increase in intra-European defense mergers and acquisitions in the post-Cold War era. The percentage of intra-European M&As increased from 43 percent in the 1980s to 55 percent in the 1990s, and the percentage of EU–US M&As decreased from 55 percent in the 1980s to 32 percent in the 1990s. European defense firms have been nearly twice as likely to pursue M&As with each other than with American defense firms, and nearly three times as likely to pursue M&As with each other than with firms from other regions.

The changing structure of the international system explains the shift to intra-European defense cooperation. In a unipolar system, European Union states led by Germany, France, and Britain have collaborated in the defense industry to decrease reliance on the United States and to increase their own economic and defense power. To be clear, European states are not pursuing neorealist balance-of-power politics; the United States does not present a military threat to Europe. Rather, collaboration decreases reliance on the United States and its defense

[34] *White Paper 1985*, 360.

[35] See, for example, "Gould to Sell Unit to AEG," *New York Times*, 3 May 1988; Michael Farr, "A 'Sleeping Giant' Goes Global," *New York Times*, 12 December 1988.

[36] D.C.R. Heyhoe, *The Alliance and Europe: Part VI, The European Programme Group*, Adelphi Paper 129 (London: International Institute for Strategic Studies, 1976/1977), 1.

FIGURE 2
Post-Cold War Defense Cooperation

Coproduction and Codevelopment Projects

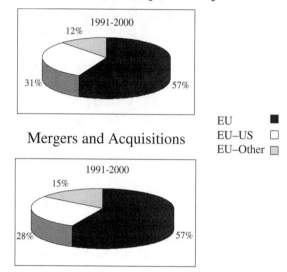

Mergers and Acquisitions

Source: Defense Budget Project's Globalization Database; thanks to Richard Bitzinger for providing access to the database.

industry, and ensures that European states have autonomous military capabilities. In addition, collaboration increases the global power of European defense firms and allows them to compete more effectively with the United States in such areas as arms sales and the spin-offs that defense industries can produce.

Creating Fortress Europe

The structural shift from bipolarity to unipolarity caused a notable shift in the procurement behavior of European states. Although most coproduction and codevelopment projects during the Cold War were transatlantic and geared toward NATO cooperation, there was a substantial increase in the number and percentage of intra-European projects in the 1990s. In the absence of the Soviet threat, EU states became increasingly concerned about U.S. dominance of the arms market. British and French leaders concluded at the 1998 St. Malo summit: "The European Union needs to be in a position to play its full role on the international stage. ... To this end, the Union must have the capacity for *autonomous* action, backed up by credible military forces, the means to decide to use them and a readiness to do so, in order to respond to international crises."[37]

---

[37] Text of a joint statement by the British and French governments, Franco-British summit, St. Malo, France, 4 December 1998. Emphasis added.

The risk of not collaborating was high. The European Advisory Group on Aerospace, which included such participants as the EU High Representative for Common Foreign and Security Policy and European aerospace industry chairmen, argued in a report titled *Strategic Aerospace Review for the 21st Century* that the failure to pursue intra-European collaboration would lead to U.S. dominance of the European arms market. "Unless Europe maintains these capabilities and develops them further," it contended, "there is a real risk that Europe's ability to act will be determined by the US through its dominance over the supply of certain types of equipment, or support to systems already delivered."[38] A similar report concluded that "there is a danger that European industry could be reduced to the status of sub-supplier to prime US contractors, while the key know-how is reserved for US firms."[39]

In France, the DGA played the central role in pushing for intra-European collaboration. As laid out in its yearly *Rapport d'activité*, the DGA argued that collaboration was important to increasing European power and military effectiveness.[40] The power of the U.S. defense industry also provided a critical impetus. As the Ministry of Defense's *Projet de loi* explained: "[The U.S.'s] global intention demands a massive reinforcement of the defense effort, which in turn benefits research and development of new defense systems, increasing the technological and military gulf between Europe and the United States." In response to U.S. power, it continued, France and Europe needed to "include an increase in defense effort" in such areas as weapons production.[41] This made projects such as the Galileo global navigation satellite system important so that, in the words of France's transport minister, "the European Union [could] liberate itself from dependence on the American GPS system."[42] Consequently, the DGA worked closely with the governments of Britain and Germany to coordinate long-term procurement planning, future preparedness, and research and technology.[43] Examples of French involvement in intra-European projects in the post-Cold War era included Galileo, the 140-mm tank gun, the PAAMS main missile system, the Europatrol combat ship, the MU-90 torpedo, and the Horizon frigate.

In Britain, Ministry of Defence officials also pushed for intra-European collaboration to build economic and military power. As the Ministry of De-

---

[38] European Advisory Group on Aerospace, "Strategic Aerospace Review for the 21st Century: Creating a Coherent Market and Policy Framework for a Vital European Industry" in Burkhard Schmitt, ed., *European Armaments Cooperation: Core Documents*, Chaillot Paper 59 (Paris: Institute for Security Studies, 2003), 152.

[39] *Towards an EU Defence Equipment Policy*, COM (2003) 113 Final (Brussels: Commission of the European Communities, 2003), 11.

[40] *Rapport d'activité 2000* (Paris: Délégation générale pour l'armement, 2000), 38.

[41] *Projet de loi de programmation militaire 2003-2008* (Paris: Ministère de la Défense, 2002).

[42] Ian Black, "European Satellite Plan Ruffles US Feathers," *Guardian*, 27 March 2002, 17; Thomas Fuller, "EU Positions Its Challenge to GPS," *International Herald Tribune*, 27 March 2002, 1.

[43] *Rapport d'activité 2001* (Paris: Délégation générale pour l'armement, 2001), 48–51.

fence's *Defence Industrial Policy* argued: "The US is the most important creator of new defence technology, and there is an increasing disparity between its defence spending and that of Europe." In response to U.S. power and to the U.S. government's establishment of barriers to entry into its defense market, the British Ministry of Defence argued that "there are significant potential benefits to be gained from a better functioning European market, a more efficient supplier base, and better prioritization of research and technology budgets in Europe."[44] Although British policymakers supported transatlantic collaboration during the Cold War, and have engaged in some projects with U.S. firms, they have favored European codevelopment and coproduction projects in the post-Cold War era. Ministry of Defence documents have been explicit about this.[45] Examples of British involvement in intra-European weapons collaboration included the Storm Shadow land attack cruise missile, the MRAV armored vehicle, and the Europatrol maritime patrol aircraft.

German leaders likewise advocated European procurement cooperation to aggregate power, and they pushed for greater intra-European collaboration.[46] As former German Chancellor Gerhard Schroder argued:

> Europe would not have an internationally successful aircraft industry had not some countries shown the will to challenge US dominance. Airbus's success shows the importance of setting strategic priorities. Galileo, the European satellite system agreed at the recent Barcelona European summit, is another such example. In short, Europe needs to become better at pooling resources and working towards a strategic vision.[47]

German Ministry of Defense documents have explicitly argued that intra-European weapons collaboration is critical to improving European economic and military power—particularly in light of the creation of a Common Foreign and Security Policy and a European Security and Defense Policy.[48] The army report *Bundeswehr 2002: Sachstund und Perspektiven* contends that European weapons cooperation is an integral part of the Common Foreign and Security Policy and "occupies a key position in the efforts to consolidate the political unification of Europe."[49] Indeed, Germany has been one of the strongest supporters of European armaments collaboration, and German de-

---

[44] *Defence Industrial Policy*, Paper No. 5 (London: Ministry of Defence, 2002), 9.

[45] See, for example, *European Defence Policy*, Paper No. 3 (London: Her Majesty's Stationery Office, 2001); *The Defence White Paper, 1999*, Cmnd. 4446 (London: Her Majesty's Stationery Office, 1999), para. 99–103; *The Strategic Defence Review, 1998*, Cmnd. 3999 (London: Her Majesty's Stationery Office, 1998), para. 162–168.

[46] See, for example, Mary Elise Sarotte, *German Military Reform and European Security*, Adelphi Paper 340 (London: International Institute for Strategic Studies, 2001), 48–52.

[47] Gerhard Schroder, "Shaping Industry on the Anvil of Europe," *Financial Times*, 29 April 2002, 21.

[48] *The Bundeswehr—Advancing Steadily into the 21st Century* (Berlin: The Federal Minister of Defence, 2000), para. 48; *White Paper 1994* (Bonn: Federal Minister of Defence, 1994), para. 594.

[49] *Bundeswehr 2002: Sachstand und Perspektiven* (Berlin: Bundesministerium der Verteidigung, 2002), 22.

fense firms have been involved in almost every major coproduction and co-development project in the post-Cold War era. Examples include the Galileo global navigation satellite system, the Eurofighter combat aircraft, the Taurus precision-guided weapon, the A400M strategic lift, and the Trigate anti-tank guided missile.

In addition, two projects neatly illustrate how the changing structure of the international system created a strong incentive for intra-European collaboration: Galileo and the A400M strategic lift.

European governments began development of the Galileo global navigation satellite system in the late 1990s to aggregate power and decrease reliance on the United States.[50] European governments could have continued relying on the U.S.'s global positioning system (GPS) for navigation, but they became increasingly concerned about the security of supply. "Only the USA (GPS) and Russia (Glonass) currently have this technology, both being financed for military purposes, with the result that the signals can be blocked or jammed at any moment to protect these countries' own interests," noted a European Commission's *White Paper* on European transport policy. "This happened during the Kosovo war, when the United States cut the GPS signal. ... Europe cannot afford to be totally dependent on third countries in such strategic areas."[51] Consequently, in 1999, European governments began development of Galileo, which is composed of thirty satellites and ground stations that provide information on the positioning of users in such sectors as defense and transport.

European governments agreed to develop and produce the A400M strategic transport plane in the late 1990s to facilitate the undertaking of European military operations. In the early 1990s, policymakers initiated a study of alternative options for replacing their aging fleets of C-130 Hercules and C-160 Transall strategic transport planes. One possibility was to purchase Boeing C-17s and updated Lockheed Martin C-130s, but European military leaders did not want to rely on the United States for security of supply. Consequently, the armaments directors of several European countries—including France, Germany, and Britain—began a series of feasibility studies to develop a European transport plane. In June of 2001, they signed a memorandum of understanding to develop the A400M because "it generates the necessary potential for harmonizing operational and support arrangements" and "paves the way for greater task sharing in meeting European military air transport demands."[52] The A400M was specifically designed for European operations to

---

[50] On Galileo and transatlantic relations, see David Braunschvig, Richard L. Garwin, and Jeremy C. Marwell, "Space Diplomacy," *Foreign Affairs* 82 (July/August 2003): 156–164.

[51] *White Paper—European Transport Policy for 2010: Time to Decide* (Luxembourg: Office for Official Publications of the European Communities, 2001), 94–95. Also see *Inception Study to Support the Development of a Business Plan for the GALILEO Programme*, TREN/B5/23-2001 (Brussels: PricewaterhouseCoopers, 2001).

[52] "Press release for the signature ceremony of the A400M program," 19 June 2001, Ministère de la défense de la France, accessed at www.defense.gouv.fr, 21 April 2006.

include all equipment—such as European armored vehicles, missile systems, helicopters, and trucks—likely to be needed for joint rapid reaction forces.[53] In sum, European governments were the primary proponents of the A400M because it decreased reliance on the United States and increased EU power.

In addition, in 2004, the European Council established the European Defense Agency to improve European military capabilities, consolidate defense research and technology, and promote armaments cooperation. It is leading or managing several current initiatives:

- UAVs and ISTAR—Developing technology demonstration work on long-endurance unmanned aerial vehicles (UAVs), in the context of the development of wider intelligence, surveillance, target acquisition, and reconnaissance (ISTAR) capabilities.
- Command, control, and communication—Finding solutions to current European Security and Defense Policy operational shortfalls and developing capacity and interoperability for the future.
- Armored fighting vehicles—Developing proposals for collaborative technology development and procurement programs based on a review of future requirements and the relevant technological and industrial base.
- Commercial and military off-the-shelf equipment—Developing proposals for a European market in commercial off-the-shelf/military off-the-shelf equipment, including a feasibility study of an "electronic market place."[54]

The Race for Critical Mass

The structural shift from bipolarity to unipolarity at the end of the Cold War also marked a significant shift in European M&A activity. European states adopted a procurement policy that stressed intra-European collaboration in the post-Cold War era to decrease reliance on the United States and increase European power abroad. As one study concluded, in the post-Cold War era, "the perception of an American 'threat' was widespread in politico-industrial circles in Europe. ... Faced with the new American giants, national champions in Europe were obliged to launch into a race for critical mass."[55] Perhaps the most significant example was the creation of the European Aeronautic, Defense, and Space (EADS) company. It included the merger of Germany's Daimler-

[53] "Hoon Welcomes Progress on A400M," December 18, 2001, accessed at www.mod.uk/dpa/pressoffice, 21 April 2006.

[54] Council Joint Action on the Establishment of the European Defense Agency, 2004/551/CFSP, 12 July 2004; *Agency in the Field of Defense Capabilities Development, Research, Acquisition, and Armaments* (Brussels: Council of the European Union, 2004); *EDA Work Programme for 2005* (Brussels: European Council, 2004); Nick Witney, "Closing the Capability Gap: The EDA's Role as Catalyst and Coordinator" (presentation at the Royal Institute for International Affairs, London, 6 December 2004).

[55] Burkard Schmitt, *From Cooperation to Integration: Defense and Aerospace Industries in Europe* (Paris: Institute for Security Studies, 2000), 25–26.

Chrysler Aerospace, Spain's Construcciones Aeronáuticas SA, and France's Aérospatiale Matra. Again, national governments played a pivotal role in pushing for a transnational European weapons industry. European defense firms were almost twice as likely to pursue M&As with each other than with American firms, and nearly three times as likely than with firms from other regions.

A significant part of this rationale was the creation of several giant and globally competitive U.S. defense firms. The U.S. defense industry consolidated in the early 1990s and produced a number of firms led by Lockheed Martin and Boeing that threatened to dominate the global arms market and jeopardize other states' security of supply. During what has been referred to as the "Last Supper," Secretary of Defense Les Aspin and Deputy Secretary William Perry invited a small number of defense industry executives to dinner at the Pentagon in 1993. After the dinner, Aspin and Perry announced that at least half the companies at the dinner would not be needed in five years, and warned that the Department of Defense was ready to see some firms exit the market. Because the U.S. defense budget was steadily decreasing in the wake of the Soviet collapse, U.S. government leaders pushed for consolidation to increase efficiency in the U.S. defense market and augment greater global competitiveness. Lockheed acquired the Fort Worth division of General Dynamics in 1993 and then merged with the missile manufacturer Martin Marietta in 1995 to form Lockheed Martin. Grumman was salvaged from near bankruptcy and acquired by Northrop in 1994. Boeing purchased McDonnell Douglas.[56] By the late 1990s, Lockheed Martin and Boeing were the dominant arms-producing firms in the world, with arms sales of $18.5 billion and $14.5 billion, respectively.[57] Furthermore, U.S. defense firms were the most technologically advanced in the world, and, as one scholar warned: "For the first time in modern history, one country [was] on the verge of monopolizing the international arms trade."[58]

U.S. consolidation in the 1990s caused deep concern in European capitals. As Thomas Enders, then CEO of defense and security systems at EADS, argued: "By 1996, in view of the mega-mergers in the US, it was clear to European industry leaders that national consolidation and joint ventures were inadequate counters to the competitive challenge being posed by US industry."[59]

---

[56] Erik Pages, "Defense Mergers" in Ann R. Markusen and Sean S. Costigan, eds., *Arming the Future: A Defense Industry for the 21st Century* (New York: Council on Foreign Relation, 1999), 207–223; Michael Oden, "Cashing In, Cashing Out, and Converting" in Markusen and Costigan, eds., *Arming the Future*, 74–105.

[57] *SIPRI Yearbook 1999: Armaments, Disarmament and International Security* (New York: Oxford University Press, 1999), 413.

[58] Ethan B. Kapstein, "America's Arms-Trade Monopoly," *Foreign Affairs* 73 (May/June 1994): 13. Also see Jens Van Scherpenberg, "Transatlantic Competition and European Defence Industries: A New Look at the Trade-Defence Linkage," *International Affairs* 73 (January 1997): 99–122.

[59] Thomas Enders, "Defense Industry Restructuring and the Implications of ESDI/DCI" (paper presented at the XVIIth International Workshop: On Political-Military Decision Making in the Atlantic Alliance, Berlin, Germany, 2–5 June 2000).

In a December 1997 message to European defense firms, French President Jacques Chirac, British Prime Minister Tony Blair, and German Chancellor Helmut Kohl argued that they shared "a vital political and economic interest in an efficient and globally competitive European aerospace industry. This [would] help to improve Europe's position in the global market, to promote European security, and ensure that Europe [would] play a full role in its defense." One important step in this direction, they contended, was consolidation of the defense industry along European lines: "We are agreed on the urgent need to restructure the aerospace and defense electronics industries. This should embrace civil and military activities in the field of aerospace, and should lead to European integration based on balanced partnership."[60] A year later, the defense ministers of France, Germany, Britain, Italy, Spain, and Sweden signed the Letter of Intent to facilitate the restructuring of the European defense industry.[61] Furthermore, the European Advisory Group on Aerospace argued, in its *Strategic Aerospace Review for the 21st Century*, of the critical need to compete with the United States:

> As regards international competition, US companies operate in the world's single largest home market and benefit from a highly supportive operation framework which is designed to underpin a declared policy aim to maintain US supremacy in aerospace. ... This situation poses a constant challenge to European industry and cannot but affect its competitive position. ... Within Europe major restructuring has taken place in recent years, leading to an industry organized on a European scale, as a competitor and partner of its powerful US counterpart.[62]

As Table 2 highlights, by 2005, Europe had four of the top ten largest defense firms in the world: BAE Systems, Thales, EADS, and Finmeccanica. This marked a notable change from 1993, when Europe had only two of the top ten firms.

In France, the DGA played the central role in encouraging defense industry consolidation along European lines. As laid out in its *Rapport d'activité*, the DGA argued that intra-European defense consolidation had occurred "with the encouragement of heads of State and government" to aggregate European power.[63] The power and impetus to pursue European consolidation

---

[60] "Joint Statement by the President of the Republic and the French Prime Minister, the Chancellor of the Federal Republic of Germany, and the Prime Minister of the United Kingdom," 9 December 1997. Published in Burkard Schmitt, ed., *Between Cooperation and Competition: The Transatlantic Defence Market* (Paris: Institute for Security Studies, 2001), 144.

[61] "Letter of Intent between the Minister of Defense of the French Republic, the Federal Minister of Defense of the Republic of Germany, the Minister of Defense of the Republic of Italy, the Minister of Defense of the Kingdom of Spain, the Minister of Defense of the Kingdom of Sweden, and the Secretary of State for Defense of the United Kingdom of Great Britain and Northern Ireland Concerning Measures to Facilitate the Restructuring of the European Defense Industry," 6 July 1998. Schmitt, ed., *Between Cooperation and Competition*, 146, 149.

[62] "Strategic Aerospace Review for the 21st Century," 131.

[63] *Rapport d'activité 2000*, 43.

TABLE 2

Top Ten Largest Arms-producing Companies, 2005

Company	Country	Arms Sales (US$ Million)
Lockheed Martin	United States	24,910
Boeing	United States	24,370
Northrop Grumman	United States	22,720
BAE Systems	UK	15,760
Raytheon	United States	15,450
General Dynamics	United States	13,100
Thales	France	8,350
EADS	France, Germany, Spain	8,010
United Technologies	United States	6,210
Finmeccanica	Italy	5,290

Source: SIPRI Yearbook 2005: Armaments, Disarmament and International Security (New York: Oxford University Press, 2005).

came from the government, which held shares in several major defense firms, such as Dassault and SNECMA, and exercised decisive clout.[64] French Prime Minister Lionel Jospin noted, following the creation of EADS, that "in view of the formation of very large-scale international groups, particularly American ones, it was becoming vitally important to group together the European forces."[65] Examples of French involvement in intra-European M&As included Thomson-CSF's acquisition of the defense electronics business of the Philips group and the British firm Racal Electronics. Other examples included SNECMA's acquisition of the Belgian firm FN Moteurs, the Norwegian firm Norsk Jet Motors, and British TI Group's landing gear business. In short, as French Defense Minister Alain Richard summed up, intra-European defense consolidation increased Europe's ability "to gain shares in a highly competitive market."[66]

British Ministry of Defence documents in the post-Cold War era also noted the desire to increase power. The 1999 *White Paper*, for example, stated that the governments of France, Germany, Italy, Spain, and Sweden were coordinating policies to develop a consistent approach to restructuring in order to harmonize European military requirements.[67] Furthermore, it argued that European consolidation would lead to greater military effectiveness. British

[64] See the comments by Philippe Humbert, Vice President for International Development of SNECMA, in *European Defense Industrial Consolidation: Implications for U.S. Industry and Policy* (Washington DC: Center for Strategic and International Studies, 2001), 8. Also see Frédérique Sachwald, *Defence Industry Restructuring: The End of an Economic Exception* (Paris: Institut Francais des relations internationals, 1999), 45.

[65] "Jospin: Aerospatiale Matra-DASA Merger 'Powerful Tool,'" *Paris AFP*, 14 October 1999.

[66] Alain Richard, "European Defense" (speech given at the Annual Defence Dinner of the London Chamber of Commerce and Industry, London, 17 May 2001).

[67] *White Paper 1999* (London: Ministry of Defence, 1999), para. 100.

Aerospace (renamed BAE Systems in 1999) was particularly active, acquiring a number of European companies, such as Heckler & Koch (Germany), a 30 percent stake in Saab (Sweden), and Muiden Chemie (Netherlands).

In Germany, defense officials advocated European M&As as a way to increase power.[68] The establishment of the transnational EADS in 1999 left Germany with *no major domestic defense company*. Rheinmetall, which produced ammunition and other defense equipment, was Germany's largest national firm measured in arms sales. That placed it twenty-third among firms from the Organisation for Economic Cooperation and Development and developing countries, well behind Europe's major defense giants such as British Aerospace, EADS, and France's Thales.[69] As German Defense Minister Rudolf Scharping argued, European governments had taken "major steps to establish new political and military structures and [to] develop more effective military capabilities for the full range of conflict prevention and crisis management tasks defined in the EU Treaty." One of the most important steps, he continued, was "the intensification of co-operation with the European defense industry, with the merger of DASA, Aerospatiale and CASA to form EADS lending the key impetus."[70]

Indeed, two M&A examples highlight the desire of EU states to aggregate resources to decrease reliance on the United States and increase European power. First, the establishment of EADS in 2000 was a significant step toward defense consolidation in creating a transnational European defense giant capable of competing with U.S. firms Boeing and Lockheed Martin. It could also produce a variety of advanced armaments, such as the Eurofighter combat aircraft, Eurocopter, A400M transport aircraft, and strategic weapons. As EADS joint executive chairmen Rainer Hertrich and Philippe Camus acknowledged: "Let us dare to assert it: EADS has, right at its birth, the scale of a European Boeing."[71] Moreover, French Defense Minister Alain Richard and Economy Minister Laurent Fabius jointly noted that the establishment of EADS "goes in line with the European policy promoting an autonomous defense industry that is globally competitive."[72]

Following the December 1997 declaration by French, German, and British leaders for regional consolidation, government and industry negotiations commenced regarding the creation of a European defense company. The defense ministers of Britain, France, Germany, Italy, Spain, and Sweden asked

---

[68] Martin Agüera, "German Arms Exporters Eye Mergers for Survival," *Defense News*, 17–23 September 2001, 32.

[69] *SIPRI Yearbook 2005: Armaments, Disarmament and International Security Studies* (New York: Oxford University Press, 2005), 406–407.

[70] Rudolf Scharping, "Euro-Atlantic Security and Regional Stability in the 21st Century" (Eisenhower lecture, NATO Defense College in Rome, 11 January 2000).

[71] Rainer Hertrich and Philippe Camus, "EADS or the Ambition to Make Europe Win," *Le Monde*, 8 June 2000.

[72] "Europe to Create World No. 2 Missiles Firm," *Xinhua General News Service*, 27 April 2001.

several of Europe's major defense companies to submit a series of reports in March and November of 1998 outlining plans for the creation of a European aerospace and defense company.[73] The successive reports submitted by industry officials argued that the target should be a single, integrated European company that could produce weapons in a number of key defense sectors. Although the British government placed substantial pressure on British Aerospace to join EADS, company executives defied the government and merged with Marconi. This left German, French, and Spanish companies and government officials to negotiate a merger. In the summer of 1999, secret negotiations between the shareholders of Daimler-Chrysler the Spanish state holding company Sociedad Estatal de Participaciones Industriales, the Lagardère Group, and their respective governments eventually led to the creation of EADS.[74] French government officials such as Finance Minister Dominique Strauss-Kahn played a particularly important role in the negotiations. The result was the creation of one of Europe's largest defense companies, which produces a number of weapons and systems in such sectors as civil and military transport aircraft, combat and military mission aircraft, helicopters, space launchers, satellites, guided weapons, and defense and aerospace systems.

Second, the creation of MBDA in the late 1990s was a significant step toward consolidating European missile production under one roof and challenging the U.S. missile producer Raytheon.[75] As former chief executive Fabrice Brégier argued: "Raytheon is the world leader, and we respect that. But we believe we can challenge that position."[76] In 2002, it was the second-largest missile firm in the world behind Raytheon. MBDA produces guided weapons for land-based, naval, and airborne requirements such as the Meteor and ASRAAM air-to-air missiles, the Storm Shadow/Scalp long-range cruise missile, the Brimstone anti-armor weapon, and the Exocet anti-ship missile. European governments began pushing for consolidation in missile production in the late 1990s to improve interoperability and decrease reliance on the United States. These benefits were particularly important because of the increased prospects for intra-European military cooperation. Following negotiations between executives from British, Italian, and French missile companies and their respective governments, MBDA was established in 1999.

---

[73] Schmitt, *From Cooperation to Integration*, 29–56.

[74] A number of government officials were involved in the secret negotiations. John Rossant, "Birth of A Giant," *Business Week*, 10 July 2000, 170; Pierre Sparaco, "EADS Completes Europe's Long-Awaited Restructuring," *Aviation Week & Space Technology,* 24 July 2000, 103–109; Yolande Baldeweck and Vianney Aubert, "Aerospatiale Matra et Dasa fusionnent," *Le Figaro*, 15 October 1999.

[75] See, for example, Katia Vlachos-Dengler, *From National Champions to European Heavyweights: The Development of European Defense Industrial Capabilities Across Market Segments* (Santa Monica, CA: RAND, 2002), 63–74.

[76] Daniel Michaels, "European Missile Firm Targets Raytheon," *Wall Street Journal*, 1 August 2000, A18. Also see "Interview, Fabrice Brégier: 'Nous avons cree l'Airbus des missiles,'" *Les Echos*, 27 April 2001, 14.

In sum, European M&A activity is best explained by a desire to decrease reliance on the United States and to increase European power. This marks a striking contrast with the Cold War, when transnational M&As occurred primarily along transatlantic lines. It also contrasts with M&A activity in non-defense sectors, since European companies concentrated more on global than regional consolidation in the post-Cold War era. As with coproduction and codevelopment projects, consolidation has been more frequent in aerospace than in land or naval systems.

The Future of Transatlantic Relations

There has been deep skepticism in the United States about the viability of European defense cooperation. Some of this has been warranted. European states spend far fewer resources on defense than does the United States, including in such areas as research and development programs. The defense spending gap between the United States and Europe has increased over the last several years from approximately $144 billion in 1999 to $224 billion in 2005.[77] In addition, European states continue to possess shortfalls in some areas, such as suppression of enemy air defense.

However, Europe has gradually established a more integrated and globally competitive defense industry. European states have been motivated by a desire to decrease reliance on the United States and to build European economic and defense power. As the historical evidence demonstrates, the structural shift to unipolarity has caused deep concern in European capitals about U.S. power. The transatlantic friction caused by the U.S.-led war in Iraq has only increased the European desire to develop independent defense capabilities. These have included the construction of European Union battle groups, a military planning capability independent of NATO, an EU military committee, and an EU military staff.

Will these developments in the defense industry continue in the future? If so, what will be the implications for transatlantic relations? Much depends on the structure of the international system. The current evidence suggests that the United States will remain the preponderant global power for the foreseeable future—including in the defense industry. As William Wohlforth and others have argued, the international system is unambiguously unipolar. The United States has an unprecedented quantitative and qualitative margin of superiority over the next most powerful state. It enjoys decisive preponderance in all major underlying components of power: economic, defense, technological, and geopolitical.[78] Even if one accepts the argument that the

---

[77] Accessed on the SIPRI Military Expenditure database at www.sipri.org, 21 April 2006. These figures are in U.S.$ millions at constant 2000 prices and exchange rates.

[78] William C. Wohlforth, "The Stability of a Unipolar World," *International Security* 24 (Summer 1999): 5–41.

United States will inevitably decline in power, as great powers have historically done, it is difficult to conceive of this happening anytime soon.

Assuming that the United States remains the preponderant global power, this structural condition will cause EU states to continue collaborating in the defense industry. Indeed, the European defense industry will likely become more integrated over the next decade. For example, European states will likely continue to develop all-weather, precision-guided weapons, such as the Storm Shadow/Scalp cruise missile and the Taurus long-range stand-off missile. They will also likely place significant resources into space-based systems and technologies that will provide EU states with military capacities—such as monitoring troop movements, facilitating logistics planning, and improving targeting and munitions guidance—that can be performed independently of the United States. Many of these projects are currently in the research and development stage, and will provide European states a greater ability to jointly project power over the next decade. One of the biggest questions over the long run is whether European states can collaborate their procurement strategies through a robust and well-resourced European Defense Agency. This would mean that the European Union would have significant power to develop capabilities requirements; determine and promote defense research; and manage land, aerospace, and naval defense programs. The answer is not entirely clear. But recent trends suggest that Europe is moving in this direction.

The preponderance of U.S. power and the European response will likely speed up a drifting apart of the transatlantic relationship. This does not mean that the United States and Europe will become enemies. But it does mean that the stronger the EU becomes as a global international political, economic, and defense power, the more likely it is that it will be willing to stand up to the United States when it disagrees. For example, the establishment of a globally competitive defense industry and a more independent Europe may increase the likelihood that European firms will sell military-use systems and technologies to countries such as China, where the United States and Europe have different strategic interests. These developments would cause transatlantic frictions to increase even further. As Jacques Chirac has argued: "We want to live in a multipolar world, one with a few large groups enjoying as harmonious relations as possible with each other, a world in which Europe, among others, will have its full place."[79] What is significant is not that a French president would like to see a multipolar international system and an integrated Europe. Rather, it is that European states more broadly are making an integrated defense industry a reality.

---

[79] Peter Ford, "Europe's Fears of US Domination," *Christian Science Monitor*, 14 March 2003, 6.

Part II:
THE NEOCONSERVATIVE HERITAGE
AND ITS FLAWS

"The Civilization of Clashes": Misapplying the Democratic Peace in the Middle East

PIKI ISH-SHALOM

A specter is haunting American neoconservatism—the specter of promoting democracy.[1] It exorcises whatever prudence conservatism might otherwise espouse; it drives neoconservatives' grand strategy to experimentalism that otherwise they would condemn as "social engineering." The neoconservatives' role in shaping the Bush doctrine makes it important to understand this obsession with promoting democracy, and to analyze its viability. Prior scholarly explanations of the Bush doctrine and the strategic thinking of neoconservatism emphasized power seeking in light of the 11 September 2001 terror attacks and the attendant threats of global terrorism, rogue states, and weapons of mass destruction (WMD);[2] the philosophy of Leo Strauss;[3] visions of national exceptionalism and imperial aspirations;[4]

---

[1] The term in the title was used by Niall Ferguson to characterize the culture of the Middle East in *Colossus: The Price of America's Empire* (New York: Penguin Press, 2004), 106.

[2] Jacques E.C. Hymans, "The Roots of the Washington Threat Consensus" in Betty Glad and Chris J. Dolan, eds., *Striking First: The Preventive War Doctrine and the Reshaping of U.S. Foreign Policy* (New York: Palgrave Macmillan, 2004), 33–45; Douglas Kellner, "Preemptive Strikes and the War on Iraq: A Critique of Bush Administration Unilateralism and Militarism," *New Political Science* 26 (September 2004): 417–440; Stephen Peter Rosen, "An Empire, if You Can Keep It," *The National Interest* 71 (Spring 2003): 51–61.

[3] Anne Norton, *Leo Strauss and the Politics of American Empire* (New Haven, CT: Yale University Press, 2004); Shaida B. Drury, *Leo Strauss and the American Right* (New York: St. Martin's Press, 1997).

[4] Michael Cox, "The Empire's Back in Town: Or America's Imperial Temptation—Again," *Millennium* 32 (February 2003): 1–27; G. John Ikenberry, "America's Imperial Ambition," *Foreign Affairs* 81 (September/October 2002), 44–60; Niall Ferguson, "Hegemony or Empire?" *Foreign Affairs* 82 (September/October 2003), 154–161; Robert Jervis, "The Compulsive Empire," *Foreign Policy* 137 (July/August 2003): 83–87; Jack Snyder, "Imperial Temptations," *The National Interest* 71 (Spring 2003): 29–40.

PIKI ISH-SHALOM is a lecturer in the Department of International Relations, the Hebrew University of Jerusalem. He has published articles in *International Studies Quarterly, International Studies Review*, and in the *European Journal of International Relations*.

ideological and religious articles of faith;[5] and the drive to control the oil market.[6] The role played by certain international relations theories, however, was mostly left out of the picture.

This article will demonstrate the role of the structural theories of the democratic peace thesis in generating the neoconservative grand strategy.[7] These are theories that try to explain the absence (or near absence) of war between democracies by pointing to the structural attributes of democracies, such as checks and balances, division of powers, and periodic elections. I argue that those theories played—and still play—multiple and crucial roles in shaping and in marketing the neoconservative agenda of promoting democracy abroad. The democratic peace thesis helped neoconservatives overcome their post-Cold War identity crisis and the demise of their old archenemy, communism. The strategic program of promoting democracy revived neoconservatism and gave it new coherence and purpose.

A decade after the Cold War ended, the neoconservatives faced yet another identity crisis when confronted with the apparent incompatibility between two major conservative theoretical frameworks: the pessimism and relativism of Samuel Huntington's *The Clash of Civilizations* and the optimism and universalism of Francis Fukuyama's *The End of History*. The structural theories of democratic peace offered the neoconservatives a middle ground between the two, along with a political platform that is both cautiously optimistic and mildly relativist. The political platform consists of three major premises: first, expanding democracy will enlarge the zone of peace and overcome the threats of civilizational wars, global terrorism, and rogue states; second, democracy should be understood structurally rather than culturally and morally; and third, building the structures of democracy is also possible in civilizations whose cultures and moralities are incompatible with those of the democratic West.

Those three premises explain neoconservatives' preoccupation with promoting democracy abroad, particularly in the Middle East, and by force if necessary. In other words, endorsing the structural theories of democratic peace resolved some of the neoconservatives' major difficulties, and generated the grand strategy of forceful democracy promotion. Moreover, by insisting on the scientific validity of the claim that democracies do not fight each other, the

---

[5] Michael Boyle, "Utopianism and the Bush Foreign Policy," *Cambridge Review of International Affairs* 17 (April 2004): 81–103; Michael J. Mazarr, "George W. Bush, Idealist," *International Affairs* 79 (May 2003): 503–522; Jonathan Monten, "The Roots of the Bush Doctrine: Power, Nationalism, and Democracy Promotion in U.S. Strategy," *International Security* 29 (Spring 2005): 112–156.

[6] Edward Nell and Willi Semmler, "The Economic Consequences of the Peace in Iraq," *Constellations* 10 (September 2003): 425–436; Stephen Pelletiere, *America's Oil Wars* (Westport, CT: Praeger, 2004); Research Unit for Political Economy, "Behind the War on Iraq," *Monthly Review* 55 (May 2003): 20–49; Research Unit for Political Economy, *Behind the Invasion of Iraq* (New York: Monthly Review Press, 2003).

[7] See also Piki Ish-Shalom, "Theory as a Hermeneutical Mechanism: The Democratic Peace and the Politics of Democratization," *European Journal of International Relations* 12 (December 2006): 565–598.

neoconservatives successfully marketed their agenda to the American public and to the administration of George W. Bush, proclaiming the proved strategic merits of exporting democracy. These thus constitute one of the sources of influence for the Bush doctrine and its preoccupation with democracy promotion.

A word of caution is in order. As will become clear below, not all neoconservatives endorsed the structural theories of the democratic peace, nor do all of them advocate democracy promotion. However, some prominent neoconservative thinkers did endorse the theories and the policy of promoting democracy. Furthermore, this policy came to be identified with neoconservatism. For this reason and the sake of brevity, I will use the general form of "the neoconservatives" throughout the article, rather than the more accurate but cumbersome terminology "some prominent neoconservative thinkers."

The article has four sections. The first outlines the major reasons for the neoconservatives' endorsement of the structural theories of democratic peace. The second explores the democratic peace thesis and its various theories to explain why the neoconservatives choose the structural theories rather than the normative ones. The third section demonstrates the strategic outcomes of adopting those theories, maintaining that it turned neoconservatism into what I metaphorically term the "civilization of clashes," an ideology of endless military crusades to spread democracy. The last section offers both a critique of the neoconservative grand strategy, pointing to two acute internal incoherencies, and an outline of an alternative theory of world affairs and democratization.

THE REASONS FOR ENDORSING THE STRUCTURAL THEORIES OF DEMOCRATIC PEACE

Five factors contributed to the neoconservatives' adoption of the structural theories of democratic peace:

- The end of the Cold War;
- Neoconservatives' affiliation with Israeli politicians such as Benjamin Netanyahu and Natan Sharansky, who, in the latter half of the 1990s, made use of the democratic peace thesis in attempting to delegitimize the Oslo Accords;
- The long-standing neoconservative agenda of toppling Saddam Hussein;
- The terror attacks of 11 September 2001;
- The intellectual perplexity resulting from the conflicting theoretical frameworks of two major conservative works: Fukuyama's *The End of History* and Huntington's *The Clash of Civilizations*.[8]

---

[8] The two sets of writings started their life as articles and three years later were published as books: Francis Fukuyama, "The End of History? *The National Interest* 16 (Summer 1989): 3–18; Francis Fukuyama, *The End of History and the Last Man* (New York: Free Press, 1992); Samuel P.

In the late 1980s and early 1990s, American foreign policy, following what was seen as its greatest success with the collapse of the Soviet Union and the end of the Cold War, underwent a phase of bafflement. The loss of the archrival brought the collapse of the purpose and coherence of a well-institutionalized foreign policy. What was bafflement for some verged on existential crisis for others, primarily the neoconservatives, for whom the main—almost sole—raison d'être was fierce anticommunism.

This crisis manifested itself in various ways. In 1989–1990, one of the flagship neoconservative journals, *The National Interest*, published a series of articles, mostly by conservatives and neoconservatives, on America's purpose after the Cold War. Irving Kristol, one of the godfathers of neoconservatism, wrote:

> It is very difficult for a great power—a world power—to articulate a foreign policy in the absence of an enemy worthy of the name. It is, after all, one's enemies that help define one's "national interest," in whatever form that definition might take. Without such enemies, one flounders amidst a plentitude of rather trivial, or at least marginal, options. That, it seems to me, is the condition of the United States today, as we enter the post-Cold War era.[9]

In their search for a new rationale, some prominent neoconservative thinkers such as Joshua Muravchik and Carl Gershman, and later also Charles Krauthammer, William Kristol, and others, adopted the relatively new theories of democratic peace, calling for a revived Wilsonian commitment to democracy promotion. As Muravchik wrote in his 1991 book *Exporting Democracy*: "The more democratic the world, the more peaceful it is likely to be. *Various researchers have shown that war between democracies has almost never occurred in the modern world.*"[10] These thinkers claimed that the democratic peace thesis showed that there is no real gap between morality and interest in foreign policy, that it was high time to stop supporting local dictators in the name of stability, and that promoting democracy would broaden the zone of peace. Moreover, as Michael Williams points out, it was also the neoconservative vision of American exceptionalism that provided

---

Huntington, "The Clash of Civilizations?" *Foreign Affairs* 72 (Summer 1993): 22–49; Samuel P. Huntington, *The Clash of Civilizations and the Remaking of World Order* (New York: Simon & Schuster, 1996).

[9] Irving Kristol, "Defining Our National Interest," *The National Interest* 21 (Fall 1990): 16–25. Even though Kristol opposes democratization policies, his bafflement is typical.

[10] Joshua Muravchik, *Exporting Democracy: Fulfilling America's Destiny* (Washington DC: American Enterprise Institute Press, 1991), 8 (emphasis added). See also Carl Gershman, "Freedom Remains the Touchstone," *The National Interest* 19 (Spring 1990): 83–86. On the endorsing of the new agenda of democracy promotion, see also John Ehrman, *The Rise of Neoconservatism: Intellectuals and Foreign Affairs 1945–1994* (New Haven, CT: Yale University Press, 1995), 184; Stefan Halper and Jonathan Clarke, *America Alone: The Neo-Conservatives and the Global Order* (Cambridge, UK: Cambridge University Press, 2004), 76.

the reasoning for the idea of promoting democracy.[11] By drawing the connection of the American present to the past, and especially to the founding era of the American republic, the neoconservatives were able to lend some continuity and coherence during the time of the identity crisis that succeeded the Cold War.

It is worth stressing, however, that neoconservatism is not a monolithic creed. Furthermore, not all neoconservatives endorsed the democratic peace thesis. As Stefan Halper and Jonathan Clarke rightly argue, with the end of the Cold War—and especially during the second half of the 1990s—an ideological gap, based mainly on generational lines, divided the neoconservatives.[12] The older cohorts of the neoconservatives, most notably Irving Kristol and Nathan Glazer, aligned themselves with the realist cause, thus abandoning the Cold War rhetoric of anti-totalitarianism and pro-democratization. The younger cohorts, including Muravchik, Gershman, Krauthammer, and Kristol, aligned themselves with the interventionist cause of promoting democracy as a way to stabilize regions plagued by authoritarianism and war, although, as the example of Norman Podhoretz demonstrates, this ideological divide is not purely generational. While belonging to the older cohorts, Podhoretz did endorse, as we will see below, the democratic peace thesis. Many of the young cohorts even opted for a short-lived cooperation with Bill Clinton in the 1992 presidential campaign, as they judged President George H.W. Bush to be a pragmatist and realist in foreign affairs. As can be learned from Muravchik's public endorsement of Clinton, it was the issue of promoting democracy abroad that became the point of convergence between Clinton and the neoconservatives.[13] Soon thereafter, however, the same issue drove them apart; the neoconservatives blamed Clinton for being a pragmatist and realist and for failing to commit the United States to promoting democracy.[14]

Following the 1993 Oslo Accords, two prominent Israeli rightist politicians mobilized the democratic peace thesis to delegitimize the agreements.

[11] Michael C. Williams, "What is the National Interest? The Neoconservative Challenge in IR Theory," *European Journal of International Relations* 26 (September 2005): 307–337.

[12] Halper and Clarke, *America Alone*, 98–103.

[13] Joshua Muravchik, "Conservatives for Clinton," *The New Republic*, 2 November 1992, 22.

[14] Joshua Muravchik, "Lament of a Clinton Supporter," *Commentary* 96 (August 1993): 15–22. The neoconservative commitment to the agenda of democracy promotion was reaffirmed again in 1997 with the establishment of The Project for a New American Century. This neoconservative think tank, chaired by William Kristol, declared in its statement of principles the "need to promote the cause of political and economic freedom abroad." See "Statement of Principles," 3 June 1997, accessed at http://www.newamericancentury.org/statementofprinciples.htm, 7 March 2006. The think tank kept calling for democracy promotion, and, furthermore, linked this cause to the democratic peace. Its September 2000 report, "Rebuilding America's Defenses," called for "secure[ing] and expand[ing] the 'zones of democratic peace'" (p. 2). See "Rebuilding America's Defenses: Strategy, Forces and Resources for a New Century," September 2000, accessed at http://www.newamericancentury.org/RebuildingAmericasDefenses.pdf, 7 March 2006.

Netanyahu, who was soon to become prime minister, and Sharansky—the famous Soviet dissident and prisoner of the Gulag, associate of Andre Sakharov, recipient of the Congressional Gold Medal, and future cabinet minister—criticized Oslo on the grounds that peace with the Palestinians would be impossible until they had democratized. Netanyahu attributed his argument to Immanuel Kant,[15] and Sharansky credited Sakharov with the origins of his thinking.[16] Both of them, however, also relied on the democratic peace thesis.[17]

The neoconservatives lauded Netanyahu and Sharansky's position.[18] This led to a revival of their interest in the democratic peace thesis and particularly its application to the Middle East, specifically, the Palestinian Authority. The result was a neoconservative demand, adopted by President Bush in his roadmap announcement of 24 June 2002, that the Palestinians democratize prior to any Israeli concessions.

Toppling Saddam Hussein had long been on the neoconservative agenda, at least since the first Gulf War and—as they saw it—its untimely ending.[19]

---

[15] Benjamin Netanyahu, *A Place among the Nations: Israel and the World* (New York: Bantam Books, 1993), 243; Benjamin Netanyahu, "Fighting Terrorism" (presented at the eighteenth annual John M. Ashbrook memorial dinner, Ashbrook Center for Public Affairs, Ashland University, Ashland, Ohio, 3 May 2002), accessed at http://www.ashbrook.org/events/memdin/netanyahu/home_speech.html, 21 November 2005.

[16] See, for example, Natan Sharansky, "Only Democracy Brings Peace," *Wall Street Journal*, 30 October 2000; Natan Sharansky with Ron Dermer, *The Case for Democracy: The Power of Freedom to Overcome Tyranny and Terror* (New York: Public Affairs, 2004), xix, 3.

[17] See, especially, Netanyahu's address as Prime Minister to the joint session of Congress on 10 July 1996, in which he declared: "I am not revealing a secret to the Members of this Chamber when I say that modern democracies do not initiate aggression. This has been the central lesson of the 20th century. States that respect the human rights of their citizens are not likely to provoke hostile action against their neighbors." "Address by His Excellency, Binyamin Netanyahu, Prime Minister of Israel," 10 July 1996, accessed at http://frwebgate.access.gpo.gov/cgi-bin/getpage.cgi?position=all&page=H7161&dbname=1996_record, 9 March 2006.

[18] See, for example, Charles Krauthammer, "Peace through Democracy," *The Washington Post*, 28 June 2002; Ira Stoll, "Israel's Reagan? Natan Sharansky Understands that Liberty Is the Only Guarantee of Peace," *The Wall Street Journal*, 13 December 2002. The praises for Sharansky increased following his 2004 book, *The Case for Democracy*, which had a significant impact on President Bush. See Arch Puddington, "Liberty for All," *Commentary* 118 (November 2004): 72–75; Meirav Wurmser, "Democracy Defended: Natan Sharansky Explains Why Democracy Makes the World Safer," *The Weekly Standard*, 6 December 2004, 28–29.

[19] For example: "The United States, which had mustered the world's most awesome military force to expel Saddam Hussein from Kuwait, failed to see that mission through to its proper conclusion: the removal of Saddam from power in Baghdad." William Kristol and Robert Kagan, "Introduction: National Interest and Global Responsibility" in Robert Kagan and William Kristol, eds., *Present Dangers: Crisis and Opportunity in American Foreign and Defense Policy* (San Francisco, CA: Encounter Books, 2000), 6. It should be noted that the neoconservative views were not monolithic; Irving Kristol, for example, was a fierce opponent of continuing the war. See Irving Kristol, "Tongue-Tied in Washington," *The Wall Street Journal*, 15 April 1991.

Initially, though, their demand for regime change in Iraq meant changing the leader and not necessarily the regime itself. But when the prospects for another war in Iraq increased in the early 2000s, the neoconservatives called for a regime change that went beyond personal cosmetics: they now championed the democratization of Iraq. For example, Gary Schmitt, executive director of the neoconservative think tank Project for the New American Century, declared: "A decade ago, the first Bush administration decided that leaving Saddam Hussein in power was acceptable. Now, a new Bush administration insists not only that Saddam's regime must go, but that, in its place, a decent, tolerant and representative government need arise."[20]

The neoconservatives adopted Netanyahu and Sharansky's creed: democracy was the antidote to terror. This notion does not stem directly from the democratic peace thesis,[21] but, rather, is an extension and, to some degree, a distortion of it, propelled by ideological reading and political needs. Looking for persuasive arguments to overthrow Saddam, the neoconservatives used the extended democratic peace thesis to proclaim that occupying and democratizing Iraq was vital for stabilizing the Middle East and defeating global terrorism. After the Iraq occupation was accomplished and other arguments for it, especially pertaining to WMD, were discredited, they only redoubled their use of the democratic reasoning.[22] Put differently, once WMD were not found in Iraq, a supplementary political value was added to the democratic peace thesis, namely that of post-facto rationalization and legitimization.

The effects of the 11 September 2001 terror attacks on U.S. soil resembled, to some extent, those of the end of the Cold War: both were viewed as a sea change that necessitated new paradigms of strategic thinking. As Lawrence Kaplan and William Kristol argued, "We thought it [the Cold War] would always be with us. And when we found during the 1990s that it no longer was, we took a holiday from history, presuming that we could rely on commerce and globalization to achieve peace and stability. But the complacent assumptions of the post-Cold War era were destroyed on September 11. That day brought

---

[20] Gary Schmitt, "A Case for Continuity," *The National Interest* 69 (Fall 2002): 11–13.

[21] For Sharansky's linkage between democratization and the end of terror, see Natan Sharansky, "Democracy for Peace," 20 June 2002, accessed at http://www.aei.org/publications/pubID.15187, filter.all/pub_detail.asp, 3 May 2006. For Netanyahu's linkage, see Benjamin Netanyahu, "The Root Cause of Terrorism Is Tyranny," *The Wall Street Journal*, 19 April 2002. For the neoconservatives' linkage, see Gerecht's remark: "The spread of democracy in the Muslim Middle East remains the only cure for the sacred terror of 9/11." Reuel Marc Gerecht, "Going Soft on Iraq," *The Weekly Standard*, 8 March 2004, 26–29. See also Joshua Muravchik, "Freedom and the Arab World," *The Weekly Standard*, 31 December 2001/7 January 2002, 15–16; Fred Barnes, "A Real Peace Process," *The Weekly Standard*, 5 May 2003, 9; Amir Taheri, "After the Arab League," *The Weekly Standard*, 3 May 2004, 20–22.

[22] See, for example, columns by Krauthammer: Charles Krauthammer, "Hoaxes, Hype and Humiliation," *The Washington Post*, 13 June 2003; Charles Krauthammer, "Iraq: A Moral Reckoning," *The Washington Post*, 16 May 2003.

us to a new era, for which we need a new roadmap."[23] Reuel Marc Gerecht, a former CIA specialist and prolific neoconservative writer, clarified the essence of this roadmap: "the spread of democracy in the Muslim Middle East remains the only cure for the sacred terror of 9/11."[24]

The search for a new paradigm of international politics was prompted by yet another source of perplexity: a debate among conservative intellectuals. Two famous works symbolize the end points of the conservative spectrum concerning international relations. At one point is the universalism and optimism of Francis Fukuyama's *The End of History and the Last Man*; at the other, the relativism and pessimism of Samuel Huntington's *The Clash of Civilizations and the Remaking of World Order*. Whereas Fukuyama claims the victory of Western/ U.S. capitalism and liberal democracy, Huntington foresees the decline of the West/United States, and the rise of China with its civilization. And whereas Fukuyama believes in universal truth and morality, Huntington maintains that the various civilizations' systems of truth and morality are incompatible.

These two works represent not only the end points of conservative thinking but also the beginning and end of an era. Fukuyama's book (and the article that preceded it) stemmed from the end of the Cold War and the resultant sense of euphoria. Huntington's book (and preceding article), while published before 11 September 2001, reflected the awakening from this euphoria. According to Huntington, Fukuyama was not only optimistic to argue that perfection was *near*;[25] what was happening instead was a deterioration in international relations. It was not the Kantian eternal peace that was imminent, but a reversion to a Hobbesian state of affairs, this time even worse because it would involve the most fundamental human attachments, those of identities and civilizations, so that the wars would be even harsher than before. Indeed, the happy 1990s ended even before they really began, when the Balkans erupted in yet another round of their eternal conflicts.[26]

It was hard to reconcile these two modes of thought. It was even harder to come up with a strategy to counter the pessimism and sense of determinism (although there is also a sense of determinism in Fukuyama's works) of *The Clash of Civilizations*. The price of not finding such reconciliation, however, might have been too high in terms of the neoconservative self-identity and internal cohesiveness. Huntington and Fukuyama are both major thinkers of the

---

[23] Lawrence F. Kaplan and William Kristol, *The War over Iraq: Saddam's Tyranny and America's Mission* (San Francisco, CA: Encounter Books, 2003), vii. See also William Kristol, "The 9/11 Election: Editorial," *The Weekly Standard*, 1 November/8 November 2004, 9.

[24] Gerecht, "Going Soft," 27. See also Reuel Marc Gerecht, "Not a Diversion," *The Weekly Standard*, 12 April/19 April 2004, 23–27.

[25] Huntington was one of the early critics of Fukuyama; see Samuel Huntington, "No Exit—The Errors of Endism," *The National Interest* 17 (Fall 1989): 3–11.

[26] Josef Joffe made this point in *Commentary* in criticizing Fukuyama's position; see Josef Joffe, "Bosnia: The Return of History," *Commentary* 94 (October 1992): 24–29.

American right, and their arguments found much resonance. Indeed, both books made the *New York Times* bestseller list, a rarity for academic works.

Moreover, each of their theses fits well with certain conservative and neoconservative premises. Fukuyama's position is palatable to the conservative belief in a teleological history that actualizes a historical scheme devised by some higher rationality. It also reinforces the belief in the supremacy of the free market. Huntington's thesis jibes with the conservative conviction that individuals are circumscribed by their communities and that those communities evolve historically and gradually—that is, as civilizations; and it resonates with Edmund Burke's philosophy of historical rights and, even more so, with the Fichteian conflictual version of Johann Gottfried von Herder's historiography. Huntington's thesis is also amenable to the neoconservative view of international politics as a Manichean battle between the democratic world and the world of terror. Hence, neoconservatives are torn between these two thinkers and their conflicting theses.

As evident in many of their writings, the neoconservatives indeed accept Huntington's arguments. They deem the values and norms of the various civilizations incompatible with their own, including their democratic norms. This is especially true with regard to the Islamic or Arabic civilization. William Kristol, for example, gives a Straussian reading of President Bush. He quotes Bush: "'Anyone in the world, including the Arab world, who works and sacrifices for freedom has a loyal friend in the United States,'" and then adds: "Why 'including the Arab world'? Because that world—or better, perhaps, the Middle East or the Islamic world—is the heart of the problem."[27] Kristol asserts that this is the true meaning of Bush's declaration, despite Bush's need to conceal it for political reasons. Thus, through a Straussian methodology, Kristol seeks to rescue Bush's true, esoteric meaning—to which Kristol himself subscribes—of the cultural and normative incompatibility between the West and the Islamic world.

Cultural incompatibility is also a theme in Muravchik's writings. As he asserted in *Commentary*: "[the Middle East] region [is] characterized by paranoia, apocalypticism, tyranny, and violence, a region where differences are settled by the sword."[28] This cultural clash is a common motif in neoconservative writings.[29]

[27] William Kristol, "The End of the Beginning," *The Weekly Standard*, 12 May 2003, 9. In a similar spirit, Stanley Kurtz asserted: "Islamic society may still adapt itself to democracy and capitalism. Yet at this point, to ignore the incompatibility between Islam and modernity is willful blindness." See Stanley Kurtz, "The Terror of Islam," *The Weekly Standard*, 27 May 2002, 37–38.

[28] Joshua Muravchik, "The Bush Manifesto," *Commentary* 114 (December 2002): 29. See also Joshua Muravchik, "Hearts, Minds, and the War against Terror," *Commentary* 113 (May 2002): 25–30; Joshua Muravchik, "The Richard Clarke Show," *Commentary* 117 (May 2004): 32–41.

[29] Norman Podhoretz, "How to Win World War IV," *Commentary* 113 (February 2002): 19–29; Ephraim Karsh, "Making Iraq Safe for Democracy," *Commentary* 115 (April 2003): 22–28; Kurtz, "Terror of Islam," 38.

But while accepting this aspect of Huntington, neoconservatives refused to surrender to his pessimism and vision of the "decline of the West/United States."[30] They kept heeding Fukuyama's optimism about the expected—if not determined—victory of the West led by America. This emerged most clearly when neoconservatives compared the two works. For example, in his 1997 *Commentary* review of Huntington's book, Richard Pipes claims it was written in response to Fukuyama's argument.[31] He then asserts that whereas Huntington is right in stressing the role of civilizations in world politics,[32] his pessimism is misplaced because the West is not declining.[33] Pipes's concluding remarks are especially enlightening: "I suspect that the truth lies somewhere between Fukuyama and Huntington: the two books complement each other. Fukuyama seems to be correct in predicting the ultimate triumph of westernization, but he is oblivious of the immense difficulties which the west will have to overcome—difficulties which Huntington spells out in a very persuasive manner."[34]

Five and a half years later, in September 2002, Pipes's more theoretical perspective took a political and strategic turn in an article by former *Commentary* editor Podhoretz. Podhoretz praises the strategic shift that President Bush underwent following 11 September 2001, defining it as a shift from realism to idealism—namely, Bush's new endorsement of democracy promotion. Analyzing the series of addresses in which Bush reacted to the terror attacks and presented a new U.S. strategy, Podhoretz writes:

> Then, in a fascinating leap into the great theoretical debate of the post-cold-war era (though without identifying the main participants), Bush came down squarely on the side of Francis Fukuyama against Samuel Huntington.... Having endorsed Fukuyama's much-misunderstood view of "the end of history," Bush now brushed off Huntington's rival theory of a "clash of civilizations."... All this was fully consistent with the two previous speeches Bush had made on September 20 and January 29. But—a very big but—it was not consistent with the realities on the ground in the Middle East. In the Islamic world, and particularly the Arab countries (including such of our "friends" as Saudi Arabia and Egypt), mothers and fathers were *celebrating* Palestinian children (including their own) who blew themselves up as a way of killing as many Israeli Jews as possible.[35]

---

[30] This is also evident in the February 24, 1997, special issue of the *The Weekly Standard* devoted to the rising power of China. The issue immediately followed a harsh review article on Huntington's determinism and pessimism that embodied the neoconservatives' disagreements with him; see Robert Kagan, "Harvard Hates America," *The Weekly Standard*, 9 December 1996, 24–27.

[31] Richard Pipes, "The West and the Rest," *Commentary* 103 (March 1997): 62–65.

[32] Ibid., 63–64.

[33] Ibid., 64.

[34] Ibid., 65.

[35] Norman Podhoretz, "In Praise of the Bush Doctrine," *Commentary* 114 (September 2002): 19–28 (emphasis in original).

Podhoretz further argues that Bush understands that these tendencies stem from hatred of the freedoms practiced in the United States.[36] Here, using the same Straussian methods as Kristol, Podhoretz claims that despite maintaining publicly that there is no real clash of civilizations, Bush is well aware that it indeed exists, and his political constraints prevent him from saying what he really thinks. This interpretational maneuver puts Bush in a kind of middle ground between Fukuyama and Huntington—the same place where, as I claim, the neoconservatives now stand as they try to reconcile the two viewpoints.

THE DEMOCRATIC PEACE THESIS

Yet, however necessary for self-identity and internal cohesiveness, the question remains: how it is possible to hold such a middle ground between conflicting viewpoints? One way to reconcile Huntington's relativism and pessimism with Fukuyama's universalism and optimism is via the democratic peace thesis, and more specifically, its structural theories. I will briefly describe the various democratic peace theories, including the structural ones, before explaining how these offer relief to the neoconservatives' perplexities.

During the 1970s and 1980s, international relations researchers iden-tified an interesting empirical phenomenon: democracies never (or, in a qualified version, rarely) go to war with one another.[37] Although over the years many harsh criticisms were leveled at the validity of this claim,[38] it steadily gained supporters, and two major theories tried to explain it. The

---

[36] Ibid.

[37] A useful, although not updated, historical background can be found in Nils Petter Gleiditsch, "Democracy and Peace," *Journal of Peace Research* 29 (November 1992): 369–376. Milestones in the early development of the democratic peace thesis are: the neglected first article by the criminologist Dean V. Babst, "Elective Governments: A Force for Peace," *The Wisconsin Sociologist* 3 (January 1964): 9–14; his second and somewhat more widely circulated article, although in a popular journal, Dean V. Babst, "A Force for Peace," *Industrial Research* 14 (April 1972): 55–58; and the first major publications in the international relations discipline: Peter Wallenstein, *Structure and War: On International Relations 1820–1868* (Stockholm: Raben & Sjogern, 1973); Rudolph J. Rummel, *Understanding Conflict and War*, vol. 4, *War, Power, Peace* (Los Angeles, CA: Sage, 1979); Rudolph J. Rummel, *Understanding Conflict and War*, vol. 5, *The Just Peace* (Los Angeles, CA: Sage, 1981); Rudolph J. Rummel, "Libertianism and Interstate Violence," *Journal of Conflict Resolution* 27 (March 1983): 27–71; Michael Doyle, "Kant, Liberal Legacies, and Foreign Affairs, Part I," *Philoso-phy and Public Affairs* 12 (Summer 1983): 205–235; Michael Doyle, "Kant, Liberal Legacies, and Foreign Affairs, Part II," *Philosophy and Public Affairs* 12 (Autumn 1983): 323–353; Michael Doyle, "Liberalism and World Politics," *American Political Science Review* 80 (December 1986): 1151–1169; Zeev Maoz and Bruce Russett, "Normative and Structural Causes of Democratic Peace, 1946–1986," *American Political Science Review* 87 (September 1993): 624–638.

[38] See, for example, Christopher Lane, "Kant or Cant: The Myth of the Democratic Peace" in Michael E. Brown, Sean M. Lynn-Jones, and Steven E. Miller, eds., *Debating the Democratic Peace: An International Security Reader* (Cambridge, MA and London: MIT Press, 1996), 157–201; David E.

first explained the democratic peace phenomenon by focusing on the structural dimensions of democracy, claiming that the division of power, checks and balances, and the leaders' accountability to the public cause the decision-making process to be complex and slow, allowing the decision makers of democratic states to reach peaceful resolutions of the conflicts between them. The second theory highlights the normative dimensions of democratic societies, claiming that the norms of tolerance and openness within these states transcend into the level of the relations between them. Consequently, there is more willingness to reach compromises, and conflicts are settled peacefully.[39]

Spiro, "The Insignificance of the Liberal Peace" in Brown, Lynn-Jones, and Miller, *Debating the Democratic Peace*, 202–238; Henry S. Farber and Joanne Gowa, "Polities and Peace" in Brown, Lynn-Jones, and Miller, *Debating the Democratic Peace*, 239–262; Ido Oren, "The Subjectivity of the 'Democratic Peace': Changing U.S. Perceptions of Imperial Germany" in Brown, Lynn-Jones, and Miller, *Debating the Democratic Peace*, 263–300; Joanne Gowa, *Ballots and Bullets: The Elusive Democratic Peace* (Princeton, NJ: Princeton University Press, 1999); Kurt T. Gaubatz, *Elections and War: The Electoral Incentive in the Democratic Politics of War and Peace* (Stanford, CA: Stanford University Press, 1999), 1–3, 16–20, 104–124, 138–140; Raymond Cohen, "Pacific Union: A Reappraisal of the Theory that 'Democracies Do Not Go to War with Each Other,'" *Review of International Studies* 20 (July 1994): 207–223; Sebastian Rosato, "The Flawed Logic of Democratic Peace Theory," *American Political Science Review* 97 (November 2003): 585–602.

[39] The division of the democratic peace theories into two major theories (or paradigms) holds true even when we examine specific explanatory variables shared by theories within the two different paradigms. Let us examine, for example, the explanatory reasoning operating in the variable of the abilities of the public in a democracy to translate their preferences into policies, and in our case, into peaceful resolution of conflict between democracies. This translation process is interpreted by structural theoreticians as incentives facing the elites, or better, as checks on the menu of policies available to the ruling elites. Hence, we find structuralists arguing that the survival of political leaders with large winning coalitions (namely, democracies) is dependent on successful policies. This means that democratic leaders will make larger efforts than will non-democratic leaders and hence, more often than not, will win against non-democrats and will not fight against other democrats. It should be noted that in this explanation, the preferences of the public are being translated into leaders' incentives via structural considerations. See Bruce Bueno de Mesquita, James Morrow, Randolph M. Siverson, and Alastair Smith, "An Institutional Explanation of the Democratic Peace," *American Political Science Review* 93 (December 1999): 791–807. James Fearon, who conceptualizes the same elites' incentives by the term 'audience costs,' employs a similar structural logic. See James D. Fearon, "Domestic Political Audiences and the Escalation of International Disputes," *American Political Science Review* 88 (September 1994): 577–592. Alternatively, the normative explanation of the democratic peace operationalizes the same translation process by focusing on its normative foundation, that is, transparency and bounded nature. The important elements in democracy, with regard to the translation from preferences to policies, are both the bounded nature of competition involved in deciding what policies will be chosen and executed, as well as the transparency of the process; both are democratic norms. Furthermore, this transparency is not limited to the democratic polity itself but is freely communicated between democratic polities. The translation of the public preferences to policies therefore causes pacification among democracies and is based on the democratic norms of the bounded and transparent nature of the political conflict. See William J. Dixon, "Democracy and the Peaceful Settlement of International Conflict," *American Political Science Review* 88 (March 1994): 14–32.

What is of interest here is the association of the structural democratic peace theories with the more conservative understanding of democracy that defines it in structural terms of checks and balances, rather than in cultural terms of democratic political culture; in procedural terms of elections, rather than normative terms of democratic values; as an elite project (that is, of the elected elite) of leading the people, rather than a polity run by its deliberating citizens. The minimal structural definition of democracy is embedded in a conservative skepticism about human faculties. In this view, it is not rationality that drives human action but a mix of perennial desires, instincts, and communal traditions. This mix is extrarational and compels humans to strive for power. Two major consequences follow. First, because every person seeks power, there is a perpetual danger of destabilization of social and political organizations. Second, there is the opposite, constant danger of a dictatorial concentration of power in the hands of those individuals who succeed in gaining it. The conservative solution for these two dangers is a minimal, structural democracy. On the one hand, by regular elections, democracy guarantees that no power lasts forever, and no dictatorial concentration of power is available. On the other hand, by confining political participation to elections, democracy precludes political and social destabilization.

Related, more-practical questions arise concerning democratization, such as what qualifies as democratization and what sort of democratization is effective? The alternative paradigms of democracy, namely, structural versus normative, not only exist in the abstract; each of them can also lead to a discrete policy. Once one accepts that democracies do not fight each other, the policy implication should be to support democratization abroad. Allegedly, each state that becomes a democracy is no longer a security threat to other democracies. To enlarge the number of democracies is to enlarge the zone of peace.[40]

But how can other countries and societies be democratized? Broadly speaking, democratization policies can be divided into two types that derive directly from the definitions of democracy. If democracy means a structure of elections, division of powers, and checks and balances, democratization will mean *building this structure*; that is, emphasizing the formal, the procedural, and the structural. It will also mean investing efforts in the state apparatus, in the "old" or institutional politics. If, however, democracy means a culture and morality of the sort that create a civic community, democratization will mean *constructing this community*. It will mean the socialization and dissemination of democratic values so as to foster a democratic society and culture, mainly by facilitating domestic agents of political and social transformation in the target

[40] Yet, as Edward Mansfield and Jack Snyder argue, democratization is not necessarily the surest way to achieve stabilty and peace. If democratization is pursued in the absence of proper political institutions, it might lead to both domestic and international violence. See Edward D. Mansfield and Jack Snyder, *Electing to Fight: Why Emerging Democracies Go to War* (Cambridge, MA: MIT Press, 2005).

country. It will mean investing efforts on the social and individual levels, trying to construct a civil society of informed, involved, and participating citizens.

Understood thus, the structural theories of democratic peace and their ensuing policies of structural democracy promotion might seem neatly compatible with the conservative concept of democracy. If so, these theories can be well accommodated in the neoconservative understanding of world politics. Thus, they could be the remedy to the intellectual perplexity by offering a way to reconcile relativism and universalism, optimism and Huntington's warnings of decline. The democratic peace thesis implies that democratization, if somehow possible, can save us from the dangers of war, including civilizational war. As Krauthammer asserts, "To extend the peace by spreading democracy and free institutions ... is an unassailable goal and probably the most enduring method of promoting peace.... The zone of democracy is almost invariably a zone of peace."[41] And if democratization is *structural* rather than *normative*, then these enlarged zones can even encompass other civilizations.

STRATEGIC OUTPUTS AND POLICY OUTCOMES

The neoconservatives, endorsing democratic peace, preached democracy promotion for the sake of security. This was true of Krauthammer's "democratic realism,"[42] and also of the more global version favored by Kristol, who argued, along with Lawrence Kaplan, that "the strategic value of democracy is reflected in a truth of international politics: Democracies rarely, if ever, wage war against one another."[43]

Thus, neoconservatives view democratization as a tool to enhance U.S. security, but consider *structural* democratization the only viable option.[44] They assume that structural democratization can be grafted onto any civilization, any

[41] Charles Krauthammer, "The Bush Doctrine: ABM, Kyoto, and the New American Unilateralism," *The Weekly Standard*, 4 June 2001, 21.

[42] Charles Krauthammer, "In Defense of Democratic Realism," *The National Interest* 77 (Fall 2004): 15–25.

[43] Kaplan and Kristol, *War over Iraq*, 104. See also Puddington, "Liberty for All," 74; Adam Wolfson, "The Two Faces of Liberalism," *The Weekly Standard*, 18 October 2004, 20–22; Clifford Kupchan, "Real Democratik," *The National Interest* 77 (Fall 2004): 26–37; Max Boot, "What Next? The Bush Foreign Policy Agenda beyond Iraq," *The Weekly Standard*, 5 May 2003, 27–33; Charles Lane, "The Democracy Wave: Has It Crested?" *The Weekly Standard*, 17 January 2000, 29; Lawrence F. Kaplan, "Leftism on the Right," *The Weekly Standard*, 9 February 1998, 29; Lawrence F. Kaplan, "Dictatorship and No Standards," *The Weekly Standard*, 8 February 1999, 27–29; Todd Lindberg, "The Referendum on Neoconservatism," *The Weekly Standard*, 1 November/8 November 2004, 16–18; William E. Odom, "NATO's Expansion: Why the Critics Are Wrong," *The National Interest* 39 (Spring 1995): 38–49.

[44] Again, Krauthammer is a case in point: "until this administration conceived a radical war plan, executed it brilliantly, liberated the country and created from scratch the *structures* of democracy." Charles Krauthammer, "The Afghan Miracle: Why Isn't This Stunning U.S. Success Appreciated?" *The Washington Post*, 10 December 2004 (emphasis added).

set of norms and values. This is based on the belief that democracy embodies the only truly universal human aspiration—for freedom; and that freedom can be guaranteed only in the structure of democracy, which limits state involvement in people's lives.[45] Both conservatives and neoconservatives assume that this universal aspiration for freedom is the sole normative foundation of democracy, and that the other foundations are structural: separation of powers, checks and balances, and periodic elections. And this structure can be transplanted to any civilization without affecting or damaging its cultural foundation.[46]

As noted earlier, this structural definition of democracy jibes well with the neoconservative view of human nature and politics, a view grounded in the traditional pessimism of conservatism. It also dictates adopting structural rather than normative theories of democratic peace. Thus, the neoconservatives can reconcile pessimism and optimism, relativism and universalism, with a cautious optimism and mild relativism, while also arming themselves against the despair of a deterministic process that supposedly dooms the United States to decline.

A further point, however, is the aggressiveness of the implied policies. Up to now, we have dealt with democratization as a goal, related to security concerns. But endorsing the structural theories of democratic peace also affects the means of achieving democratization; it entails using the military. If democratizing other countries is a vital U.S. interest, drawing them into the zone of peace, then this interest has to be attained even against severe resistance.

If, however, democratization is conceived of as a lengthy, intrasocietal process of learning and socialization, norm dissemination and consolidation—as it is understood by the normative paradigm of democracy and the normative theories of democratic peace—then imposing democratization from the outside is illegitimate and futile. For the neoconservatives, their conservative understanding of democracy as mainly a structure and an elite-driven set of responsible political behaviors, along with their acceptance of Huntington's civilizational relativism, affects their view of democratization; they see it as viable only in its elitist, institutional, and structural dimensions. They see it, in other words, as regime change, reforming the existing structure into one in which periodic elections take place and there is a type of checks and balances. And that structure can be built according to general guidelines that are applied from above and outside.

Hence, it is reasonable to expect the success of democratization at bayonet point.[47] It should not even take much effort. After all, the occupation unleashes the

---

[45] Charles Krauthammer, "Free to Dance in Iraq," *The Washington Post*, 4 February 2005. See also Paula Dobriansky, "Advancing Democracy," *The National Interest* 77 (Fall 2004): 71–78.

[46] Dobriansky, "Advancing Democracy"; see also Peter Wehner, "The Wrong Time to Lose Our Nerve," *The Wall Street Journal*, 4 April 2006.

[47] See Boot, "What Next?" 29–30; Tom Donnelly and William Kristol, "More Caissons Rolling Along," *The Weekly Standard*, 9 February 2004, 7–8.

universal aspiration to freedom, as the occupied people seize the opportunity to lock up their former oppressors and realize their yearnings. They will cooperate with the occupation in building the structure of democracy, and the occupying army will create the conditions for these reforms. This army may delegate more responsibility to local elites, or import an elite from the outside (such futile efforts are epitomized by the tragicomic experience of Ahmed Chalaby). Thus, the occupying army can graft democratic structure onto a nation that while readily welcoming it (or doing so with the help of a tamed elite), maintains what cannot be changed: its civilizational identity, norms, and culture.

Many neoconservatives were well positioned inside the Bush administration and as public intellectuals to market their agenda in the wake of the terror attacks of 11 September 2001. The self-proclaimed neorealist President Bush reemerged after the attacks as an idealist president with a new understanding of America's security problems, seeking a new strategy to fit it. The neoconservatives used the democratic peace thesis to convince him, along with the American public, that democratization is the key to security. They kept emphasizing the academic verification of the thesis, rhetorically invoking scientific objectivity in pressing their ideological agenda.[48]

To be sure, good marketing and a neoconservative persuasion were not the sole reasons for the wars in Afghanistan and Iraq. Neither were these the only source of influence on President Bush and the formation of his doctrine, as is evident from his many speeches on these topics. In these speeches, we can identify themes that derive directly from the neoconservative persuasion, such as the unity of values and interests, the global appeal of freedom, and, not least, the power of freedom and democracy to bring peace. As he declared on 16 November 2005 in Kyoto, "Free Nations are peaceful nations, free nations do not threaten their neighbors, and free nations offer their citizens a hopeful vision for the future. By advancing the cause of liberty throughout this [Asia-Pacific] region, we will contribute to the prosperity of all—and deliver the peace and stability that can only come with freedom."[49] At the same time, some beliefs and views reflected in Bush's speeches transcend the neoconservative convictions, framing democracy in broader terms than the purely structural and elitist conceptualization. Bush discusses, for example, such themes as broad political participation, democratic reform from within, respect for rights and for minority rights, and the culture of reconciliation.[50]

---

[48] Kaplan and Kristol, *War over Iraq*, 104; Puddington "Liberty for All," 74; Wolfson, "The Two Faces of Liberalism," 20–22; Kupchan, "Real Democratik," 35; Boot, "What Next," 27; Lane, "The Democracy Wave," 29; Kaplan, "Leftism on the Right," 29; Kaplan, "Dictatorship and No Standards," 27–29; Lindberg, "Referendum on Neoconservatism," 16–18; Odom, "NATO's Expansion," 43.

[49] "President Discusses Freedom and Democracy in Kyoto, Japan," 16 November 2005, accessed at http://www.whitehouse.gov/news/releases/2005/11/20051116-6.html, 6 March 2006.

[50] See, for example, "Remarks by the President at 2002 Graduation Exercise of the United States Military Academy," 1 June 2002, accessed at http://www.whitehouse.gov/news/releases/2002/06/

However, the democratic peace thesis, with its objective reputation (as advocated by neoconservatives), together with President Bush's self-proclaimed democratic commitment and a sense of confusion, rage, and urgency, combined to help democracy promotion become the backbone of the new Bush doctrine. Democracy promotion became the new creed, especially in the Middle East, as evident not only in the Afghanistan and Iraq wars but also in the roadmap, with its insistence on structural democratic reforms in the Palestinian Authority; in the Greater Middle East and North Africa project of building a democratic alliance; and in the U.S. National Security Strategy promulgated on 17 September 2002, which institutionalized democracy promotion as the main strategy in fighting global terrorism, aiming "to create a balance of power that favors human freedom."[51] No wonder William Kristol could boast, along with Tom Donnelly, in a *Weekly Standard* editorial, that "U.S. forces will be active and present in the region, in the service of furthering a decent alternative to the violent, corrupt, and anti-American status quo. Afghanistan and Iraq are the beginning, not the end, of what National Security Advisor Condoleezza Rice described as a 'generational commitment.'"[52]

In sum, we have seen how the neoconservatives' attempts to reconcile Fukuyama's *The End of History* and Huntington's *The Clash of Civilizations* brought them to endorse the structural theories of democratic peace, and how their reading of these theories was conducive to ushering in a new grand strategy of forceful democratization. This has turned neoconservatism into what I metaphorically term the "civilization of clashes." A good marketing strategy succeeded, and their creed is now reflected in the Bush doctrine, and in an endless military crusade designed as a democratizing project.

CRITIQUE

Many criticisms can be raised against the Bush administration's current creed of democratization. The policies could be labeled as imperialistic, as

---

20020601-3.html, 6 March 2006; "Remarks by the President at the 20th Anniversary of the National Endowment for Democracy," 6 November 2003, accessed at http://www.whitehouse.gov/news/releases/2003/11/20031106-2.html, 6 March 2006; "Remarks by the President on Winston Churchill and the War on Terror," 4 February 2004, accessed at http://www.whitehouse.gov/news/releases/2004/02/20040204-4.html, 6 March 2006; "Inauguration 2005," 20 January 2005, accessed at http://www.whitehouse.gov/news/releases/2005/01/20050120-1.html, 6 March 2006; "State of the Union Address," 2 February 2005, accessed at http://www.whitehouse.gov/news/releases/2005/02/20050202-11.html, 6 March 2006; "President Discusses War on Terror and Upcoming Iraqi Elections," 12 December 2005, accessed at http://www.whitehouse.gov/news/releases/2005/12/20051212-4.html, 6 March 2006; and "State of the Union Address," 31 January 2006, accessed at http://www.whitehouse.gov/stateoftheunion/2006/index.html, 6 March 2006.

[51] White House, "The National Security Strategy of the United States of America," 17 September 2002, accessed at http://www.whitehouse.gov/nsc/nss.html, 1 October 2007.

[52] Donnelly and Kristol, "More Caissons," 7.

paternalistic, as destabilizing crusades, as cynical demagogy masking self-aggrandizing interests, and as unlawful warmongering. Criticism can also be leveled at the futile efforts to democratize at bayonet point, and at the neoconservatives' misunderstanding of the essence of democracy. Additionally, critics can point to the unjust distribution of the burdens in American society of fighting and financing the war, as well as the unequal distribution of the profits arising from oil revenues and the reconstruction of Afghanistan and Iraq, or they can point to the immorality of aggressiveness, invasions, and occupations.

These criticisms, however, are mainly external: their origins and rationale, their philosophical and moral premises, differ from those that drive the neoconservatives. Although it may be morally more significant and philosophically more interesting to engage in heated ideological debates about neoconservatism and Bush's policies, such arguments will only reemphasize how unbridgeable are the premises of the neoconservatives and their adversaries. The persuasive potential of such external criticism is weak in regard to publics that fail to question the underlying premises or share them, or are not committed to any ideological camp.

A stronger criticism, therefore, is internal, and entails exposing the incoherencies in the idea-structure. Such incoherencies may prove irremediable, invalidating the ideology and destabilizing the strategy based on it. Then and only then is the path cleared to presenting an alternative. Two powerful internal criticisms of neoconservative ideology and aggressive democracy promotion are first, the conservative belief in the power of culture and tradition and their distrust of "social engineering," and second, the conservative fear of dictatorial concentration of power.

Conservatives and neoconservatives alike look askance at "social engineering." They believe in the gradual evolvement of societies, trusting the wisdom of what already exists, as in Georg F.W. Hegel's "what is rational is actual and what is actual is rational."[53] Conservative programs of change rely on incremental reforms that take into account the historical—even organic—nature of society. Dismantling the structure of society in a quick attempt at change is seen as radicalism based on the hubris of the Enlightenment, and on excessive belief in human rationality, leading inevitably to destabilization. In this light, neoconservatives view welfare policies and other centrist governmental programs as "social engineering" that is bound to fail and cause damage.

Does not the project of democratizing other countries entail at least as much trust in rationalism and "social engineering" as the domestic welfare state? Is not the idea of building democracy, in a country that has never experienced anything like it, founded on the same Enlightenment presumptions? Is this not an exercise in radicalism and hastiness, involving hubris of the worst sort? If true to their creed, conservatives can only answer these questions

---

[53] Georg F.W. Hegel, *Philosophy of Right*, trans. T.M. Knox (Oxford: Clarendon Press, 1952), 10.

affirmatively. Indeed, Fukuyama was quick to criticize the neoconservative democracy-promotion agenda along these lines, pointing to its incoherence and the need to return to conservative humility.[54] Pursuing further this line of argumentation brought Fukuyama in 2006 to renounce his allegiance with neoconservatism.[55]

It is the aforementioned conservative fear of unchecked power that underlies their minimalist, elitist concept of democracy. Indeed, in the domestic arena, they uphold the virtues of checks and balances, and in the global arena, of the balance of power. Supposedly, these structures counteract dictatorial concentrations of power and foster prudence in politics. Nevertheless, the neoconservatives show a reluctance to respect other global powers, and not only call on the United States to act unilaterally, but favor unipolarity, a world in which the United States is the sole hegemon, unchecked and unbalanced.[56] The Bush doctrine followed suit, with a concentrated effort to prolong the unipolar moment,[57] ensuring America's ability to build structural democracies around the world that would liberate their citizens from unbalanced and unchecked domestic rulers, thus enhancing U.S. security by forging democratic zones of peace.

The internal contradiction is evident and did not escape the notice of the conservative Huntington[58] and of realist theoreticians.[59] If one wishes to build domestic checks and balances to prevent concentrated power, one should aspire to similar precautionary mechanisms globally, ensuring that no single power can rule without prudence-inducing restraints. After all, the logic of Lord Acton's warning that "power tends to corrupt, and absolute power corrupts absolutely"[60] applies globally as well as domestically.

---

[54] Francis Fukuyama, "The Neoconservative Moment," *The National Interest* 76 (Summer 2004): 57–68.

[55] Francis Fukuyama, *America at the Crossroads: Democracy, Power, and the Neoconservative Legacy* (New Haven, CT and London: Yale University Press, 2006).

[56] In an earlier article, Krauthammer called for "nothing short of universal dominion": Charles Krauthammer, "Universal Dominion: Toward a Unipolar World," *The National Interest* 18 (Winter 1989): 48–49. Since then, he has somewhat moderated his aspirations: Krauthammer, "In Defense of Democratic Realism," 15–25; Krauthammer, "Bush Doctrine," 21; see also Boot, "What Next?" 27–33.

[57] White House, *National Security*, 29.

[58] Samuel Huntington, "The Great American Myth," (paper presented at the Grano Lecture Series on American Empire, Toronto, 10 February 2005), accessed at http://www.macleans.ca/topstories/politics/article.jsp?content=20050214_100487_100487, 21 November 2005. Neither was it hidden from the conservative analysts of the Cato Institute; for their critique of the Bush administration's democracy promotion, see, for example "Rebuilding Iraq: Prospects for Democracy," September/October 2003, accessed at http://www.cato.org/pubs/policy_report/v25n5/iraq.pdf, 1 October 2007.

[59] Prominent realist theorists, including Kenneth Waltz, Stephen Walt, and John Mearsheimer, formed the Coalition for a Realistic Foreign Policy to argue against the policies promoted by neoconservatism. See http://www.realisticforeignpolicy.org, accessed 1 October 2007.

[60] See his famous letter to Mandell Creighton published in John E.E. Dalberg-Acton, ed., *Historical Essays and Studies* (London: Macmillan, 1907), 504.

These two internal incoherencies emerge once we understand how the neoconservatives came to adopt the democratic peace thesis, what they mean by it, and what roles it has played in shaping and marketing the democracy-promotion agenda. This grand strategy of promoting democracy so as to attain security, based on the academic structural theories of democratic peace, suffers from acute internal incoherencies. When identifying these internal incoherencies, we should expect some critical problems in implementing this grand strategy.

Beyond the internal criticism, two alternative—and more viable—strategies offer a better approach to current world affairs and the issue of democratization. The first alternative is to mend neoconservatism's incoherencies and steer it back to a prudent and conservative reliance on gradual reform and on the global balance of power—that is, to heed the realist critique. The second involves a more optimistic worldview, a more comprehensive understanding of democracy, a more rigorous concept of change, and a search for a global structure based on multilateral activism—in other words, a critical theory of both domestic and world affairs.

Realism shares many features with conservatism, including the fear of disorder, the fear of dictatorial concentration of power, the emphasis on prudence, and the reliance on multipolar structures as fostering prudence. In applying these tenets to the global arena, the realist remedy to the neoconservatives' strategy is a global balance of power in which the United States concentrates on its own vital interests while respecting the sovereignty and interests of other states and powers. This could generate prudent American policies while preventing the rise of an imperial power (including the United States) that would impose its wishes on other states, interfere with their sovereignty, and subvert their freedom of action. Under the realist critique, the United States must abandon its current policy of democracy promotion.

This realist vision, then, favors a nondictatorial, multipolar world order that prevents chaos and provides the conditions of global justice. Realists, of course, are the first to admit that this global justice is minimal. They assert, however, that it is the only kind that is viable in the international sphere, and that any attempt to advance a more comprehensive notion of justice will compromise states' sovereignty and produce war, chaos, and the danger of world dictatorship, even further dissipating the minimal justice that is sustainable under conditions of sovereignty and the balance of power.

The realist approach indeed remedies neoconservatism's internal incoherencies, steering it back from experimentalism and aggressiveness to conservative prudence. However, realism has its own democratic, moral, and political drawbacks. It propounds a minimal concept of democracy, defining it narrowly as a structural, procedural, and elite project that precludes participatory citizenship and the serious consideration of normative democracy. Morally speaking, realism espouses an overly restricted view of morality and justice, and of their importance and plausibility in world affairs. Consequentially, realists show indifference to the political fortunes and misfortunes of others, proclaiming that whether they live under democracy or autocracy is not our concern. This moral indifference gives rise to a political drawback in that it leaves the neoconservatives, with their talk of democratization, holding the rhetorical high ground.

The other opponents of neoconservatism, those espousing more-progressive and leftist visions of world order, are pushed into a corner where they—out of disdain for the neoconservatives' policies—advocate pacifism at any cost, including abandoning others to their political misfortunes no matter how severe. Today, the radical left preaches isolationism and, even more disturbing, a moral relativism that eschews any international effort at democratizing authoritarian regimes. Again, this leaves the neoconservatives to salvage the rhetoric of morality and project an image as defenders of democracy.[61] In other words, dictators can entrust their survival to the realists' moral indifference, the leftists' pacifism and relativism, and the neoconservatives' inadequate unilateral policies.

Therefore, an alternative strategy is needed that can address the inadequacies of neoconservatism; that is based on different philosophical premises and political commitments; that simultaneously and *coherently* favors deliberative democracy, notions of global morality and justice, and multilateral approaches to international problems; and that, furthermore, does not shy away from actively promoting domestic and international change. In other words, we need to elaborate a critical theory of both domestic and global realities. In the following I will outline a sketch of such a critical theory worthy of further exploration.

On the democratic front, this theory should endorse participatory paradigms of democracy that respect the citizen, her rationality, and her understanding of her self-interest and of collaborative democratic activity. These paradigms are congruous with global notions of morality and justice, meaning we should seek to spread human and political rights to those who lack them, entailing, among other measures, democracy promotion around the world. However, spreading democracy and human rights should not be done unilaterally, disrespecting the concerns of the democratized people and of other states; it should be done in ways that value democratic values, norms, and procedures. It should not be the province of any single power, no matter how mighty it is, how globally it views its interests, and how unipolar it believes the world to be. Democratization should be done multilaterally, involving inter-governmental organizations, nongovernmental organizations, and social movements, as well as individuals from the democratized countries.

Moreover, as argued earlier, the normative and cultural concepts of democratization (which are the same as the deliberative and participatory ones)

---

[61] A notable exception is Michael Ignatieff, who calls on the United States to meet its moral obligations, including by resorting to force. See Michael Ignatieff, *Empire Lite: Nation-Building in Bosnia, Kosovo and Afghanistan* (London: Vintage, 2003).

call for constructing a democratic society and culture primarily by facilitating domestic agents of political and social transformation in the target country. Constructing a civil society of informed, involved, and participating citizens is a long process that involves profound social and political changes. In that sense, democratization is a radical process aiming at the foundational level of society, its most deep-seated roots and attributes, and attempting to drastically change them. Forcing democratization from the outside and dictating a rapid tempo of superficial transformation may result in a backlash dynamic. It may lead to the rise to power—sometimes by means of elections—of fundamentalist and xenophobic groups. The sweeping victory of Hamas in the Palestinian elections of 25 January 2006 is a case in point. Neither can democratization be implemented via military occupation, as laid out in the ineffective neoconservative strategy. The military can be employed to intervene in humanitarian crises, but not in the hope that it will become the agent of democratization or that occupation will quickly and easily result in democracy.

The critical theory, then, opens a political space between an international Hobbesian reality and a dictatorial neoconservative empire. In that space, it is possible to promote the institutionalization of international organizations and of a world order that respects the rights of individuals, the merits of social movements, and the sovereignty of states. Clearly, such a world does not yet exist, and our belief in actualizing it rests on our belief in the human capacity to ameliorate the current international reality.

Nevertheless, the inadequacies of the neoconservative strategy of regime change based on the structural theories of democratic peace, and the moral and political drawbacks of both realist moral indifference and leftist moral relativism, leave us no option but to further develop this critical theory that coherently seeks to spread democracy domestically and globally. This is a morally worthwhile goal, regardless of the academic validity or strategic value of the democratic peace theories.*

*Earlier versions of this paper were presented at the 47th annual meeting of the International Studies Association, San Diego, CA, on 23 March 2006, and at the Belfer Center for Science and International Affairs at Harvard University, Cambridge, MA, on 3 March 2005. I would like to thank Emanuel Adler, Katty Ish-Shalom, Sean M. Lynn-Jones, Steven E. Miller, Assaf Moghadam, Lien-Hang Nguyen, Martín Plot, David Ricci, Doron Shultziner, and the two anonymous reviewers for their most useful comments. I also benefited from the financial support and the intellectual communities of the Belfer Center for Science and International Affairs at Harvard University, and the John M. Olin Institute for Strategic Studies at Harvard University.

Credibility and the War on Terror

CHRISTOPHER J. FETTWEIS

Credibility is a nation's greatest asset in international affairs. It is the hardest to earn and the most difficult to maintain, but once possessed it makes it possible to compel changes in behavior.

—John McCain[1]

Were the United States to withdraw prematurely from Iraq, warned Donald Rumsfeld in August 2006, the consequences for global stability would be catastrophic. Dominoes would fall across the region, and then beyond. "The enemy would tell us to leave Afghanistan and then withdraw from the Middle East," he told the Senate Armed Services Committee. Then "they'd order us and all those who don't share their militant ideology to leave what they call the occupied Muslim lands from Spain to the Philippines." The harm to the credibility of the United States would be nearly irreparable, and before long, the American people would be forced "to make a stand nearer home."[2]

Clearly, Henry Kissinger's decades-old observation that no serious policymaker doubts the importance of prestige, honor, and credibility still applies today.[3] Experienced practitioners of foreign policy take for granted the notion that actions taken today can affect (and perhaps prevent) the crises of tomorrow. The messages sent by foreign policy actions can sometimes seem to be more important than the actions themselves, since other states—including current and potential enemies—are watching every move, making judgments about the credibility of U.S. threats and promises. To question the wisdom of the imperative may seem terribly naïve, and perhaps even dangerous.

This "credibility imperative," in historian Robert McMahon's words, has occupied a central position in every major foreign policy debate in the last

---

[1] John McCain, "No Time to Sleep," *The Washington Post*, 24 October 2002.
[2] "The Sound of One Domino Falling," *The New York Times*, 4 August 2006.
[3] Henry Kissinger, *The White House Years* (Boston, MA: Little, Brown & Co., 1979), 228.

CHRISTOPHER J. FETTWEIS is assistant professor of political science at Tulane University and is author of *Losing Hurts Twice as Bad: The Four Stages to Moving Beyond Iraq*.

50 years.[4] However, many scholars remain, for the most part, unconvinced. Since the war in Vietnam, a competing conventional wisdom has been building momentum in scholarly circles, one that considers the obsession with credibility to be an illusory waste of time at best, and a producer of profoundly destructive misguidance at worst. Few issues currently separate the policy community from scholars in a more profound and important way. Resolving this curious disconnect between the beliefs of scholars and those of practitioners could hardly be more urgent. For better or for worse, the credibility imperative will probably have an enormous effect on U.S. foreign policy throughout the "long war" on terror, shaping all of the most vital decisions that will have to be made.

At first glance, Islamic fundamentalists appear to pose a difficult challenge to the credibility imperative's many academic skeptics. Osama bin Laden and his allies apparently considered the United States to be a feckless, cowardly "paper tiger," which is a perception that may have emboldened them to strike. When attacked, effete Americans sue; they send lawyers, not soldiers. September 11 might even have been prevented, so this logic goes, if Washington had responded to previous al Qaeda attacks with a more determined show of force. Perhaps the war on terror will prove the conventional wisdom of the practitioner regarding the lessons of credibility to have much more value than scholars think. Did a lack of American "credibility" lead al Qaeda to believe that it could strike the United States with impunity? Would a reputation for resolve keep a country safer during the war on terror?

Surely it behooves both policymakers and scholars to re-assess occasionally the wisdom of even their most closely held assumptions. Few beliefs are more deeply ingrained in the foreign policy conventional wisdom, and more in need of re-examination, than the nearly universal belief in the vital importance of national credibility. This paper investigates this curious divergence between scholars and practitioners when it comes to credibility. It reviews conventional wisdoms and speculates on how they developed. After making a series of observations about the effect that the "credibility imperative" has on the foreign policy debates, the paper discusses the uses and abuses of the concept in the war on terror. In the end, it is hard to escape the conclusion, even during the current era, that credibility is an illusion—and an exceptionally dangerous illusion at that. Since it remains impossible for any state to control the perceptions of others, the continuing concern with credibility and reputation in the post-Cold War world is deeply misguided, and likely to cause many more problems than it solves. Keeping an eye on the future, although natural and comforting, often creates profound myopia in the present.

---

[4] Robert J. McMahon, "Credibility and World Power: Exploring the Psychological Dimension in Postwar American Diplomacy," *Diplomatic History* 15 (Fall 1991), 455–471.

The Credibility Imperative in U.S. Foreign Policy

The term "credibility" has been used in so many contexts that it can at times seem to mean all things to all people. The credibility of a state is a mixture of its competence, legitimacy, resolve, trustworthiness, willingness to take casualties, and/or rigidity of purpose. In perhaps its most central and common usage, however, credibility is simply the capability to be believed or trusted. Perhaps most crucially for policymakers, credibility is often used as a code word for the prestige and reputation of a state.[5] It is, in Kissinger's words, "the coin with which we conduct our foreign policy," an intangible asset without which a state cannot influence the actions of others.[6] In periods of high credibility, a state can deter and compel behavior and accomplish goals short of war; when credibility is low, skeptical adversaries and allies may be tempted to ignore a state's threats and promises. To policymakers, therefore, solid credibility is worth many divisions at the negotiating table.

The credibility of a state forms the basis of its reputation, which is little more than an impression of fundamental national character that serves as a guide for others trying to anticipate future actions.[7] Classical deterrence theory holds that if a state fails to rise to a challenge or pursue a goal with sufficient resolve, it risks earning a reputation for weakness, which might encourage aggression from enemies and discourage the loyalty of allies.[8] Threats made by a state without credibility may not be believed, setting off a cascading "domino effect" of aggression from emboldened rivals, possibly until they challenge an interest that is truly vital, making a major war unavoidable. The credibility imperative is also clearly related to the post-war Western obsession with "appeasement," which is, of course, a code word for a show of weakness that inadvertently encourages an aggressor.

Credibility is a unique and complicated national asset. Perhaps some of the profound insecurity that some policymakers display regarding their credibility may be tied to the fact that its status is ultimately beyond their control. No state owns its reputation—it can be affected by the actions of a state to be sure, but

---

[5] Ibid., 455.

[6] Dan Williams and Ann Devroy, "U.S. Policy Lacks Focus, Critics Say: Bosnia Cited as Prime Case," *The Washington Post*, 24 April 1994.

[7] Jonathan Mercer, *Reputation and International Politics* (Ithaca, NY: Cornell University Press, 1996), 6.

[8] Thomas C. Schelling, *The Strategy of Conflict* (Cambridge, MA: Harvard University Press, 1960); Thomas C. Schelling, *Arms and Influence* (New Haven, CT: Yale University Press, 1966); Glenn H. Snyder, *Deterrence and Defense: Toward a New Theory of National Security* (Princeton, NJ: Princeton University Press, 1961); Alexander L. George and Richard Smoke, *Deterrence in American Foreign Policy: Theory and Practice* (New York: Columbia University Press, 1974); Robert Jervis, *Perception and Misperception in International Politics* (Princeton, NJ: Princeton University Press, 1976); Richard Ned Lebow, *Between Peace and War* (Baltimore, MD: Johns Hopkins University Press, 1981); and Robert Jervis, Richard Ned Lebow, and Janice Stein, eds., *Psychology and Deterrence* (Baltimore, MD: Johns Hopkins University Press, 1985).

in a very real and important sense, it exists in the minds of others. "Credibility exists," John McCain has noted, "only in the eye of the beholder."[9] Given this complexity, perhaps it is little wonder that scholars often omit the credibility imperative from their otherwise-parsimonious explanatory models of U.S. foreign policy behavior. All psychological variables are difficult to measure and inherently unquantifiable; credibility is no different. However, U.S. foreign policy is impossible to understand without it.

The Origin and Development of the Credibility Imperative, in Theory and Policy

A variety of explanations have been proposed to account for the power that the credibility imperative has had over U.S. policymakers since World War II. First, it is possible that concerns about reputation go hand in hand with great-power status.[10] Perhaps small powers, whose basic security is often not assured, have less need to worry about the messages that their actions send to potential enemies and allies. The weak do not fear the credibility of their commitments to the strong—no dominoes will fall if a small state fails to keep a promise. According to this explanation, as the power of the United States grew over the years, perhaps it was quite natural for its leaders to become more concerned with intangible assets. Credibility might be a concern only for those participating in geopolitics on a global scale.

Second, the nature of the Cold War surely helped the imperative to take root. Since both sides were for the most part interested in avoiding direct conflict, the contest for global supremacy was fought in nontraditional arenas. In a very important sense, the Cold War was a battle of ideas, pitting competing systems of socioeconomic organization against each other in the minds of the masses as much as on the field of battle. Intangible, psychological factors took on increased importance for security and stability, with success and failure often measured by perception as much as reality. Credibility for the United States was therefore also a measure of the viability of the system it espoused, so when it was low, policymakers worried that others might get the impression that history was on the side of the Soviets and communism. Walt Rostow, who was the director of policy planning in John F. Kennedy's State Department, was perhaps the strongest advocate of this argument. Rostow felt that since it was vitally important to convince the third world to follow a capitalist model of development, reverses in the periphery could be strategic disasters.[11] More than merely the "coin with which we run our foreign policy," credibility became the measuring stick by which to judge which side was winning the

[9] McCain, "No Time to Sleep."

[10] McMahon, "Credibility and World Power," 469.

[11] John Lewis Gaddis, *Strategies of Containment: A Critical Appraisal of Postwar American Security Policy* (New York: Oxford University Press, 1982), 208–209.

struggle, and which camp the wise third parties would join. On the Cold War scorecard, credibility points were won each time Washington kept its commitments, and lost whenever it did not.

The dominant weaponry of the Cold War also enhanced the imperative to remain credible. The nuclear revolution changed not only how states acted, but also how policymakers thought about international relations.[12] Since much about the use of nuclear weapons seemed irrational—after all, only "madmen" would contemplate nuclear war—security professionals were forced to deal with basic questions about sanity and insanity. The psychology of the opponent, in particular, became a much more important point of emphasis. As McMahon has argued, "The very essence of security in the nuclear era has been based on conjectures about the cognitive process of others."[13] The wise policymaker took all possible steps to influence those cognitive processes in productive ways. Maintaining credible commitments was perhaps the most obvious way to do so.

Third, some scholars have suggested that there may be something in U.S. political culture that makes it particularly susceptible to the credibility imperative.[14] While all states are concerned to some degree about their reputations, no country seems to have taken the imperative to remain credible as seriously as has the United States since the Second World War. Scholars have not been able to detect similar levels of concern over credibility in any other state, even in the Soviet Union, which presumably faced many of the same challenges during the Cold War without exhibiting a similar influence of the imperative.[15] Jerome Slater has argued that "it does not occur to ordinary states to imagine that their 'vital interests' are integrally linked to outcomes of local wars in tiny countries thousands of miles away from their borders."[16] The United States, of course, has never been an "ordinary" state.[17]

Finally, the prevailing conventional wisdom in academia has helped to provide an intellectual justification for the belief in the importance of credibility. Deterrence theory, which was, of course, one of the major intellectual orthodoxies of the early Cold War, preached the essential *interdependence* of foreign policy actions across time and space. Since the actions of a state send messages to others about its probable behavior in the future, irresolution in crises can teach rivals and allies alike that the state is unlikely

---

[12] See Michael Mandelbaum, *The Nuclear Revolution: International Politics Before and After Hiroshima* (Cambridge, UK: Cambridge University Press, 1981).

[13] McMahon, "Credibility and World Power," 469.

[14] Ibid., 471.

[15] Gaddis, *Strategies of Containment*; McMahon, "Credibility and World Power," 471.

[16] Jerome Slater, "The Domino Theory and International Politics: The Case of Vietnam," *Security Studies* 3 (Winter 1993/94), 218.

[17] Robert H. Johnson, *Improbable Dangers: U.S. Conceptions of Threat in the Cold War and After* (New York: St. Martin's Press, 1994); and Frances Fitzgerald, *Way Out There in the Blue: Reagan, Star Wars and the End of the Cold War* (New York: Touchstone, 2001).

to respond to any challenges anywhere.[18] Emboldened by such perceptions, adversaries would be likely to press their advantage and engage in adventurism elsewhere. If, instead, the state is resolute in honoring its commitments, even in cases of seemingly small importance, potential aggressors will take note and serious future crises will be less likely. "Essentially," explained Thomas Schelling, "we tell the Soviets that we have to react here because, if we did not, they would not believe us when we say that we will react there."[19] The imperative to remain credible was part of the training of nearly every American foreign policy professional for decades. Its importance was taken as a given, almost as the political science equivalent of settled law.

Cold War policymakers often had deep backgrounds in academic theories of international relations. Indeed no policymaker provides a better example of the interdependence belief in practice than Henry Kissinger, a former academic who often seemed to interpret all international events through zero-sum, interdependent lenses. Kissinger was but the most visible of a brand of foreign policy generalist who, along with such men as Dean Acheson, John Foster Dulles, Robert McNamara, Paul Nitze, Richard Nixon, and Zbigniew Brzezinski, tended to fit every event, no matter how local or peripheral it might have seemed, into a tightly knit framework of global competition. When India intervened in the Pakistani civil war in 1971, for example, Kissinger saw the hidden hand of the Soviets, which underlined the importance of maintaining the credibility of U.S. threats. "Had we acquiesced in such a power play," he wrote, "we would have sent a wrong signal to Moscow and unnerved all our allies, China, and the forces for restraint in other volatile areas of the world. This was, indeed, why the Soviets had made the Indian assault on Pakistan possible in the first place."[20] When the Soviets threatened to construct a submarine base in Cienfuego in 1970, Kissinger thought that "the Kremlin had perhaps been emboldened when we reacted to the dispatch of combat troops to the Middle East by pressing Israel for a cease-fire."[21] The Soviet invasion of Afghanistan was only possible, thought Brzezinksi, Kissinger's successor and former academic, because the United States had lost credibility by not responding more forcefully to communist adventurism in the Horn of Africa, which, in turn, was a result of the abandonment of Saigon.[22] The belief in the importance of credibility may have partially begun in the academy—but the current skepticism of scholars, which began in earnest during the war in Vietnam, has not had similar real-world traction.

---

[18] Schelling, *Arms and Influence*, 35–91.

[19] Ibid., 55.

[20] Kissinger, *White House Years*, 913–914.

[21] Ibid., 641.

[22] Zbigniew Brzezinski, *Power and Principle* (New York: Farrar, Strauss and Giroux, 1983), 429.

The Point of Divergence: Vietnam

The credibility imperative had become firmly embedded in the psyche of the U.S. foreign policy establishment by the time some of the crucial decisions regarding the war in Vietnam needed to be made. Without the imperative, the war would not have been fought. More than any other single factor, a fear of the message that a communist victory would send to the neighboring (and not-so-neighboring) states compelled the United States to try to prop up the corrupt, unpopular, Roman Catholic South Vietnamese rulers. In a 1965 memo released with the *Pentagon Papers*, Secretary of Defense John McNaughton described the reasons that the United States was in Vietnam as 70 percent "to avoid a humiliating U.S. defeat (to our reputation as guarantor)," 20 percent to prevent communism from overtaking South Vietnam, and only 10 percent to help the people of South Vietnam.[23] The damage that a failure in Vietnam could do to the reputation of the United States was potentially catastrophic. President Lyndon Johnson warned his cabinet that "if we run out on Southeast Asia, there will be trouble ahead in every part of the globe—not just in Asia, but in the Middle East and in Europe, in Africa and Latin America. I am convinced that our retreat from this challenge will open the path to World War III."[24] Kissinger agreed, warning that if South Vietnam were allowed to fall, it would represent a "fundamental threat, over a period of time, to the security of the United States."[25] Only when framed inside the prism of the credibility imperative did victory in Vietnam become a vital national interest.

Skepticism grew steadily as the war dragged on, and as the credibility imperative drove policymakers to believe that withdrawal from what seemed to be an unwinnable war would lead to national catastrophe. Intellectuals in the anti-war movement led the way, expressing moral outrage that a war would be fought primarily for the messages it would send to our enemies and allies.[26] Academic skepticism about the importance of credibility grew alongside questions about the tangible interests at stake, especially after it became clear that the costs in blood and treasure were not proportional to any potential benefits that could conceivably be gained from the survival of an anti-communist South Vietnam. To prominent realists such as Hans Morgenthau and Kenneth Waltz, intervention in isolated, resource-poor Vietnam was irrational, "moralistic," and mistaken. Only "if developments in Vietnam might indeed tilt the world's balance in America's disfavor,"

---

[23] Quoted by Bruce W. Jentleson, "American Commitments in the Third World: Theory vs. Practice," *International Organization* 41 (Autumn 1987), 676.

[24] Lyndon Baines Johnson, *The Vantage Point* (New York: Holt, Rinehart and Winston, 1971), 147–148.

[25] Quoted by Barbara W. Tuchman, *March of Folly: From Troy to Vietnam* (New York: Random House, 1984), 375.

[26] Jonathan Schell, *The Time of Illusion* (New York: Knopf, 1976), 337–387.

argued Waltz, would the war be worthwhile.[27] They did not, of course, since from a purely material perspective, Vietnam was next to irrelevant to U.S. national security. The cost of a loss to U.S. credibility, however, appeared incalculable.

The war in Vietnam marked the beginning of the current debate over the importance of credibility, and the point of divergence between scholars and practitioners. Despite dire warnings from many of its leaders, the United States not only withdrew its forces from Southeast Asia but also cut back on its aid and watched North Vietnamese troops overrun Saigon in 1975. Since this "cut-and-run" and subsequent loss of an ally were undoubtedly unmitigated disasters for the credibility of the United States, presumably a string of foreign policy setbacks should have followed. If international actions are truly interdependent, as policymakers believe, then the 1970s would probably have seen evidence of allies beginning to question U.S. commitments, dominoes falling where the reputation of the United States maintained the status quo, and increased levels of Soviet activity in the third world. The conventional wisdom suggests that the humiliating rooftop helicopter evacuation of the U.S. embassy in Saigon should have heralded a dark period for U.S. foreign policy.

However, no such string of catastrophes took place. Perhaps most obviously, there is no evidence that any allies of the United States were significantly demoralized, or that any questioned the wisdom of their allegiance. If anything, many of Washington's closest allies seemed relieved when the war ended, since many of them had doubted its importance in the first place and had feared that it distracted the United States from other, more pressing issues.[28] Certainly no state, not even any "client" states in the third world, changed its geopolitical orientation as a result of Vietnam.

The damage to U.S. credibility also did not lead to the long-predicted spread of communism throughout the region, as even Kissinger today grudgingly acknowledges.[29] On the contrary, in the ten years that followed the fall of Saigon, the non-communist nations of Southeast Asia enjoyed a period of unprecedented prosperity.[30] The only dominoes that fell were two countries that were even less relevant than Vietnam to the global balance of power—Cambodia and Laos, both of which were hardly major losses for the West,

---

[27] Kenneth N. Waltz, "The Politics of Peace," *International Studies Quarterly* 11 (September 1967), 206. See also Hans J. Morgenthau, *Vietnam and the United States* (Washington DC: Public Affairs Press, 1965).

[28] Johnson, *Improbable Dangers*, 160–161.

[29] Henry Kissinger, *Ending the Vietnam War: A History of America's Involvement in and Extrication from the Vietnam War* (New York: Simon and Schuster, 2003), 561. See also Shiping Tang, "Reputation, the Cult of Reputation, and International Conflict," *Security Studies* 14 (January–March 2005), 34–62; and Slater, "The Domino Theory and International Politics."

[30] George C. Herring, *America's Longest War: The United States and Vietnam, 1950-1975*, 2nd ed. (New York: Knopf), 270.

especially given the tragedies that followed. Nationalism proved to be a bulwark against the spread of communism that could not be overcome by any loss of confidence in U.S. commitments.

Most importantly, the Soviet Union apparently failed to become emboldened by the U.S. withdrawal, and did not appreciably increase its "adventurism" in the third world, compared to the 1950s and '60s, when U.S. credibility was high.[31] In an important and convincing study, Ted Hopf examined over 500 articles and 300 leadership speeches made by Soviet policymakers throughout the 1970s, and found that their public pronouncements did not show evidence of a belief that U.S. setbacks in the third world signaled a lack of resolution. "The most dominant inference Soviet leaders made after Vietnam," concluded Hopf, "was not about falling regional dominoes or bandwagoning American allies, but about the prospects of détente with the United States and Western Europe."[32] Soviet behavior did not change, despite the perception of incompetence that many Americans feared would inspire increased belligerence. Kissinger has referred to Soviet decisions to intervene in Angola and Ethiopia as evidence of the negative effect of Vietnam, but Hopf found no evidence that perceptions of U.S. credibility affected Soviet decision makers. It appears as if those interventions—which, of course, were in strategically irrelevant countries anyway—were independent events that probably would have occurred no matter what had happened in Vietnam. Other negative events in the 1970s, such as the fall of the Shah, seem even more independent of the catastrophe, despite half-hearted efforts to link them together.[33] As it turns out, Vietnam was all but irrelevant to international politics, which is of course exactly what critics of the war had maintained all along.

The immediate post-Vietnam era actually contains a good deal of evidence to bolster a conclusion opposite to the presumptions of deterrence theorists. Robert Jervis has argued that states often act more aggressively in periods of "low" credibility following a reversal, or in response to the perception of irresolution. The Soviets might well have expected the United States to act like a wounded animal, perhaps even more willing to defend its interests than before the withdrawal from Vietnam. "A statesman's willingness to resist," Jervis argued, "may be inversely related to how well he has done in the recent past."[34] Indeed, U.S. policymakers, believing that

---

[31] Ted Hopf, *Peripheral Visions: Deterrence Theory and American Foreign Policy in the Third World, 1965-1990* (Ann Arbor: University of Michigan Press, 1994).

[32] Ted Hopf, "Soviet Inferences from their Victories in the Periphery: Visions of Resistance or Cumulating Gains?" in Robert Jervis and Jack Snyder, eds., *Dominoes and Bandwagons: Strategic Beliefs and Great Power Competition in the Eurasian Rimland* (New York: Oxford University Press, 1991), 167.

[33] Kissinger, *Ending the Vietnam War*, 561.

[34] Robert Jervis, "Domino Beliefs and Strategic Behavior" in Jervis and Snyder, eds., *Dominoes and Bandwagons*, 37.

the national credibility had been damaged, seemed eager to reverse such perceptions abroad. The seizure of the *Mayaguez*, which occurred immediately after the fall of Saigon, provided the opportunity to do so. The response of the administration of Gerald Ford was rapid, decisive, and belligerent. As the President said at the time, "I have to show some strength in order to help us ... with our credibility in the world." Kissinger had told reporters off the record that "the United States must carry out some act somewhere in the world which shows its determination to continue to be a world power." He wanted to react rapidly, arguing that "indecision and weakness can lead to demoralized friends and emboldened adversaries." Even though a rapid military response might have put the captured crew at risk, their lives were unfortunately a "secondary consideration," argued Kissinger, since the "real issue was international credibility and not the safe return of the crew."[35] As will be argued below, the credibility imperative rarely supports negotiated solutions. This was by no means an isolated incident. The invasion of Grenada, for example, cannot be understood without reference to the perceived loss of credibility that followed the removal of troops from Lebanon after the bombings of the embassy and Marine barracks. The intervention in Somalia was in large part a response to and cover for U.S. inaction in Bosnia.[36]

Since Vietnam, scholars have been generally unable to identify cases in which high credibility helped the United States achieve its goals. The short-term aftermath of the Cuban Missile Crisis, for example, did not include a string of Soviet reversals, or the kind of benign bandwagoning with the West that deterrence theorists would have expected. In fact, the perceived reversal in Cuba seemed to harden Soviet resolve. As the crisis was drawing to a close, Soviet diplomat Vasily Kuznetsov angrily told his counterpart, "You Americans will never be able to do this to us again."[37] Kissinger commented in his memoirs that "the Soviet Union thereupon launched itself on a determined, systematic, and long-term program of expanding *all* categories of its military power .... The 1962 Cuban crisis was thus a historic turning point—but not for the reason some Americans complacently supposed."[38] The reassertion of the credibility of the United States, which was done at the brink of nuclear war, had few long-lasting benefits. The Soviets seemed to learn the wrong lesson.

[35] Christopher Jon Lamb, *Belief Systems and Decision Making in the Mayaguez Crisis* (Gainesville: University of Florida Press, 1989), 68, 72, 73, 81, 149.

[36] David Halberstam, *War in a Time of Peace: Bush, Clinton, and the Generals* (New York: Scribner, 2001), 250–252.

[37] Michael R. Beschloss, *The Crisis Years: Kennedy and Khrushchev, 1960-1963* (New York: Edward Burlingame Books, 1991), 563; and Charles E. Bohlen, *Witness to History 1929-1969* (New York: W.W. Norton and Co., 1973), 495–496.

[38] Kissinger, *White House Years*, 197 (emphasis in original).

There is actually scant evidence that other states ever learn the *right* lessons. Cold War history contains little reason to believe that the credibility of the superpowers had very much effect on their ability to influence others. Over the last decade, a series of major scholarly studies have cast further doubt upon the fundamental assumption of interdependence across foreign policy actions. Employing methods borrowed from social psychology rather than the economics-based models commonly employed by deterrence theorists, Jonathan Mercer argued that threats are far more *independent* than is commonly believed and, therefore, that reputations are not likely to be formed on the basis of individual actions.[39] While policymakers may feel that their decisions send messages about their basic *dispositions* to others, most of the evidence from social psychology suggests otherwise. Groups tend to interpret the actions of their rivals as *situational*, dependent upon the constraints of place and time. Therefore, they are not likely to form lasting impressions of irresolution from single, independent events. Mercer argued that the interdependence assumption had been accepted on faith, and rarely put to a coherent test; when it was, it almost inevitably failed.[40]

Mercer's larger conclusions were that states cannot control their reputations or level of credibility, and that target adversaries and allies will ultimately form their own perceptions. Sending messages for their consideration in future crises, therefore, is all but futile. These arguments echoed some of the broader critiques of the credibility imperative that had emerged in response to the war in Vietnam, both by realists like Morgenthau and Waltz and by so-called area specialists, who took issue with the interdependence beliefs of the generalists. As Jervis observed, a common axis of disagreement in American foreign policy has been between those who focus on the specific situation and the particular nations involved (often State Department officials or area experts), and those who take a global geopolitical perspective (often in the White House or outside foreign policy generalists). The former usually believe that states in a region are strongly driven by domestic concerns and local rivalries; the latter are predisposed to think that these states look to the major powers for their cues and have little control over their own fates.[41]

Throughout most of the Cold War, since those who argued that events are interdependent won most of the policy debates, U.S. foreign policy was obsessed with credibility.

A series of other studies have followed those of Hopf and Mercer, yielding similar results. The empirical record seems to suggest that there have been few instances of a setback in one arena influencing state behavior in a second arena.[42]

---

[39] Mercer, *Reputation and International Politics*.

[40] Ibid., 28–42.

[41] Jervis, "Domino Beliefs and Strategic Behavior," 26.

[42] Paul Huth and Bruce Russett, "What Makes Deterrence Work? Cases from 1900 to 1980," *World Politics* 36 (July 1984): 496–526. Also James D. Fearon, "Signaling versus the Balance of Power and

Daryl Press began his recent study expecting to find that perceptions of the opponent's credibility would be an important variable affecting state behavior.[43] He chose three cases in which reputation would presumably have been vital to the outcome—the outbreak of the First World War, the Berlin Crisis of the late 1950s, and the Cuban Missile Crisis—and found, to his surprise, that in all three cases, leaders did not appear to be influenced at all by prior actions of their rivals, for better or for worse. Crisis behavior appeared to be entirely independent; credibility, therefore, was all but irrelevant. Mercer's conclusions about reputation seem to have amassed a good deal more supporting evidence in the time since he wrote.

Today the credibility imperative's academic defenders are small in number and influence.[44] In the policy world, however, the obsession with credibility lives on undiminished, and doubters are clearly in the minority. Shiping Tang considers the continued existence of the credibility imperative in spite of the overwhelming evidence to the contrary to be evidence of almost cultish behavior among policymakers.[45] The longevity of this cult seems to derive from a couple of foundations. First, since foreign policy is by necessity a worst-case-scenario business, prudence often counsels leaders to hedge against the most negative potential outcomes.[46] Since a loss of credibility offers a presumably plausible route to national ruin, the sagacious policymaker will often be very wary of damage to the reputation of the state, no matter what logic and the empirical evidence suggest. After all, while incorrect academics face virtually no consequences, missteps by leaders can be catastrophic.

Second, the current academic conventional wisdom is counterintuitive, and in some senses contradictory to normal daily experience. Individuals certainly develop reputations in their daily lives that influence the way that others treat them. Parents understand that they must carry through on their threats and promises if they want their children to take their future instructions seriously, and we all have friends whose repeated failures to deliver on past promises make us skeptical of their future assur-

---

Interests: An Empirical Test of a Crisis Bargaining Model," *Journal of Conflict Resolution* 38 (June 1994): 236–269.

[43] Daryl G. Press, *Calculating Credibility: How Leaders Assess Military Threats* (Ithaca, NY: Cornell University Press, 2006), vii–viii.

[44] Recent defenders include Vaughn P. Shannon and Michael Dennis, "Militant Islam and the Futile Fight for Reputation," *Security Studies* 16 (April–June 2007): 287–317; Michael Lind, *Vietnam. The Necessary War: A Reinterpretation of America's Most Disastrous Military Conflict* (New York: Free Press, 1999); Dale C. Copeland, "Do Reputations Matter?" *Security Studies* 7 (Autumn 1997): 33–71; and Paul K. Huth, "Reputations and Deterrence: A Theoretical and Empirical Assessment," *Security Studies* 7 (Autumn 1997): 72–99.

[45] Tang, "Reputation, the Cult of Reputation, and International Conflict."

[46] Jack Snyder, "Introduction," in Jervis and Snyder, eds., *Dominoes and Bandwagons*, 9–12.

ances.[47] However, international relations differ drastically from interpersonal. As Press explains,

> Children use past actions when they evaluate their parents' credibility to punish them, and perhaps we all use past actions to assess whether a friend will show up at the movies. But there is no logical basis to generalize from these mundane situations to the most critical decisions made by national leaders during crises. In fact it would be odd—even irrational—if people relied on the same mental shortcuts that they use to make unimportant split-second decisions of daily life when they confront the most important decisions of their lives—decisions on which their country's survival depends.[48]

Press argues that national capabilities and interests—not past behavior—provide the foundation for the formation of perceptions. However, the credibility imperative has a powerful intuitive logic behind it, based upon lifetimes of interpersonal experience. There are therefore significant impediments in front of those who would challenge the wisdom of the policymaker's obsession with reputation.

This divergence in conventional wisdom between policy and scholarship would not be a major issue for twenty-first-century international politics if policies that are primarily based upon the need to appear credible were not often counterproductive, costly, and dangerous. The imperative has clear effects upon policy, and is employed in debates in predictable, measurable, and uniformly unhelpful ways.

The Post-Cold War Credibility Imperative

Today there is no competing superpower poised to take advantage of perceived U.S. irresolution, no revisionist state probing the "new world order" for weaknesses. Presumably, the credibility imperative should have waned in importance with the collapse of the Soviet Union, as neutrals were robbed of bandwagoning alternatives and as allies were relieved of any lingering fears that the United States might fail to come to their rescue in a crisis. But concerns for reputation have lingered throughout the post-Cold War period, and have returned with renewed vigor to misguide policymakers waging the war on terror.

The Soviet Union collapsed; the national obsession with credibility lived on, in defiance of logic and evidence. It has been difficult for the imperative's defenders to identify an instance in which a post-Cold War state (or independent actor) was either encouraged by a discredited United States or discouraged by its apparent resolution. Of course, one can always respond that such counterfactual argument is impossible. Successful deterrence is hard to

---

[47] Press, *Calculating Credibility*, 12.
[48] Ibid., 23.

measure, since the analyst can never be sure that the aggressor was deterred from attacking or simply never planned to attack in the first place.[49] But the evidence thus far suggests that there is little reason to believe that post-Cold War international events are any more interdependent than were their predecessors.

Although many observers have argued that the administration of Bill Clinton damaged U.S. credibility in a number of ways, it is hard to identify a rival (or an opportunistic local leader) who took advantage of such an impression. When a semi-organized mob prevented the disembarkation of U.S. troops in Haiti in October of 1993, for example, critics like James Baker predictably accused the Clinton administration of "debas[ing] the currency of U.S. credibility."[50] Senator Tom Harkin worried that "if we can't stand up for democracy and human rights in our own hemisphere, then what do the Serbs have to fear? What do the Chinese have to fear?"[51] Less than a year later, however, a multinational force led by U.S. marines enforced a negotiated and peaceful resolution to the crisis without losing a single American life. No perceptible change in the behavior of any other state occurred, despite what Dick Cheney labeled the "abject national embarrassment" at the docks of Port-au-Prince.[52]

Kosovo proved to be an equally independent event. Administration officials routinely defended their actions there in terms of the risks to global order that a damaged credibility would entail. NATO's "fundamental strategic objectives" in Kosovo, as identified by a classified strategy report that was leaked to the *Washington Post*, were to "promote regional stability and protect our investment in Bosnia; prevent resumption of hostilities in Kosovo and renewed humanitarian crisis; [and] preserve U.S. and NATO credibility."[53] Senator McCain worried that "Pyongyang and Baghdad and Tripoli," were paying "close attention" to NATO actions, and that "if a military establishment that was defeated by the Croatian Army prevails, one led by a Balkan thug prevails, then we will be vulnerable to many challenges in many places."[54] It is, however, hard to sustain the argument that NATO's display of resolution in defense of its credibility affected the calculations of any other state. Just as no enemy stood waiting to take advantage of low U.S. credibility, none was cowed into acquiescence when Washington was resolute.

[49] George and Smoke, *Deterrence in American Foreign Policy*, 516–517.
[50] Ann Devroy and Daniel Williams, "GOP Attacks Clinton, Claims Incompetence in Foreign Relations," *The Washington Post*, 28 July 1994.
[51] Williams and Devroy, "U.S. Policy Lacks Focus."
[52] Devroy and Williams, "GOP Attacks Clinton."
[53] Barton Gellman, "The Path to Crisis: How the United States and Its Allies Went to War," *The Washington Post*, 18 April 1999.
[54] Alison Mitchell, "McCain Keeps Pressing Case for Troops," *The New York Times*, 4 April 1999.

Credibility in Practice

The evidence seems to fall heavily on one side of the divide between scholars and practitioners over the importance of credibility. This division is not merely of academic interest. The credibility imperative has distinct and profound effects upon policymaking, all of which are apparent during the current war on terror. In order to assess more accurately the true value of a healthy reputation for resolve, policymakers ought to be aware of the following general rules about how the credibility imperative shapes national debate. Three such effects are presented below, more as arguments rather than testable hypotheses, owing to the nature of the subject. Although the supporting evidence is by necessity somewhat anecdotal, the arguments themselves should not be very controversial.

First, the credibility imperative is almost always employed to bolster the most hawkish position in a foreign policy debate. Cries of appeasement (and of the need to maintain credibility) arise almost every time the use of force is debated in the United States. Critics warned that U.S. credibility would be irreparably harmed if Washington failed to get involved in Vietnam, and then if it did not stay until the war was won; if it did not use air strikes against the Soviet missiles in Cuba; if it did not respond to Bosnian Serb provocations with sufficient force; if it failed to attack the leaders of the military coup in Haiti in 1994; and, of course, if it does not "stay the course" today in Iraq. At other times, hawks have employed the credibility imperative to urge two presidents to use military force to prevent nuclear proliferation in North Korea and to punish the recalcitrant Saddam Hussein.[55] The reputation of the United States is always endangered by inaction, not by action, no matter how peripheral the proposed war might be to tangible national interests. The reputation for good policy judgment never seems to be as important as the reputation for belligerence.

The credibility imperative not only urges the use of military force, but it encourages hawkish behavior at the negotiating table as well, supporting rigidity and decrying all compromise as demonstrations of weakness. Only victory can legitimate diplomacy; compromised settlements only encourage further challenges, and are synonymous with appeasement. Madeleine Albright reported a typical example in her memoirs, explaining that during Bosnia negotiations "the ordinarily hawkish Jamie Rubin urged me to compromise on a particular measure. I glared and said, 'Jamie, do you think we're in Munich?'"[56] After Jimmy Carter's now-famous mission helped find common

---

[55] On the former, see the floor speeches of Senator John McCain, such as "The Nuclear Ambitions of North Korea," 7 October 1994, accessed at http://www.fas.org/spp/starwars/congress/1994/s941007-dprk.htm, 22 May 2006; on the latter, see Eliot A. Cohen, "Sound and Fury," *The Washington Post*, 19 December 1998; and Charles Krauthammer, "Saddam: Round 3," *The Washington Post*, 13 November 1998.

[56] Madeleine Albright, *Madame Secretary* (New York: Miramax, 2003), 382.

ground between Pyongyang and Washington in 1994, McCain worried that the deal "will have changed the balance of power in Europe and the Middle East. That it will have changed for the worse is obvious."[57] *Washington Post* columnist Charles Krauthammer labeled the compromise on the same peninsula in 2003 "an abject cave-in," which would prove to be a "threat to American credibility everywhere."[58]

This is not meant to suggest, of course, that individual cases of belligerence or intervention were not warranted; however, it is important to recognize that, for better or for worse, the credibility imperative is the rhetorical instrument of the hawk. The actors employing the imperative are not always the same, but their prescription never waivers. Many of the doves of the 1980s had become hawks by the 1990s, warning of the potential loss of credibility if strong action were not taken in Bosnia, Rwanda, Kosovo, and Haiti. For example, the *New York Times* cited "United States diplomats" warning President Clinton that a failure to act in Bosnia in 1993 would "badly damage U.S. credibility abroad."[59] Anthony Lake told the Council on Foreign Relations that among the reasons to act in Haiti was the need to defend American credibility in world affairs.[60] In general, the more a policymaker or strategist saw the credibility of the United States in peril, the more willing he or she was to use force to prevent its erosion.

The second observation on the use of the credibility imperative in policy debate is perhaps related to the first: the imperative often produces astonishing hyperbole, even in otherwise sober analysts. If the United States were to lose credibility, the floodgates would open to a variety of catastrophes, setting off dominoes that would eventually not only threaten vital interests and make war necessary, but perhaps even lead to the end of the Republic itself. The credibility imperative warns that momentum toward disaster can begin with the smallest demonstration of irresolution, thus sustaining the vision of an interdependent system in which there are no inconsequential events. In the words of Dale Copeland, "It is easier to stop a snowball before it begins to roll downhill than to intervene only after it has started to gain momentum."[61] Therefore, even the smallest of slips can lead to large-scale disaster.

Thus, although Quemoy and Matsu might have seemed like irrelevant, uninhabitable rocky atolls, if they fell to the Chinese without action from the United States, the resulting loss of credibility for the United States would enable the communists "to begin their objective of driving us out of the western Pacific, right back to Hawaii and even to the United States," according to John

---

[57] McCain, "Nuclear Ambitions."

[58] Charles Krauthammer, "Korea Follies," *The Washington Post*, 17 January 2003.

[59] R.W. Apple, Jr., "Testing a Commitment," *TheNew York Times*, 19 September 1993.

[60] Paraphrased by Jim Hoagland in "Don't Do It," *The Washington Post*, 15 September 1994.

[61] Copeland, "Do Reputations Matter," 43.

Foster Dulles.[62] Ten years later, Dean Rusk wrote that if U.S. commitments became discredited because of a defeat in Vietnam, "the communist world would draw conclusions that would lead to our ruin and almost certainly to a catastrophic war."[63] Ronald Reagan told Congress that if the United States failed in Central America, "our credibility would collapse, our alliances would crumble, and the safety of our homeland would be put at jeopardy."[64] The examples are legion—indeed, the tendency toward hyperbole seems almost irresistible. In a world where threats are interdependent, the loss of credibility in one area threatens U.S. goals everywhere. The fall of Vietnam, thought Nixon, "would spark violence wherever our commitments help maintain the peace—in the Middle East, in Berlin, eventually even in the Western Hemisphere."[65] Credibility is apparently the glue holding together the international system of dominoes.

Audiences often seem distressingly willing to accept such statements at face value. Rarely are policymakers or analysts asked to justify these visions, or pressed to examine the logic connecting the present decisions to such catastrophic future consequences. Could interdependence alone set off such enormous strings of disasters? Why should anyone believe that the loss of credibility would result in an unprecedented string of disasters? For those under the spell of the credibility imperative, the logic behind these statements seemed less relevant than establishing the potential, however slim, for catastrophe. Since foreign policy is a worst-case-scenario business, the sagacious policymaker hedges against disaster, no matter how absurdly remote the risk may seem. Who would oppose the defense of Quemoy and Matsu, if that defense might prevent a "catastrophic war"? Similarly, it was difficult to argue that aid to the Contras was not in the national interest once it became linked to the survival of NATO and the safety of "our homeland." Once policymakers accept the imperative to remain credible, logic and reason can become casualties of fear.

The third and final observation is that there is a loose inverse relationship between the rhetorical employment of the credibility imperative and the presence of vital, more tangible national interests. Franklin D. Roosevelt did not make reference to the reputation of the United States when he asked Congress for a declaration of war against Japan in 1941. Similarly, Winston Churchill's stirring speeches rallying his countrymen at their darkest hour did not mention the importance of maintaining the credibility of the realm. When a clear national interest is at stake, policymakers have no need to defend (or sell) their actions with reference to the national reputation or credibility. Simply

---

[62] Quoted by Gaddis in *Strategies of Containment*, 144.

[63] Ibid., 240.

[64] Steven R. Wiesman, "President Appeals before Congress for Aid to Latins," *The New York Times*, 28 April 1993.

[65] McMahon, "Credibility and World Power," 467.

put, the more tangible the national interest, the smaller the role that intangible factors will play in either decisions or justifications for policy. The United States was willing to use force to ensure that Korea, Lebanon, Vietnam, Grenada, El Salvador, and Nicaragua stayed in the camp of free nations despite the fact that none had any measurable impact upon the global balance of power. "El Salvador doesn't really matter," one of Ronald Reagan's foreign policy advisers admitted in 1981, but "we have to establish credibility because we are in very serious trouble."[66]

When credibility is the primary justification for action, the interest is usually not vital to the United States. Since Washington had no strategic interests at stake in the Balkans in the 1990s, for example, it was forced to invent some. Rather than sell the policy based solely on what it was—predominantly a humanitarian intervention—the Clinton administration repeatedly linked the fate of the Muslims of southeastern Europe to the credibility of the United States and NATO. By doing so, according to Owen Harries, the administration "managed to create a serious national interest in Bosnia where none before existed: an interest, that is, in the preservation of this country's prestige and credibility."[67] The credibility imperative rose to prominence precisely because no tangible U.S. interest in Bosnia existed.

In sum, when the credibility imperative drives policy, states fearful of hyperbolic future consequences are likely to follow hawkish recommendations in order to send messages that other states are unlikely to receive. Policymakers are thus wise to beware of the credibility imperative when devising policy, questioning the assumptions that it contains and remaining skeptical of the catastrophes of which it warns. They must recognize that the imperative is typically employed when no tangible national interest exists, used as a rhetorical smoke screen to win over otherwise-peaceful masses. Most importantly, it should perhaps give them pause that scholars can supply virtually no evidence supporting the conventional wisdom about its importance.

It might seem blasphemous, or at least dangerously naïve, to suggest that the blood and treasure spilled over the past six decades to preserve the credibility of the United States has been in vain. However, history offers little evidence to support one of the most deeply held beliefs of the makers of U.S. foreign policy. States cannot control their reputations or their credibility, since target adversaries and allies will ultimately form their own perceptions, often learning incorrect lessons. Even the best efforts to bolster the credibility of the United States ultimately serve little purpose.

---

[66] Quoted by William M. LeoGrande, "A Splendid Little War: Drawing the Line in El Salvador," *International Security* 6 (Summer 1981): 27.

[67] Owen Harries, "An Anti-Interventionist No More: America's Credibility is Now at Stake," *The Washington Post*, 21 April 1994.

THE CREDIBILITY IMPERATIVE AND THE WAR ON TERROR

Does the preceding discussion remain relevant for the "war on terror"? Some observers have argued that concerns for credibility are justified in this post–September 11 era, since the United States faces an enemy that repeatedly refers to American irresolution as inspiration for its actions.[68] The current administration clearly believes in the importance of credibility, and often repeats that importance mantra-like in its talking points. Even a brief examination of the current challenges facing the United States, however, should be sufficient to demonstrate that there is no reason to believe that the credibility imperative will provide guidance to current policymakers any more sage than it gave to those of eras past.

Credibility and Terrorism

The leadership of al Qaeda has repeatedly cited a lack of resolution in Washington as inspiration for its actions. Bin Laden has accused America of being a "paper tiger," a state that will back away at the slightest use of force. "We have seen in the last decade," he has argued, "the decline of the American government and the weakness of the American soldier who is ready to wage Cold Wars and unprepared to fight long wars. This was proven in Beirut when the Marines fled after two explosions. It also proves they can run in less than 24 hours, and this was also repeated in Somalia."[69]

Some scholars have argued that if al Qaeda has drawn inspiration from perceptions of American irresolution, then the conclusions of Mercer and others regarding the ultimate unimportance of reputation and credibility are demonstrably false.[70] If decreased U.S. credibility has altered the calculations of militant fundamentalist groups, then indeed, states combating terrorism would be justified in worrying about the messages that their actions send, and should consider the probable impact that current decisions will have on future crises.

However, there are good reasons to doubt this conclusion. First of all, it is not clear that the United States can control the perceptions of non-state actors in the current era any more easily than it could those of states during the Cold War. It is quite a stretch to believe that if U.S. troops had not been pulled out of Lebanon or Somalia, al Qaeda would have acted any differently throughout the 1990s. Did the U.S. withdrawals really embolden al Qaeda? In order for the policymaker's conventional wisdom about the importance of credibility to be correct, al Qaeda's behavior would have to have been different if the United

---

[68] Shannon and Dennis, "Militant Islam."

[69] Osama bin Laden, in an interview with John Miller, in Laura Egendorf, ed., *Terrorism: Opposing Viewpoints* (San Diego, CA: Greenhaven Press, 1999), 125.

[70] Shannon and Dennis, "Militant Islam."

States had not pulled out of Somalia when it did. If the terrorists would have attacked either way—and it is certainly plausible to think that they would have—then concerns for reputation are still irrelevant, and it remains unwise for policymakers to look beyond the current crisis.

Second, there are good reasons to believe that al Qaeda's perceptions will remain unaffected by Washington's attempt to control them. In fact, it may well be that a strategy like that pursued by Islamic fundamentalists is almost necessary for the smaller participant in a case of extreme power asymmetry. Since they lacked the power to force a retreat, the *mujahadeen* in Afghanistan needed to preach that the Soviet Union would prove irresolute in order to convince its fighters that resistance was not utterly pointless; likewise, Bin Laden must paint the United States as a paper tiger or no one will rally to his cause. The strategy of a weak actor in extreme asymmetry must be based on the premise that although it may not be able to employ tangible assets to win the war, intangible, moral elements will prove decisive. Therefore, no matter what the behavior of the strong actually is, the weak are likely to accuse it of being irresolute. Since *jihadists* have no hope of success without a certain degree of superpower irresolution, it is unlikely that any amount of credibility will cause them to abandon that belief (or hope). Once again, Washington will probably not be able to control its reputation in the eyes of others. The future actions of these groups will probably remain unaffected by their perceptions of U.S. credibility.

Finally, it is quite possible that Bin Laden's pronouncements of American irresolution are less explanations for his behavior than tools for attracting new recruits. Although al Qaeda took credit for the Somalia adventure, for example, it disavowed any participation in the embassy bombings, perhaps since those incidents did not cause any change in U.S. behavior and therefore would not serve as well in recruitment.[71] Their preposterous exaggeration of both their involvement in and the scale of the battles in Somalia lend credence to the argument that the true importance of the event was for propaganda rather than for the actual formulation of strategy. Although there is little evidence that the battle in Mogadishu was fought by anyone other than Somalis, to listen to Bin Laden, one would think that the *mujahadeen* from all over the region had converged to oust the imperialists. He has repeatedly claimed that 300,000 Americans turned tail and fled after the battle, which is more than 10 times the number that were ever in the country and almost 100 times the number that actually left after Mogadishu. No matter what the United States did in Somalia, al Qaeda would probably have continued its tangible and intangible assaults, which even in extreme exaggeration, would have found eager ears among the disaffected, angry masses.

---

[71] Ibid., 36.

Might resolute, credible superpowers be able to prevent *jihadists* from recruiting new generations of terrorists? Probably not, since al Qaeda and its allies have shown no particular interest in the accuracy of their statements. No matter what the United States and its allies do, Bin Laden is likely to twist the truth and argue that each succeeding action is further proof of his claims. Many regions of the world have populations quite sympathetic to the argument that despite its apparent strength, the United States is actually a weak, feminized, immoral, corrupt paper tiger. The Middle East, where conspiracy theories often find wide audiences, is seemingly fertile ground for Bin Laden's interpretation of U.S. irresolution. In other words, U.S. actions are not likely to have direct bearing on the interpretation of U.S. credibility in the region, or on the outcome of the war on terror, for better or for worse.

Credibility and the Post–September 11 Wars

The credibility imperative has affected debates about the response to the attacks of September 11 exactly as the preceding analysis would have predicted. It was almost entirely absent in the discussion leading up to the war in Afghanistan, since few disputed the belief that the terrorist leadership and training camps that were given sanctuary by the Taliban represented a clear and present danger to international security. It is hard to imagine that any president (or any leader of any country, for that matter) would have failed to use military force to address these tangible interests once negotiations proved ineffective.

The war that followed 17 months later, however, was different. Although regime change in Iraq was sold to the American public in terms of very tangible, vital national interests, the war was fought to send messages and influence the future behavior of other states at least as much as it was to address any threat posed by Saddam. Although Condoleezza Rice was fond of saying, "The smoking gun could be a mushroom cloud," many observers and scholars of U.S. foreign policy felt that the real reasons for the war were much less tangible, and in some ways much more ambitious.[72] In fact, it is hard to find a serious analyst who believed Saddam to be on the verge of using weapons of mass destruction in an assault on the United States or its allies. Some of the President's advisers had, of course, long supported the removal of Saddam for other, less-tangible reasons. Saddam's very existence seemed to some to be indicative of a failure of U.S. foreign policy, one that sent the wrong messages to the vague "others" that were biding their time, waiting for signs of U.S. irresolution to begin their own anti–status quo machinations. Neoconservatives like Paul Wolfowitz, Richard Perle, and William Kristol ardently believed in a benign version of domino dynamics, in which a display of American resolve

---

[72] Todd S. Purdum, "Bush Administration Officials Say the Time has Come for Action on Iraq," *The New York Times*, 9 September 2002.

and commitment would encourage regional liberalization and democratization, and would demonstrate that the United States would not allow further weapons proliferation. The crisis of the present was managed (or, in this case, created) primarily to address those of the future; it was fought for intangible interests but sold with reference to the tangible. Positive credibility would be the engine to drive desirable changes across the region, and indeed throughout the world.

Krauthammer argued that continuing the containment of Saddam would "shatter the credibility of post-9/11 American resolve that was achieved by the demonstration of American power and will in Afghanistan." He then went on to repeat the basic outlines of the credibility imperative, which has been passed down unchanged from the Cold War generation.

> Credibility matters deeply in a world of enemies—and of fence-sitters who must decide which side to choose. Particularly after the collapse of our position on North Korea, which can only be explained away as a temporary necessity while we gird ourselves for Iraq, the entire Bush Doctrine, which sees the conjunction of rogue states, terrorists and weapons of mass destruction as the great existential challenge of our age, would collapse. You cannot march up this hill and then march back down empty-handed without undermining American deterrence everywhere.[73]

Once again, foreign policy generalists rather than regional specialists were most concerned with the impact of Iraq on U.S. reputation. By punishing the recalcitrant Saddam, the United States would demonstrate to other states that the pursuit of weapons of mass destruction in particular, and opposition to U.S. policies in general, would be self-defeating. Future challengers then would be deterred from challenging U.S. interests.

As scholars of credibility would have predicted, once again an operation fought mostly for psychological reasons has not met its objectives. Like petulant children, target states (and non-state actors) have stubbornly refused to learn the lessons they were taught. As argued above, the precedent the United States hoped to set in proliferation matters has not seemed to change the behavior of Iran or North Korea, both of whom continue along the road to weapons development. The only success that the administration can point to, although it is surely not without controversy, is in Libya, where Muammar al-Qaddafi has declared his days as an international pariah to be over and has apparently put an end to his research into the development of weapons of mass destruction. "Our diplomacy with Libya was successful only because our word was credible," argued Vice President Cheney in January of 2004. "That kind of credibility can be earned in only one way—by keeping commitments, even when they bring difficulty and sacrifice; by leaving potential adversaries with no doubt that dangerous conduct will invite certain

---

[73] Charles Krauthammer, "No Turning Back Now," *The Washington Post*, 24 January 2003.

consequences."[74] Skeptics have been quick to point out that negotiations with Qaddafi were in progress for two years before the invasion of Iraq, however, and that the two events were unrelated.[75] Presumably Qaddafi had little reason to fear a U.S. invasion. The credibility imperative, however, has no requirement for veracity.

Perhaps even more important than nonproliferation messages was the commitment to democracy and freedom that neoconservatives felt would be more credible after the invasion of Iraq. It will be some time before the results of this wager are in, for it still may be possible for Iraq to become a beacon of democracy and freedom for the region and begin a fundamental erosion of anti-American sentiment. Following that, perhaps within a few years, dominoes of democracy may fall, and the region may be fundamentally changed for the better. The terrorist swamp may yet be drained by the destruction of the Iraqi dike. But the early evidence is not encouraging. As Shibley Telhami and others have pointed out, thus far, the invasion has had quite the opposite effect—regional governments have been even more oppressive to their people than before, and levels of anti-Americanism have skyrocketed.[76] Both early reports and the recently declassified National Intelligence Estimate indicate that the war in Iraq has proved to be an aid to al Qaeda recruiting.[77] Through their attempts to distance themselves from (or find scapegoats for) a war they supported, it is clear that some leading neoconservatives share the pessimistic forecasts of the war's progress.[78] Since target audiences have once again failed to learn the right lessons, thus far, the war in Iraq seems to provide more support for the dangers in looking beyond the crisis at hand.

[74] "Remarks by the Vice President to the World Economic Forum," Davos, Switzerland, 24 January, 2004, accessed at http://www.whitehouse.gov/news/releases/2004/01/20040124-1.html, 22 May 2006.

[75] Flynt Leverett, "Why Libya Gave Up the Bomb," The New York Times, 23 January 2004.

[76] Shibley Telhami, The Stakes: America in the Middle East (Boulder, CO: Westview Press, 2002). See also Shibley Telhami, "A Growing Muslim Identity," Los Angeles Times, 11 July 2004; and Shibley Telhami, "Double Blow to Mideast Democracy," The Washington Post, 1 May 2004.

[77] Neil MacFarquhar, "Rising Tide of Islamic Militants See Iraq as the Ultimate Battlefield," The New York Times, 13 August 2003; International Institute for Strategic Studies, Strategic Survey 2004/05 (London: International Institute for Strategic Studies, May 2005); Office of the Director of National Intelligence, "Declassified Key Judgments of the National Intelligence Estimate 'Trends in Global Terrorism: Implications for the United States,'" Washington DC, April 2006, accessed at http://www.dni.gov/press_releases/Declassified_NIE_Key_Judgments.pdf, 18 October 2006.

[78] Robert Kagan and William Kristol, "Democracy Now," The Weekly Standard, 17 May 2004, accessed at http://www.weeklystandard.com/Content/Public/Articles/000/000/004/056mvrqy.asp, 4 October 2007. ; Kenneth M. Pollack, "Mourning After: How They Screwed it Up," The New Republic, 28 June 2004, accessed at http://www.brookings.edu/views/articles/pollack/20040628.htm, 4 October 2007.

Credibility and Withdrawal from Iraq

The Nixon administration made it clear that extrication from the Vietnam quagmire would proceed if and only if it could be done without damage to the national honor. The South Vietnamese had to be capable of defending themselves before a pullout would be acceptable to Washington. Were the United States to withdraw its troops from Vietnam amidst defeat, it would suffer serious harm to its credibility, and global calamity would probably follow. Kissinger had long held that the United States could not pull its troops out of Vietnam without threatening "the political stability of Europe and Japan and the future evolution of the developing countries of Latin America, Africa, and Asia," which depend on the perception of a United States "able to defend its interests and those of its friends. If the war in Vietnam eroded our willingness to back the security of free peoples with our military strength, untold millions would be in jeopardy."[79] The credibility imperative, as usual, counseled continued belligerence and warned of apocalyptic consequences that would follow a failure to pursue this course. As discussed above, however, the South Vietnamese house of cards collapsed soon after the American withdrawal, and although few policymakers seemed to notice at the time, the anticipated string of catastrophes failed to occur.

Today, the United States once again finds itself faced with decisions about how and when to withdraw from an ill-advised, increasingly unpopular, and probably unwinnable war. The credibility imperative has predictably been playing a key role in formulating those decisions regarding the endgame in Iraq. While the United States may well have tangible national interests in ensuring the successful transition to democratic governance in Iraq—surely no one stands to benefit if fundamentalists come to power in Baghdad, for instance—intangible factors will probably prove to be just as important. The "messages" that a pullout would send to future belligerents are playing an enormous role in current decision making, counseling hawkish, uncompromising behavior and threatening hyperbolic potential consequences for failure.

Once again, those in the policy community apparently believe that a string of unprecedented catastrophes would soon follow the loss of U.S. credibility. Kissinger has predictably warned that a premature pullout would be "disastrous" for "America's position in the world."

> Defeat would shrivel U.S. credibility around the world. Our leadership and the respect accorded to our views on other regional issues from Palestine to Iran would be weakened; the confidence of other major countries—China, Russia, Europe, Japan—in America's potential contribution would be diminished. The respite from military efforts would be brief before even greater crises descended upon us.[80]

[79] Kissinger, *White House Years*, 196.
[80] Henry Kissinger, "How to Exit Iraq," *The Washington Post*, 19 December 2005.

Kissinger, who is apparently a close adviser to the Bush administration, is certainly not alone in this belief.[81] Rumsfeld, as discussed above, warned the Senate Armed Services Committee that a premature withdrawal would result in a string of catastrophes that would soon force the United States to make a stand nearer to home.[82] The editor of the *National Review* warns that "the consequences of that defeat would be remarkably similar to those in the wake of Vietnam. The prestige of the U.S. government would sink around the world, emboldening our enemies and creating a period of American doubt and retreat."[83] As was the case with Vietnam, global stability appears to be at stake; bigger wars, regional chaos, the end of unipolarity, and even the collapse of democracy in the United States would soon follow a withdrawal from Iraq. Former Secretary of Defense Melvin Laird has even warned that "the stakes could not be higher for the continued existence of our own democracy."[84] Thus, despite its historical underperformance, the credibility imperative is once again having an enormous, and poisonous, influence on a vitally important national debate. When credibility takes center stage in the discussion, rationality quickly recedes.

If the history of the U.S. experience with the credibility imperative is any guide, at the very least, one must conclude that no string of catastrophes is likely to follow a U.S. withdrawal from Iraq. The credibility of U.S. commitments is not the glue that holds the world together, nor is it the bulwark preventing the fall of various harmful dominoes. The U.S. presence is also not the only force preventing a region-wide war. Presumably, the other states of the region, who have little interest in becoming embroiled in a self-defeating, self-immolating war, can imagine what specific consequences would follow. In fact, there is a case to be made that the U.S. presence is more accurately thought of as a destabilizing presence, making the spread of violence more likely.

Even if some states were to begin to doubt U.S. credibility, it is hard to believe that fundamentalism would sweep across the region somehow, or that our allies would become so disheartened that they would rethink their allegiance to the United States. During the Cold War, theoretically states had the option to "flip sides" and rely on the Soviets if they began to doubt the credibility of the United States (although none ever did so, of course). Today it is impossible to imagine that any state would flip sides in the war on terror. If anything, the perception that they could not rely on the United States would probably make other states intensify their effort to fight their local, anti-regime fundamentalists. Even if states of the region do begin to doubt the credibility of U.S. commitments, which is of course by no means inevitable,

---

[81] Bob Woodward, *State of Denial* (New York: Simon & Schuster, 2006), 406–410.
[82] "The Sound of One Domino Falling."
[83] Rich Lowry, "Bush's Vietnam," *National Review*, 15 August 2006.
[84] Melvin Laird, "Iraq: Learning the Lessons of Vietnam," *Foreign Affairs* 84 (November/ December 2005), 36.

Islamic fundamentalist victories are not likely. And while it is obviously pre-posterous to suggest that the United States would soon have to fight them "nearer home," or that the continued existence of U.S. democracy is at stake, such statements are predictable products of the credibility imperative.

The only plausible enemies positioned to benefit from a U.S. display of irresolution are fundamentalist terrorist groups. Al Qaeda and its allies were apparently encouraged to some degree by the Soviet failure in Afghanistan, and a U.S. withdrawal from Iraq might provide a similar boost to recruiting. This is probably a near-inevitable consequence of the war no matter when it ends. Since fundamentalists have shown no interest in the veracity of their statements, and since asymmetric actors need to appear indomitable, they will always claim to have been the cause of the U.S. withdrawal. Unless the United States wishes to remain in Iraq indefinitely, it will at some point have to run the risk of aiding fundamentalist recruiting. However, this risk must be weighed against the amount of inspiration that terrorists receive by the continued U.S. occupation of Arab lands.

Global stability is certainly not at stake in Iraq. The preceding analysis suggests that if the United States were to withdraw its forces, the rest of the world might well view it as a wounded animal, and be fearful of its need to regain credibility in the next crisis. The United States, after all, did not go on the offensive following the Cuban Missile Crisis, nor did the Soviets after the fall of Saigon. Despite the nearly ubiquitous warnings from policymakers, a withdrawal from Iraq would not be catastrophic for the Middle East, for U.S. foreign policy, or for international stability itself.

Actions during the war on terror that are inspired by the imperative to remain credible will probably not lead to any better outcomes than they did in previous eras. Policymakers would do well to listen to the emerging conven-tional wisdom of scholars, and avoid thinking beyond the current situation. The future will take care of itself. Even when facing enemies that may doubt the credibility of U.S. commitments, foreign policy actions designed to send mes-sages to third parties are unlikely to succeed. In the past, they have consistently marched the United States toward folly; there is little reason to doubt that they would do so again. Both logic and history suggest that the wise policymaker will disregard the worst-case, hyperbolic, belligerent advice from those under the spell of the credibility imperative.

CONCLUSION

The United States responded to the challenges of global communism and Islamic fundamentalism in many similar ways, despite obvious (if sometimes underappreciated) differences in the scale of the threats involved. Washington could once again find itself supporting a variety of unsavory regimes in the name of global competition. Fears of domestic infiltration by fifth columnists may cause domestic overreactions that restrict basic civil liberties; and a

Manichean, us-versus-them, with-us-or-against-us mentality has once again overtaken the White House. Perhaps most importantly, *ideas* lie at the center of both the Cold War and the war on terror, making "hearts and minds" of neutral parties as important as tangible national security interests. The reputation and credibility of the combatants today seem to be as central to policymakers as they were during the Cold War. As a consequence, the war on terror may also inspire ill-conceived, debilitating wars in the periphery in misguided attempts to control the perceptions of others. History never repeats itself, as Mark Twain may or may not have said, but at times it does rhyme.

Both logic and a preponderance of the evidence suggest that the current U.S. obsession with credibility is as insecure, misplaced, and malinformed as all that have preceded it. Whether it will result in the kind of counterproductive policies that accompanied the Cold War credibility imperative remains to be seen. What is more assured is that there is no clear way to control the perceptions of others, whether they are superpowers, small states, or loosely connected non-state groups. The impression that *their* thoughts can be controlled by *our* actions may be comforting, springing perhaps from basic human psychological needs, but in reality, their perception of us is largely outside of our influence. The messages we hope to send through our actions are unlikely to be successfully received. Washington would be well-advised to avoid the understandable and natural temptation to look beyond the current crisis when making decisions. As unsettling as it may be, the future is largely outside our control; the tangible interests of the present, therefore, must outweigh the intangible interests of the future.

The behavior of the United States is not driven by only tangible, material measures of power; however, perhaps it should be. When the credibility imperative drives policy, due to the inherently uncontrollable nature of this most intangible of assets, states march toward folly. "Many of the tenets underlying American security policy are held with strong but unwarranted conviction," Nancy Kanwisher sagaciously observed as the Cold War drew to a conclusion. "Further, these dubious beliefs often persist even after their flaws have been widely exposed."[85] Few dubious beliefs match the credibility imperative for both the extent of its acceptance and the depth of its flaws.

---

[85] Nancy Kanwisher, "Cognitive Heuristics and American Security Policy," *Journal of Conflict Resolution* 33 (December 1989): 652.

Part III:
HUMAN RIGHTS AND CIVIL LIBERTIES

U.S. Human Rights Policy in the Post-Cold War Era

JOHN W. DIETRICH

Historically, the implementation of U.S. human rights policy has been a case of "two steps forward, one step back." From its earliest days, the United States has attempted, at least to some degree, to include morality, the protection of individual rights, and the spread of democracy in foreign policy calculations. These efforts became more prominent after World War II. By the late 1980s, human rights concerns were firmly embedded in U.S. foreign policy rhetoric, policymaking institutions, and global actions. Despite these long-term trends, full policy implementation of human rights principles was constrained over time by lack of U.S. power, U.S. wariness of multilateral institutions and international legal commitments, competing policy priorities, and the limited institutional power of U.S. human rights advocates. The end of the Cold War and other contemporaneous international and domestic shifts appeared to finally remove these long-standing limitations. Now, a little more than a decade later, it is clear that human rights considerations have shaped recent policies in many ways. Strikingly, though, past limitations have persisted. The continuing existence of these limits shows that they were never short-term, era-specific problems, but rather deeper constraints that stem from the realities of global and domestic politics. Thus, although human rights considerations have become an important component of policy, those observers expecting a dominant role for human rights in U.S. foreign policy will always be disappointed and may fail to appreciate the progress that does occur.

HISTORIC TRENDS

Massachusetts Bay Governor John Winthrop stated in 1630, "We shall be as a City upon a Hill, the eyes of all people are upon us."[1] This early expression of

---

[1] Quoted in David P. Forsythe, *American Exceptionalism and Global Human Rights* (Lincoln: University of Nebraska, 1998), 2.

JOHN W. DIETRICH is a professor of political science at Bryant University. He has published *The George W. Bush Foreign Policy Reader: Presidential Speeches with Commentary*. This article is part of a larger project examining recent U.S. human rights policy.

American exceptionalism and moralism was followed by many similar state-ments from early American leaders.[2] These views led some of them to promote "crusading interventionism" to spread liberty; others were led to advocate "complacent withdrawal from world affairs" to keep America free from the world's impurities.[3] Either way, human rights ideas had some impact on early policymakers. Those ideas and the crusading internationalist viewpoint gained new prominence after World War II. The United States rose to superpower status and worked with other countries and the United Nations to establish new global human rights standards.[4] In the 1970s, Congress and President Jimmy Carter placed even more focus on human rights and took steps to create the legislative and institutional framework that still guides U.S. human rights policy today.[5] In the 1980s, under President Ronald Reagan, significant changes in human rights policy occurred, but the underlying focus remained.[6]

At the same time as these positive developments, full implementation of human rights principles was constrained by various factors. The limitations included an early lack of power that restricted U.S. ability to effect change. Many observers in the nineteenth century shared the opinion of John Quincy Adams, who counseled the still weak country against going out to find dragons to slay. This limitation was somewhat alleviated by the subsequent rise in U.S. power, but first the Cold War and then the Vietnam War demonstrated that the United States still did not have sufficient power, or will, to spread its ideas to all countries.

A second limitation was U.S. wariness of multilateral institutions and international legal commitments. For much of its early history, the country followed George Washington's advice against forming long-term alliances and multilateral commitments. After World War II, though, the United States responded to new global conditions by helping to establish and by joining many new institutions and treaties. Still, the country retained some wariness of formal commitment. For example, U.S. representatives played a major role in drafting the Universal Declaration of Human Rights in 1948, but promoted a

---

[2] Michael H. Hunt, *Ideology and U.S. Foreign Policy* (New Haven, CT: Yale University Press, 1987), 19–45; and Arthur Schlesinger, Jr., "Human Rights and the American Tradition," *Foreign Affairs* 57 (Review Issue 1978): 503–510.

[3] Tami R. Davis and Sean M. Lynn-Jones, "City Upon a Hill," *Foreign Policy* 66 (Spring 1997): 21.

[4] Jan Herman Burgers, "The Road to San Francisco: The Revival of the Human Rights Idea in the Twentieth Century," *Human Rights Quarterly* 14 (May 1992): 447–477.

[5] Lincoln P. Bloomfield, "From Ideal to Program to Policy: Tracking the Carter Human Rights Policy," *Journal of Policy Analysis and Management* 2 (Fall 1982): 1–12; Joshua Muravchik, *The Uncertain Crusade: Jimmy Carter and the Dilemmas of Human Rights Policy* (Lanham, MD: Hamilton Press, 1986); Gaddis Smith, *Morality, Reason and Power: American Diplomacy in the Carter Years* (New York: Hill and Wang Publishers, 1986).

[6] David P. Forsythe, "Human Rights and US Foreign Policy: Two Levels, Two Worlds," *Political Studies* 43 (Special Issue 1995): 120–124; and Tamar Jacoby, "The Reagan Turnaround on Human Rights," *Foreign Affairs* 64 (Summer 1986): 1066–1086.

document that laid out aspirations and ideals, not legally binding require-ments.[7] Subsequently, the United States remained outside of many key inter-national agreements, such as the UN Covenant on Civil and Political Rights and the Covenant on Social, Economic, and Cultural Rights. In several cases, the United States also openly disregarded decisions by the International Court of Justice (World Court).

Third, pursuit of human rights policies was limited by competing policy priorities. This problem can be seen even early in U.S. history in debates about whether to ally with France or England, but it was particularly dominant during the Cold War era. Containment of communism and security interests fre-quently outweighed human rights concerns. When human rights policies were in line with containment, for example in criticizing communist regimes, or when they could be pushed in less-strategically important areas, they were pursued. On the other hand, when anticommunist credentials and political stability were deemed necessary, the United States was willing to mute cri-ticism of pro-Western dictators.

Finally, full implementation of a human rights policy was constrained by the limited institutional power of governmental human rights advocates and by minimal domestic political support for a human rights focus. In the U.S. foreign policymaking process, an idea, no matter how worthy, will not be implemented unless it has strong and savvy supporters who are able to push it through the various bureaucratic or congressional debates. The weakness of human rights advocates was partially ameliorated by the creation of the State Department's Human Rights and Humanitarian Affairs Bureau in 1977 and the rise of nongovernmental human rights organizations (NGOs) in the 1970s. In its early years, though, the Bureau was given little respect or cooperation by other bureaucratic players.[8] The NGOs had limited funding and policy exper-tise and often were excluded from the relatively closed foreign policymaking system of the era.

Thus, although there is a long-standing American tradition of rhetorical support for human rights, and although several historical and institutional changes led to the development of a human rights policy, translating ideals into practical application was difficult. Analysts looking at any given period through the 1980s could point to new ways in which human rights were shaping policies, but were also left acknowledging, and often lamenting, the particular era's constraints on full implementation.[9]

---

[7] Forsythe, *American Exceptionalism and Global Human Rights*, 7.

[8] Edwin S. Maynard, "The Bureaucracy and Implementation of US Human Rights Policy," *Human Rights Quarterly* 11 (May 1989): 175–248; and Daniel W. Drezner "Ideas, Bureaucratic Politics and the Crafting of Foreign Policy," *American Journal of Political Science* 44 (October 2000): 733–749.

[9] The existing literature on U.S. policy is vast, but discussions showing some of these restraints include David P. Forsythe, *Human Rights and U.S. Foreign Policy: Congress Reconsidered* (Gainesville: University of Florida Press, 1988); David Forsythe, "Human Rights in U.S. Foreign Policy: Retrospect and Prospect," *Political Science Quarterly* 105 (Fall 1990): 435–454; Glenn A.

NEW FOCUS IN A NEW PERIOD

The end of the Cold War and other contemporaneous shifts appeared to finally remove all the long-standing limitations on U.S. human rights policy. Many observers felt that the United States now stood alone as a hegemon and had the power to influence decisions in countries around the globe. The collapse of communism also led many analysts to agree with Francis Fukuyama's idea that history had reached its end and liberal democracy had emerged triumphant.[10] Therefore, the United States, as the leading democracy, would just have to nudge a few recalcitrant states into line with the inevitable. Global trends also appeared favorable. Increased economic globalization seemed to enable the United States and other leading powers to use trade and other economic policies as "carrots" and "sticks" to enforce human rights.[11] Also, state sovereignty appeared to be weakening. The international community increasingly accepted the idea that powerful countries, like the United States, would lead international efforts to bring rogue states' policies into line with international norms.

The United States still retained some wariness of multilateralism and was unwilling to accept the levels of internal monitoring and joint action seen in the polices of other global human rights leaders,[12] but there were important shifts in U.S. attitudes beginning in the late 1980s. During the Cold War, U.S. officials were often hesitant to establish powerful UN agencies. They feared that the Soviet Union and its communist allies, perhaps in conjunction with newly independent states that might see some Western actions as reminders of colonial imposition, would skew UN debates and definitions of which rights should be protected. Moves toward democracy in Russia, Eastern Europe, and the developing world reduced those worries. The end of the Soviet veto in the Security Council also increased the chance of U.S.-controlled multilateral action. Finally, after the long Cold War, the United States was looking to shift some of the burden of world responsibility to its allies and multilateral institutions.

The Cold War's end also took away major competing policy priorities. With the Soviet threat gone, the United States appeared to have new flexibility in bilateral relationships and overall strategic planning. Human rights goals could rise and security considerations decline. Particular country-specific in-

---

Mower, *Human Rights and American Foreign Policy: The Carter and Reagan Experiences* (Westport, CT: Greenwood Press, Inc., 1987); and Natalie Hevener Kaufman, *Human Rights Treaties and the Senate: A History of Opposition* (Chapel Hill: University of North Carolina Press, 1990).

[10] Francis Fukuyama, *The End of History and the Last Man* (New York: Free Press, 1992).

[11] Rebecca R. Moore, "Globalization and the Future of U.S. Human Rights Policy," *Washington Quarterly* 21 (Autumn 1998): 193–212.

[12] Kathryn Sikkink, "The Power of Principled Ideas: Human Rights Policies in the United States and Western Europe" in Judith Goldstein and Robert O. Keohane, eds., *Ideas and Foreign Policy: Beliefs, Institutions, and Political Change* (Ithaca, NY: Cornell University Press, 1993): 139–170.

terests such as counternarcotics goals in Colombia, military cooperation in Turkey, or regional cooperation in Egypt remained to complicate policy priorities, but there appeared to be no global doctrine that would conflict with the pursuit of human rights.

By the late 1980s, the policymaking position of human rights advocates had been strengthened by institutional growth of both governmental and nongovernmental agencies. Also, the foreign policymaking system opened somewhat after Vietnam to allow more independent activity by Congress, the press, interest groups, and the general public. Support from nongovernmental actors became increasingly crucial, and their access to decision makers increased.

Taken together, the various changes of the late 1980s appeared to have removed the old limitations. The United States was powerful, more willing to act multilaterally, free of major competing priorities, and had stronger domestic human rights advocates. Therefore, within many government, NGO, and academic circles, there was great optimism that a new policy era had emerged and that human rights considerations could move forward unencumbered.[13]

Before examining the extent to which human rights policies in this new era have or have not matched that optimism, it is important to note a couple of methodological ideas. For the purpose of this argument, the post-Cold War era will be defined as beginning in 1991. The major policy event of that year, the Persian Gulf War, was a harbinger of policies to come, not a throwback to the Cold War era policies. Therefore, the period includes the end of George H.W. Bush's presidency and the presidencies of Bill Clinton and George W. Bush. There are differences among the viewpoints and rhetoric of these three presidents. For example, the elder Bush pursued more ad hoc policies, whereas Clinton laid out a grander vision and had more commitment to international organizations.[14] Clinton and the younger Bush have important differences on how to define rights and how to pursue objectives. For definitions, Clinton usually drew off existing international treaties and common law, whereas Bush has put more focus on the less legally binding idea of God-given human "dignity." On tactics, Clinton often acted multilaterally, while Bush is more willing to act unilaterally.[15] These differences are real, and reflect both ideo-

---

[13] This view was quite widely held, but for a sample of the arguments, see U.S. Department of State Management Task Force, *State 2000: A New Model for Managing Foreign Affairs* (Washington DC: U.S. Department of State Publications, 1992); Theodore C. Sorenson, "America's First Post-Cold War President," *Foreign Affairs* 71 (Fall 1992): 13–30; and David P. Forsythe, "Human Rights in a Post-Cold War World," *National Forum* 72 (Fall 1992): 40–44. For a competing view that the Cold War's end might lead to a less activist human rights policy, see Alan Tonelson, "Jettison the Policy," *Foreign Policy* 97 (Winter 1994–95): 121–132.

[14] Forsythe, "Two Levels, Two Worlds," 124–128.

[15] Julie Mertus, "The New Human Rights Policy: A Radical Departure," *International Studies Perspectives* 4 (November 2003): 371–384; and L. Kathleen Roberts, "The United States and the World: Changing Approaches to Human Rights Diplomacy under the Bush Administration," *Berkeley Journal of International Law* 21 (Issue 3 2003): 631–661.

logical disputes and the very different world conditions faced by each president. However, if one examines the specific country policies followed by the three presidents, there is significant and important continuity. Also, differences in presidential tactics are very often differences of degree, not kind. The human rights literature commonly analyzes policy development by administration, but this paper will focus on substantive policy trends across the three administrations.

THE STEPS FORWARD

Since the end of the Cold War, increased focus on human rights in policymaking has continued. The steps forward are diverse, but can be organized around four main themes: rhetorical support for human rights, proactive measures to spread democracy and rights, new targeted legislation, and new acceptance of international human rights treaties and legal authority.

Rhetorical Support

All three post-Cold War presidents have laid out an overall vision guiding policy. All three visions have incorporated and strengthened the idea of pursuing human rights and democracy. In justifying the Persian Gulf War, George H.W. Bush spoke of an emerging "New World Order" based on international norms and rights.[16] Clinton, and his national security advisor, Anthony Lake, looked for a vision to replace containment and spoke of "democratic enlargement" that would "foster and consolidate new democracies and market economies where possible."[17] For George W. Bush, the guiding vision has been defeating terrorism. As will be discussed later, this vision has complicated the pursuit of a human rights agenda, but Bush has also reinforced the idea that in order to defeat terrorism and ensure security, America must lead the fight for individual rights. In his 2002 State of the Union address, Bush explained, "America will lead by defending liberty and justice ... [and] will always stand firm for the non-negotiable demands of human dignity: the rule of law, limits on the power of the state, respect for women, private property, free speech, equal justice, and religious tolerance."[18] The *National Security Strategy*

---

[16] Bush first publicly used the phrase "New World Order" in an 11 September 1990 speech to Congress describing the response to Iraq's invasion of Kuwait. George Bush, "Out of These Times ... a New World Order," *Washington Post*, 12 September 1990.

[17] Anthony Lake, quoted in Douglas Brinkley, "Democratic Enlargement: The Clinton Doctrine," *Foreign Policy* 106 (Spring 1997): 116.

[18] President George W. Bush, "State of the Union Address, January 29, 2002," accessed on the White House website at http://www.whitehouse.gov/news/releases/2002/01/20020129-11.html, 24 January 2004.

of the United States of America issued in September 2000 pledged to "press governments that deny human rights."[19]

Beyond these sweeping visions, the promotion of human rights has become a regular part of arguments used to justify many policies. Crucially, it is now often argued that the United States need not choose between human rights and other interests, because defense of human rights aids other interests. This view stems partly from acceptance of the academic conventional wisdom that no two democracies have ever fought each other. Furthermore, many government officials believe that countries with good human rights records are more likely to work with the United States on transnational issues such as drugs and weapons proliferation, to engage in more trade, and, in the words of one State Department official, to be "the best partners and only true allies for our nation."[20] These statements show that human rights promotion is fully entrenched as a U.S. policy goal.

Proactive Policies

Traditionally, human rights policies have focused on criticizing violators and punishing them through a variety of symbolic, economic, and legal means. In the post-Cold War period, the United States has continued to implement such polices. For example, the State Department's Annual Report on Human Rights, whose influence is illustrated each year by the strenuous denials and counterattacks advanced by countries singled out for criticism, has been strengthened. Also, the United States has led diplomatic efforts to punish violators in places such as Serbia, Haiti, Iraq, Zimbabwe, and Burma. Importantly, though, the United States has increasingly adopted more proactive policies that attempt to stop abuses before they occur and give greater rewards for human rights progress.

One sign of this shift has been the rise of humanitarian interventions. There are always multiple interests driving major military interventions, but U.S. actions in Somalia, Haiti, and Kosovo were driven to a large degree by human rights and humanitarian priorities. Operation Restore Hope in Somalia was prompted by humanitarian desires to stop the civil war and establish order so that food relief could reach the starving population.[21] In Haiti's case, the

---

[19] *National Security Strategy of the United States of America*, 4, accessed at http://www.whitehouse.gov/nsc/nssall.html, 24 January 2004.

[20] Michael E. Parmly, Principle Deputy Assistant Secretary of State for Democracy, Human Rights, and Labor, "The UN Commission on Human Rights," testimony before the House International Relations Committee's Subcommittee on International Operations and Human Rights, *Federal News Service, Inc.*, 6 June 2001.

[21] Herman J. Cohen, "Intervention in Somalia" in Allan E. Goodman, ed., *The Diplomatic Record 1992-1993* (Boulder, CO: Westview Press, 1995), 51–80; and John L. Hirsch and Robert B. Oakley, *Somalia and Operation Restore Hope: Reflections on Peacemaking and Peacekeeping* (Washington DC: United States Institute of Peace, 1995).

refugee issue played a major role in policy calculations, but even when much of that flow had been reduced, Clinton tried a number of pressures and appeared ready to fight for democracy in Latin America.[22] Ultimately, a major invasion was headed off only by last-minute negotiations that restored to power democratically elected President Jean-Bertrand Aristide. In Kosovo, the United States led NATO efforts aimed at stopping Serbian abuses.[23] Importantly, this intervention occurred against an existing government acting in its sovereign territory. None of these interventions proved entirely successful, but what is striking is that they were made at all. They demonstrate that the United States was willing to use force to change the internal governance and conditions within other countries even when security interests were minimal.

The United States has also tried to change conditions through nonmilitary means. New focus has been put on the idea of building civil societies and stable government systems that will protect citizens' rights. These ideas are not entirely new and gained momentum with the creation of the National Endowment for Democracy during the Reagan administration, but they have reached new heights. In recent years, the United States has spent over $700 million per year on programs to promote democracy.[24] Through programs such as the Human Rights and Democracy Fund, these monies go to help monitor elections, train legislatures, develop political parties, promote judicial reform, and support trade unions. These and other programs will likely expand if Bush pursues his goal of bringing democratic reforms to the Middle East.

The proactive policies have also included efforts to encourage reform through "carrots" rather than "sticks." In March 2002, Bush announced the creation of a new development fund, the Millennium Challenge Account (MCA). The new $5 billion-per-year program will distribute aid only to countries that are "ruling justly, investing in their people, and encouraging economic freedom."[25] To be eligible, countries must meet per capita income requirements. They are then scored on sixteen data indicators: six on governing justly, four on investing in people, and six on promoting economic freedom. Countries must score above the median for their income group on at least half of the indicators in each area and above the median on corruption. The hope is that the program will lessen corruption and waste in

---

[22] Douglas Jehl, "Clinton Explains Why He Might Use U.S. Army in Haiti," *New York Times*, 20 May 1994; Pamela Constable, "Haiti: A Nation in Despair, a Policy Adrift," *Current History* 93 (1994): 108–114.

[23] Ivo H. Daalder and Michael E. O'Hanlon, *Winning Ugly: NATO's War to Save Kosovo* (Washington DC: Brookings Institution Press, 2000); and Albrecht Schnabel and Ramesh Chandra Thakur, *Kosovo and the Challenge of Humanitarian Intervention: Selective Indignation, Collective Action, and International Citizenship* (New York: United Nations University Press, 2000).

[24] Figure cited in David P. Forsythe and Barbara Ann J. Rieffer, "US Foreign Policy and Enlarging the Democratic Community," *Human Rights Quarterly* 22 (November 2000): 989.

[25] George W. Bush, "President Proposes $5 Billion Plan to Help Developing Nations, March 14, 2002," accessed on the White House website at http://www.whitehouse.gov/news/releases/2002/03/20020314-7.html, 20 November 2004.

U.S. aid programs, give countries an incentive to implement economic and political reform, reward countries that are succeeding, and help alleviate some of the causes of human rights abuse, such as poverty and excessive state control. The program has been slow to become fully operational. Implementation questions also remain, such as whether the program is so targeted that it will exclude many of the world's poorest areas, or conversely, whether it will become so broad that it risks becoming politicized in ways that have hurt past programs. Many development and human rights groups have welcomed MCA as a new tool for inducing change. The embrace of aid and human rights criteria by a conservative Republican president has been described as having a "Nixon-goes-to-China flavor"[26] and is another indication of how human rights goals have become important components of U.S. policy.

New Targeted Legislation

A third development of this new era has been a shift to targeted legislation. During the Carter period, the focus was on broad legislative restrictions on U.S. foreign aid. Often referred to as 502B restrictions, the law states that no security assistance may be provided to any country that engages in a "consistent pattern of gross violations of internationally recognized human rights."[27] In practice, however, aid has been restricted only rarely.[28] Neither the executive branch nor Congress has wanted to antagonize U.S. allies by labeling them as abusers, and even nongovernmental human rights leaders like Aryeh Neier note that 502B is "like an atom bomb; it may have more benefit before you actually use it."[29] In response to the step back of non-enforcement after the step forward of passing the legislation, congressional human rights leaders in the post-Cold War period have advanced more-targeted legislation. In some cases, this has meant new restrictions on trade with or aid to specific countries, such as Burma, Indonesia, or Colombia. In two other significant cases, the Leahy law and the International Religious Freedom Act, it has meant new global restrictions on ties with specific kinds of violators.

With an eye toward restricting U.S. aid to Colombia without having to use the all-or-nothing approach of 502B, Senator Patrick Leahy (D-VT) sponsored an amendment to the 1997 Foreign Operations Appropriations Act (P.L.

[26] Steven Radelet, "Bush and Foreign Aid," *Foreign Affairs* 82 (September/October 2003): 117.

[27] Originally offered as a sense of Congress resolution in 1974, the language was made binding in the International Security Assistance Act of 1978 (codified as amended at 22 USCS § 2304 [2004]).

[28] Numerous academic studies have shown the limited impact of the legislation. A recent example is Clair Apodaca and Michael Stohl, "United States Human Rights Policy and Foreign Assistance," *International Studies Quarterly* 43 (March 1999): 185–198.

[29] Aryeh Neier, at the time executive director of Human Rights Watch, in Carroll J. Doherty, "Human Rights," *The Congressional Quarterly Weekly Report*, 5 December 1992, 3755.

104-208) that prohibited giving U.S. counternarotics aid to any specific military unit that had committed a gross violation of human rights. The following year, the prohibition was extended to all forms of aid to security forces paid through the 1998 Foreign Operations Appropriations Act (P.L. 105-118). Then in 1999, similar language prohibiting U.S. military training of violators was added to the Defense Appropriations Act (P.L. 105-261). These terms are often referred to as the "Leahy law"; however, because they are actually appropriations riders, they must be renewed each year as part of the appropriations cycle. The Leahy language brought three significant changes. First, the law theoretically keeps U.S. aid out of the hands of actors that are among the worst violators, because it targets military units, who often lead state abuse. Second, the law promotes prosecution of violators, because aid can be continued if the recipient country is taking action to bring the offenders to justice. Third, and most crucially, it gives the United States a targeted human rights tool to supplement the blunt weapon of 502B. In 1998, the law stopped the Turkish anti-terror police from purchasing armored vehicles. Subsequently, it has affected discussions with Indonesia, Mexico, and others. In late 2002, the Bush administration announced that for the first time, it was suspending aid to a Colombian Air Force unit accused of using helicopter-launched rockets against civilians.

New targeted legislation has also been put in place to punish countries that violate religious freedom. The International Religious Freedom Act (P.L. 105-292) was signed into law on 27 October 1998, after several years of work by faith-based organizations and religious conservatives in Congress.[30] The law establishes the Office on International Religious Freedom within the State Department, led by an ambassador-at-large. The office monitors religious persecution, recommends policies to promote freedom, and compiles its own report in conjunction with the annual human rights reports. The law also provides a long list of actions the president can take to punish violators. More of the sanctions were mandated in original drafts of the legislation, but the Clinton administration pressed for flexibility in determining which countries should be targeted, what actions should be taken, and when the sanctions could be waived. Some observers have complained that this flexibility allows the administration too great a latitude to avoid criticizing allies.[31] At a minimum, though, the law adds another layer of review and potential condemnation and punishment, so that violators may be induced to change their policies.

---

[30] For more on the work of these groups and their mounting power, see Miles A. Pomper, "The Religious Right's Foreign Policy Revival," *CQ Weekly*, 9 May 1998, 1209–1210; and Miles A. Pomper, "Religious Right Flexes Muscles on Foreign Policy Matters," *CQ Weekly*, 13 July 2002, 1893–1896.

[31] Human Rights Watch, "U.S. Report on Religious Freedom is Flawed," 26 October 2001, accessed at http://www.hrw.org/press/2001/10/religious1026.htm, 24 July 2002.

International Treaties and Legal Authority

A fourth post-Cold War development was increased U.S. participation in international agreements and multilateral institutions. Since 1988, the United States has ratified four international human rights treaties that it had ignored for decades. Conventions on genocide, torture, and racial discrimination, along with the fundamental International Convention on Civil and Political Rights, were all ratified by 1994. Also, in 1998, Clinton signed an executive order stating that it was the policy and practice of the U.S. government "fully to respect and implement its obligations under international human rights treaties to which it is a party."[32] These ratifications and commitments simply brought the United States into line with much of the rest of the international community that had already ratified the agreements, but they were an important symbol of a new U.S. attitude as the Cold War ended.

The early post-Cold War years also saw the United States working much more often through the UN. The most visible sign of this new attitude was that the United States went to the UN for resolutions of support and justification for actions in the Persian Gulf, Somalia, and Haiti. In each of these cases, the decision to act was really made in Washington, but UN support was seen as politically important for reinforcing the idea of a new world of international human rights norms and cooperation. The United States has also been supportive of UN actions in Cambodia and East Timor.

U.S. efforts in the early 1990s to buttress the UN's institutional capabilities on human rights have garnered less attention, but are also important. Under George H.W. Bush, Assistant Secretary of State for Human Rights Richard Schifter pushed the UN Human Rights Commission to be more active in investigating high-profile countries.[33] Also, during the Cold War, the United States had given rhetorical support to the idea of developing a UN High Commissioner for Human Rights, but U.S. diplomats acknowledge that the idea was never given active support.[34] Under Clinton, however, the United States made the project a priority. In 1993, the office of the UN Human Rights Commissioner was established as a full-time human rights watchdog. In 2006, the United States did vote against creation of the UN's Human Rights Council, which was replacing the discredited UN Commission, but it was with an argument that the panel should be even stronger. The Bush administration also pledged to finance and support the new Council.

---

[32] Executive Order No. 13107, as quoted in Sean D. Murphy, "Contemporary Practice of the United States Relating to International Law," *American Journal of International Law* 93 (April 1999): 479.

[33] *U.S. Human Rights Policy: A 20-Year Assessment* (Washington DC: United States Institute of Peace, 1999), 8.

[34] Patrick Flood, "Human Rights, UN Institutions, and the United States" in David P. Forsythe, ed., *The United States and Human Rights: Looking Inward and Outward* (Lincoln: University of Nebraska Press, 2000): 367.

One final way in which the United States has shown support for multilateral actions and international law was by supporting formation of the International Criminal Tribunals for Yugoslavia and for Rwanda.[35] The United States also used sanctions and other pressures to encourage countries to cooperate with the tribunals. Established in 1993 and 1994, respectively, these tribunals were the first international war crimes tribunals since the post-World War II Nuremberg trials. Although their long-term impact remains to be seen, the tribunals have been important symbols of new international agreement on norms of behavior. Additionally, they have established international case law and precedents, shown that even top political leaders can face possible prosecution and punishment, and possibly deterred future abuses by those fearing punishment; however, this last point is widely contested. U.S. support for the tribunals showed that the United States would acknowledge and promote the legitimacy of international courts in certain cases.

CONTINUED LIMITS ON POWER

As the Cold War ended, the United States appeared ready to dominate the world, but the ensuing decade clearly has shown that important barriers to U.S. influence still exist. The overall local conditions of countries that the United States hopes to influence and the determination of particular leaders to act as they see fit despite international condemnation remain two great barriers to U.S. influence. These factors will not change significantly, no matter how much economic or military power the United States amasses. Too often, optimistic observers, including some U.S. government officials, assume that if the United States just focuses its attention on a particular country, and especially if it takes active steps such as sanctions or military intervention, years of local history will simply vanish as indigenous people see the light of U.S. wisdom. For example, when the United States acted in Somalia, some officials initially believed that the mission could be completed in a month's time. When the U.S. phase of the mission continued instead for five months, there was real impatience and annoyance with the UN for failing to step in to assume responsibility so that U.S. troops could withdraw. There was also a degree of shock and betrayal expressed when, in the following fall, eighteen U.S. soldiers were killed by a Somali faction that did not accept the UN's plans for a new Somali government. Similarly for Haiti, Bosnia, Chechnya, and elsewhere, critics tend to assume that anything short of total success is a sign of U.S. inattention or mistakes, not the result of complicated local histories that the United States can influence only at the margins.

Cases such as Serbia, Iraq, North Korea, Cuba, Zimbabwe, and others defined as "rogue states" also show that U.S. power to influence is severely

---

[35] Henry J. Steiner and Philip Alston, *International Human Rights in Context: Law, Politics, and Morals: Text and Materials*, 2nd ed. (Oxford: Oxford University Press, 2000), 1144–1156.

limited if leaders are determined to act despite international displeasure.[36] One must not forget that the prime goal for many leaders is to maintain power, no matter what actions that requires. Also, leaders are well aware of international standards, so their violations come not from ignorance but from policy calculations that certain steps are necessary or justified, given local conditions. When the Cold War ended, many optimists assumed that with Soviet support gone, governments would be forced to yield to U.S. power, but this view neglected to give proper weight to Representative Thomas P. (Tip) O'Neill's famous comment that "all politics is local."

Furthermore, U.S. power to bring about human rights change has been limited by four developments in the post-Cold War era. First, the spread of a global economy, at times, has constrained instead of enhanced U.S. power.[37] The United States itself is increasingly dependent on trade and access to foreign markets and investment opportunities. Therefore, if the United States threatens economic sanctions, violators can try to call the U.S. bluff, and force the United States into a decision that could hurt its own economy. Also, the global economy means that there are many other countries ready to step in to replace lost investment, imports, and export markets if a country loses U.S. business. The classic case of these economic realities is China. George H.W. Bush supported continued trade with China despite the Chinese government's actions at Tiananmen Square. In 1993, Clinton imposed human rights conditions on China's Most Favored Nation (MFN) trade status and set up a one-year game of "chicken." By the spring of 1994, China clearly had not met the conditions, but only a minority of congressmen and few in the administration were actually willing to limit U.S. trade. This hesitation was reinforced by the fact that America's European allies had long since ended their punishments of China and were actively looking to increase business in China should the United States pull out. In response to these realities, Clinton dealt the human rights community one of its greatest losses by de-linking human rights and trade and adopting a strategy of engagement with China.[38]

The European defection on China also highlights a second new limit on U.S. power; namely, the United States can no longer automatically count on the support of its allies in pressing human rights concerns. For years, international human rights alliances followed Cold War alliances. Democratic countries generally were in agreement and saved their toughest criticism for communist countries. Furthermore, it was accepted that major disagreements

---

[36] Meghan L. O'Sullivan, "Sanctioning 'Rogue States,'" *Harvard International Review* 22 (Summer 2000): 56–60.

[37] Moore, "Globalization and the Future," 193–194.

[38] David M. Lampton, "America's China Policy in the Age of the Finance Minister: Clinton Ends Linkage," *The China Quarterly* 139 (September 1994): 597–621; Joseph Fewsmith, "America and China: Back from the Brink," *Current History* 93 (September 1994): 250–255; John W. Dietrich, "Interest Groups and Foreign Policy: Clinton and the China MFN Debates," *Presidential Studies Quarterly* 39 (June 1999): 280–296.

within the alliance should be muted, so that it could remain strong against its enemies. Recently, though, with the unifying Soviet threat gone, U.S. allies have shown more independence on a host of issues, including human rights. As many countries move toward various forms of liberal and illiberal democracy, the United States and its allies are hard-pressed to agree on who deserves human rights pressure. European allies have had sharp differences with the United States on policies toward Cuba, Iran, Iraq, China, and the Middle East. There are also more differences now on tactics. Although the United States often turns to military and economic pressures, European governments more often address human rights through engagement, dialogue, and treaties.[39] Europeans also have argued that the United States has followed a unilateralist foreign policy, with little consultation. Without allied support, the United States may be powerful by some measures, but it lacks both the moral authority and the resources to challenge every violator.

The combination of the global economy giving countries multiple sources for trade and the lack of allied cooperation has led many observers to conclude that a third limit on U.S. power is that sanctions rarely achieve their intended purposes. Sanctions often appeal to those who are looking for action tougher than simple criticism. By 2001, some form of sanctions had been placed on seventy-two countries for a variety of offenses, including human rights violations.[40] Numerous academic and other studies have shown, however, that sanctions—particularly unilateral sanctions, as many U.S. human rights actions are—have a poor record of inducing policy change.[41] Furthermore, they can also hurt the U.S. economy. Business groups and coalitions such as USA Engage frequently argue that sanctions hurt the American people. Worse still is the pain that may be inflicted upon the very people the sanctions are designed to protect. In Iraq, in Haiti, and elsewhere, there are real questions as to whether the denial of food, medicines, safe water, and so on may not have been worse human rights violations than anything that the indigenous government had done. Human rights sanctions blossomed during the 1990s, but now both George W. Bush's administration and congressional figures have called for their reduction. Problematically, policymakers are thus left with few options between criticism and intervention. The net effect may be fewer punishments of any kind.

A final new development limiting U.S. power to enforce human rights policies is that the violating countries have become much more savvy and

---

[39] Robert Kagan, "Power and Weakness," *Policy Review* 113 (June/July 2002): 3.

[40] Figure cited in Miles A. Pomper, "GOP Drive to Roll Back Sanctions Promises to be Case-by-Case Struggle," *CQ Weekly*, 10 February 2001, 339.

[41] Gary Clyde Hufbauer and Jeffrey J. Schott, assisted by Kimberly Ann Elliott, *Economic Sanctions Reconsidered: History and Current Policy* (Washington DC: Institute for International Economics, 1990); Robert A. Pape, "Why Economic Sanctions Do Not Work," *International Security* 22 (Fall 1997): 90–136; and Kimberly Ann Elliot, "The Sanction's Glass: Half Full or Completely Empty?" *International Security* 23 (Summer 1998): 50–65.

active in combating U.S. and UN efforts. Countries have learned that in the human rights arena, image is very important. Rather than allowing the United States and others to paint their image, countries now go on the offensive. They release political prisoners at strategic times, challenge the State Department's annual report almost before it has been released, and raise complaints against other countries that will deflect attention away from themselves. Frequently criticized countries also realize that they can block much action if they join human rights institutions. Cuba, Syria, Sudan, and China have all found that seats on the UN Human Rights Commission and careful lobbying of members can blunt many U.S. efforts. These countries do not allow the United States to rally international pressure; they nip actions in the bud.

In fact, the recent history of the UN Human Rights Commission offers insight into many of the power problems the United States faces. Commission members are elected to represent their regions of the world. Given U.S. leadership in the human rights field, the United States had held one of the Western Europe and Others Group seats since the Commission's founding. In 2001, though, the United States came in fourth in a race for three seats. The loss has been attributed by various observers to a combination of U.S. inattention to UN diplomacy, European desire to punish U.S. unilateralism, and the power of accused violators who rallied voting countries against the United States and in favor of Austria, which itself had been criticized by international bodies.[42] In 2002, the United States was able to regain its seat, but the Commission had been much less active in the intervening year. For example, the United States could not find any country willing to sponsor a tough resolution against China. A former public member of the U.S. delegation attributed this reluctance to Chinese threats to economically punish countries that acted against China in international forums.[43]

These various limits on U.S. power and policy setbacks reinforce the idea that although there have been many changes in the international system in recent years, fundamentally it is still based on state sovereignty and the pursuit of national interests.[44] Although the United States stands as the only multidimensional power and is far ahead of its competitors, it cannot always dictate polices to either target countries or to its allies. In principle, the United States could use its power to bring regime changes and to engage in long-term, colonial-style occupations that might or might not bring about desired local changes. Such actions, however, would go against new global and American

---

[42] See Barbara Crossette, "For the First Time, U.S. Is Excluded From U.N. Human Rights Panel," *New York Times*, 4 May 2001; and Christopher Marquis, "Washington Angry Over Losing Rights Seat," *New York Times*, 4 May 2001.

[43] Nina Shea, Director of the Center for Religious Freedom, Freedom House, "The UN Commission on Human Rights: A Review of Its Mission, Operations, and History," testimony before the House International Relations Committee's Subcommittee on International Operations and Human Rights, 6 June 2001, *Federal News Service, Inc.*

[44] Stephen D. Krasner, "Sovereignty," *Foreign Policy* 122 (January/February 2001): 20–26.

norms against imperialism. Only time will tell if U.S. actions in Afghanistan and Iraq—both interventions driven by security goals but with important human rights implications—will establish a new paradigm. Early evidence from those countries, added to evidence of limits on U.S. commitments to and ongoing problems in Haiti, Somalia, and the former Yugoslavia, seems, though, to confirm American distaste for both long-term occupations and nation building and to show that local realities are the most crucial variable in determining a country's path to stability and democracy.

These limits on U.S. power suggest why U.S. human rights policies are often not successful, but they also have affected the chance that efforts would be made in the first place. The American public and many government officials want to see short-term success. If positive change is not guaranteed or occurs slowly, Americans often become frustrated or lose interest, and policies are scaled back. Therefore, U.S. human rights policy in the future likely will look much as it has in the past, with the U.S. pressuring countries from the outside and often failing in its goals.

CONTINUED RESISTANCE TO INTERNATIONAL AGREEMENTS AND ACTIONS

As was discussed earlier, the post-Cold War era has seen the United States take the forward steps of signing some international treaties and supporting international tribunals. Subsequently, though, it has followed its usual pattern of then taking steps backward. When the United States signed several treaties in the late 1980s and early 1990s, two steps were taken to limit the impact of the treaties. First, each ratification was accompanied by a series of "reservations," "understandings," and "declarations" (RUDs). These sought to clarify U.S. interpretations of particular treaty language and to lay out what actions the United States would or would not take in implementing the treaties. Taken together, the RUDs essentially said that the United States would follow the treaties as long as they were consistent with existing U.S. law and would implement the treaties without accepting any obligation to change U.S. law or policy.[45] These positions were in line with long-held beliefs that the U.S. Constitution is the highest law in the land and that it grants Congress the exclusive power to consider and create all laws. Thus, the validity of treaty guarantees that go beyond constitutional guarantees are questionable, and treaties that would require the United States to change laws are problematic.

RUDs are common international practice, but the U.S. RUDs raised the question of whether the United States was actually following the treaties at all. In November of 1994, the UN Human Rights Commission adopted a general statement on RUDs with a clear focus on the U.S. positions. In that statement, the Commission expressed "regret" over the U.S. positions and

---

[45] William A. Schabas, "Spare the RUD or Spoil the Treaty" in Forsythe, ed., *The United States and Human Rights*, 110–125.

argued that specific U.S. reservations to the Covenant on Civil and Political Rights were "incompatible with the object and purpose of the Covenant."[46] Since then, the United States has not ratified any other major human rights treaties. Given the current focus on George W. Bush's unilateralism, it is important to remember that the RUDs and the slowdown in treaty signing began before his administration.

The second U.S. move to limit the impact of the treaties brought back the idea of "Brickerism." Senator John Bricker was a fierce opponent of the UN, international legal commitments, and international human rights treaties specifically. In the early 1950s, he led a movement for a constitutional amendment that would have made treaties non-self-executing, meaning that they would only become valid once Congress passed specific legislation implementing their terms into U.S. law.[47] Bricker's amendment would have asserted a large congressional role in foreign policymaking and would have served his express purpose: "to bury the so-called Convention on Human Rights so deep that no one holding high public office will ever dare to attempt its resurrection."[48] The movement gained momentum. To ensure the measure's close defeat and to protect its own overall constitutional powers, the Eisenhower administration promised that the United States would not ratify the conventions if Bricker's amendment was defeated. Ensuing administrations moved away from that promise, but for several human rights conventions, they returned to Bricker's idea that the treaties should be non-self-executing. This requirement places an extra hurdle in the ratification process and provides a way for the United States to symbolically support human rights by ratification without having to accept any real changes in U.S. policies.

In addition to placing limits on the treaties it has ratified, the United States also has chosen not to ratify several international treaties that relate more or less directly to human rights. The United States refused to join the over-100 countries that signed the 1997 Land Mines Treaty after U.S. demands for changes in the treaty were denied. The United States has been slow to accept international efforts to stop the use of child soldiers because of its own efforts to recruit seventeen-year-olds into military service.[49] The United States has signed, but not ratified, the Convention on All Forms of Discrimination against Women and the Convention on the Rights of the Child.

A desire to limit the impact of international agreements also explains U.S. reaction to the International Criminal Court (ICC); the reaction provides a classic illustration of American views. In some ways, the Court is the culmination of years of U.S. effort to bring order to the international system and to

---

[46] Ibid., 111. "Consideration of Reports Submitted by State Parties under Article 40 of the Covenant, Comments of the Human Rights Committee."

[47] Louis Henkin, "U.S. Ratification of Human Rights Conventions: The Ghost of Senator Bricker," *American Journal of International Law* 89 (April 1995): 346–350.

[48] Ibid., 349. Senator John Bricker quoted.

[49] Kenneth Roth, "Sidelined on Human Rights," *Foreign Affairs* 77 (March/April 1998): 2–6.

find new ways of punishing violators. Clinton endorsed the goal of establishing the Court in 1995, and the U.S. delegation was active in shaping the Rome Statute of 1998 that established the Court. The ICC also seems similar to the tribunals on Yugoslavia and Rwanda, which were strongly supported by the United States. There are, however, two important differences: first, the ICC operates more independently of the UN security council and thus, in theory, more independently of great-power control; second, U.S. troops or government officials could some day face charges by the Criminal Court.

Over time, officials from both the Clinton and George W. Bush administrations have expressed other concerns about the Court.[50] For example, there has been concern that the Rome Statute's definitions of international crimes are vague, open-ended, and not subject to reservations. There have again been questions about the constitutionality of forcing U.S. adherence to laws not passed by Congress. There has also been major criticism of Article 12 of the statute, which states that the Court may assert jurisdiction over certain crimes committed on the territory of a state party, including crimes committed by nationals of a non-party. Thus, even if the United States does not ratify the statute, its soldiers could be brought before the ICC if they committed a crime while in a ratifying country. U.S. officials have stated that this article goes against treaty law by making a non-party subject to a treaty. From a practical perspective, this article only becomes a problem if the United States chooses not to ratify for other reasons.

The interrelated questions of U.S. control and possible trials of Americans have been the two central issues hindering U.S. acceptance of the ICC. During negotiations, the U.S. delegation pushed hard for UN Security Council control of the Court, which would have enabled the United States to veto politically motivated investigations of U.S. citizens. Other countries argued for an independent court. In the end, the United States accepted a compromise that gave the ICC prosecutor much independence but allows the Security Council to pass a resolution to suspend an investigation or prosecution for one year.[51] Some U.S. officials still felt the prosecutor was given too much latitude. Also, many argued that U.S. soldiers and officials were at greater risk of prosecution because of America's greater world role. Clinton officials thus pressed for several ways to limit the chance that Americans would be brought before the Court.[52] Most crucial was the principle of complementarity, which means that the ICC cannot proceed with an investigation or prosecution of a crime that is being or has been investigated or prosecuted by a state that has juris-

[50] David J. Scheffer, "Staying the Course with the International Court," *Cornell International Law Journal* 35 (November 2001): 47–98; and John R. Bolton, "The Risks and Weaknesses of the International Criminal Court from America's Perspective," *Virginia Journal of International Law* 41 (Fall 2000): 186–203.

[51] Diane Orentlicher, "Unilateral Multilateralism: United States Policy Toward the International Criminal Court," *Cornell International Law Journal* 36 (Issue 3 2004): 419.

[52] Scheffer, "Staying the Course," 73–74.

diction, unless the state is unwilling or unable to carry out a fair investigation or trial.[53] Thus, if a U.S. soldier were to be accused of a crime, the case could go to the ICC only if the U.S. judicial system failed to genuinely investigate the allegation and proceed with a fair trial. Thus, the chance of an American being put on trial was low, but still present.

Because of these concerns, the United States was one of only seven countries to vote against the Rome Statute. Clinton signed the Statute on 31 December 2000, the last day that countries could become party to the treaty without formal ratification. As he did so, however, he discussed "significant flaws in the treaty" and said that he would not submit the treaty for ratification.[54] He pledged to work for the evolution of Court rules. George W. Bush has expressed even deeper concerns about the Court and has taken more-assertive action. First, in May 2002, as the Court was about to begin operation, Bush notified the UN that the United States had no intention of becoming a party to the statute and was essentially "unsigning" the treaty. Bush administration officials argued that this unprecedented action was necessary because complementarity was "simply an assertion, unproven and untested."[55] They were worried about the potential damage if investigations of either U.S. servicemen or U.S. leaders occurred, and they opposed the idea that the ICC would ultimately decide whether a national court system had acted fairly. The administration, therefore, took steps to ensure that Americans would not be turned over to the ICC. In July of 2002, the Bush administration delayed reauthorization of the UN peacekeeping mission in Bosnia as it sought permanent immunity for peacekeeping troops from ICC prosecution. U.S. actions were sharply criticized by European and UN officials. A compromise was struck that prohibited the ICC from investigating peacekeepers from non-ratifying countries for one year. A similar resolution was passed in 2003, but the Bush administration chose not to pursue another renewal in 2004 after it became clear that such a resolution would not pass. Meanwhile, the United States pressed hard for countries to sign bilateral agreements under Article 98 of the Rome Statute. In the agreements, countries pledged not to surrender U.S. citizens to the ICC. By the summer of 2004, the United States had concluded over ninety agreements. These agreements have been sharply opposed by many U.S. allies. In August 2002, Bush signed the American Servicemembers' Protection Act (P.L. 107-206), which prohibits U.S. military assistance to countries that are party to the ICC and have not signed Article 98 agreements. The legislation also authorizes the president to use force to release any U.S. citizen held by the Court.

[53] Robert Tucker, "The International Criminal Court Controversy," *World Policy Journal* 18 (Summer 2001): 75–77.

[54] Bill Clinton, "The Right Action," *New York Times*, 1 January 2001.

[55] John R. Bolton, "The United States and the International Criminal Court," remarks to the Federalist Society, 14 November 2002, accessed on the website of the Department of State at http://www.state.gov/t/us/rm/15158pf.htm, 10 August 2003.

Taken together, these actions show that the United States supports international treaties and courts as long as they are not applied to U.S. citizens and do not interfere with either U.S. domestic policies or U.S. military operations abroad. More generally, the United States is once again demonstrating that it supports human rights efforts, but only when it can lead and control those efforts. The U.S. position seems hypocritical to many critics and may prove shortsighted if U.S. power declines in the future. For the foreseeable future, though, the U.S. position reflects international realities. As was stated centuries ago, "The strong do what they have the power to do and the weak accept what they must accept."[56] Other countries may object to U.S. actions, but, so far at least, U.S. power has allowed it to act independently without huge long-term costs. Thus, as long as the United States remains the preeminent power, it will resist efforts either to bring its policies into line with the goals of others or to place restrictions on the pursuit of what it considers national interests.

CONTINUED COMPETITION FROM OTHER POLICY PRIORITIES

As a superpower, the United States has complex global interests and thus has to choose between policy priorities. In the Cold War era, containment of communism trumped all other policy goals. With the end of the Cold War, the United States appeared to have new flexibility. In fact, the last decade has seen the emergence of two new competing priorities, namely, pursuit of global trade and antiterrorism.

Clinton did raise human rights issues in his campaign against George H.W. Bush, but it was clear that he was elected because he remembered the famous slogan "It's the economy, stupid." Throughout his eight years, Clinton never lost focus on his pursuit of a strong economy, and he embraced the idea that the United States needed access to foreign markets to continue its growth. He worked hard to promote trade pacts such as the North American Free Trade Agreement and pursued ties with the "Big Emerging Markets." When pursuit of trade conflicted with tough human rights policies, as in the case of China, trade won time and time again. Clinton spoke of democratic enlargement, but as Douglas Brinkley argues, that strategy became increasingly "econocentric" and "was about spreading democracy through promoting the gospel of geoconomics."[57]

Soon, human rights advocates were speaking of "The New Double Standard," under which action was taken against only economically unimportant countries.[58] In the abstract, such a double standard is lamentable, but in the real

---

[56] "The Melian Dialogue" in Thucydides, *History of the Peloponnesian War* (New York: Penguin Books, 1954): 402.

[57] Brinkley "Democratic Enlargement," 118, 125.

[58] Aryeh Neier, "The New Double Standard," *Foreign Policy* 105 (Winter 1996/97): 91–101.

world it is almost inevitable. Trade is a growing part of the U.S. economy, and economic strength is a growing part of what defines modern world power. Human rights must not be forgotten, but those waiting for the United States to sacrifice its perceived economic national interests for the good of humanity will have a long wait.

That wait has now been lengthened by George W. Bush's declaration of war on terrorism. Antiterrorism has replaced anticommunism as the guiding security doctrine. This shift has shaped the allocation of administration time and resources. It also has had a crucial impact on U.S. alliances and willingness to criticize human rights violators. Countries that were previously targeted as violators, but which expressed sympathy for U.S. losses and provided counter-terrorism aid, were seen in a new light. The government of Ali Abullah Salih in Yemen suddenly was negotiating the arrival of U.S. military trainers and equipment. Malaysia's Prime Minister Mahathir Mohamad, known for his sharply anti-American views and his support of a conviction against his rival, Anwar Ibrahim, in a case the State Department termed "politically motivated and patently unfair,"[59] was invited to the White House. To reward Pervez Musharraf of Pakistan for his assistance, Bush supported new legislation that allowed him to waive sanctions imposed after Musharraf's 1999 coup. The administration also turned a relatively blind eye to Pakistan's 2002 referendum that extended Musharraf's rule without competitive elections and to modifications of the Pakistani constitution that gave the military a long-term role in politics.

The war on terrorism also lessened U.S. criticism of countries cracking down on internal groups, if those groups were defined as terrorists. For example, criticism of Russia's actions in Chechnya has declined. Before September 11, State Department officials met with the foreign minister of the separatist Chechen leadership. After September 11, a message was sent to separatists in Chechnya demanding that they sever all contacts with terrorists or face American isolation. Bush and other officials subsequently have expressed sympathy with Russian President Vladimir Putin's characterization of the Chechens as Islamic terrorists.[60] The long-term civil war in Colombia also has been recast as a battle against terrorism, because leftist revolutionary forces have frequently engaged in kidnappings and bombings. In the Middle East, the focus has been on cracking terrorist cells, so the administration has not yet pushed hard for democratic reforms in Saudi Arabia and elsewhere.

The war on terrorism has also strained U.S. adherence to international treaties on the treatment of prisoners. In general, the Bush administration has felt that security concerns were paramount. Therefore, the administration

---

[59] U.S. Department of State, "Malaysia," *Country Reports on Human Rights Practice–2001*, accessed on the website of the Department of State at http://www.state.gov, 28 September 2003.

[60] Michael Wines, "Road to U.S.-Russia Alliance Is Still Unmapped," *New York Times*, 21 October 2001.

planned to hold suspected terrorists indefinitely and authorized use of tough interrogation tactics to acquire intelligence that might prevent future attacks. In the fall of 2001, top administration officials repeatedly referred to Taliban and al Qaeda detainees held at Guantanamo Bay, Cuba as "unlawful combatants" and argued that they did not qualify as prisoners of war (POWs) under the Geneva Conventions. President Bush reportedly confirmed this position on 18 January 2002 in an unreleased legal decision.[61] On 7 February 2002, Bush partially reversed this policy after pressure from allies, human rights groups, and his own State Department. He decided that while al Qaeda detainees still would not be covered, the Conventions would be applied to Taliban captives, although none of them would be granted POW status.[62] Critics suggested that Bush was misapplying definitions in the Conventions and that at a minimum, the administration was required to follow Article 5 of the third Convention, which requires a competent tribunal to determine the status of detainees whenever doubt arises as to their status.[63] The administration argued that Article 5 tribunals were not necessary because there was no doubt about the detainees' status.

Treatment of prisoners at Guantanamo Bay and elsewhere has also drawn criticism. In the wake of abuse cases at Abu Ghraib prison in Iraq, attention has focused on an August 2002 Justice Department memo written to guide Central Intelligence Agency treatment of al Qaeda detainees and a March 2003 Defense Department report that covered actions at Guantanamo. The Justice Department memo laid out a narrow definition of torture and advised the White House that torture "may be justified" and legal as part of the President's efforts "to prevent further attacks on the United States by the Al Qaeda terrorist network."[64] The Pentagon report was based partly on the Justice memo and went beyond standard military doctrine in laying out acceptable interrogation techniques, such as adjusting the temperature to uncomfortable levels, serving cold rations, and reversing sleep cycles from night to day.[65] The White House disavowed the Justice memo and took the unusual step of releasing previously classified documents in an effort to show that Bush had never approved torture. However, the overall tough policy on detainees joins the post-September 11 alliances and support for global crackdowns in rein-

---

[61] Sean D. Murphy, "Decision Not to Regard Persons Detained in Afghanistan as POWs," *The American Journal of International Law* 96 (April 2002): 475–480.

[62] Thom Shanker and Katherine Q. Seelye, "Captives: Behind-the-Scenes Clash Led Bush to Reverse Himself on Applying Geneva Conventions," *New York Times*, 22 February 2002.

[63] Ruth Wedgewood, "Al Qaeda, Terrorism, and Military Commissions," *The American Journal of International Law* 96 (April 2002): 328–335; George H. Aldrich, "The Taliban, Al Qaeda, and the Determination of Illegal Combatants," *The American Journal of International Law* 96 (October 2002): 891–898.

[64] Quoted in Dana Priest and R. Jeffrey Smith, "Memo Offered Justifications for Use of Torture: Justice Department Gave Advice in 2002," *Washington Post*, 8 June 2004.

[65] Dana Priest and Bradley Graham, "U.S. Struggled Over How Far to Push Tactics: Documents Show Back-and-Forth on Interrogation Policy," *Washington Post*, 24 June 2004.

forcing the idea that security interests, like economic interests, still trump human rights concerns and will do so as long as the United States continues to face security threats—a situation that will continue for the foreseeable future.

CONTINUED WEAKNESS OF HUMAN RIGHTS ADVOCATES

Human rights seemed well-positioned at the start of the post-Cold War era from the standpoint of bureaucratic and NGO power. The State Department's Bureau on Democracy, Human Rights and Labor was now institutionalized.[66] Offices focusing on human rights or the promotion of democracy were being established at the National Security Council, the Agency for International Development, the Pentagon, and in the economic agencies. Furthermore, particularly during the Clinton administration, key positions were filled with long-time human rights advocates. Clinton's Secretary of State, Warren Christopher, had been active on the issue during the Carter administration. Assistant Secretaries of State for Human Rights John Shattuck, and after him Harold Hongju Koh, were both well-known and well-respected human rights advocates. These leaders and many of the staff they brought with them had close connections to private human rights groups such as Human Rights Watch and Amnesty International. They established much closer working relationships between government and nongovernment actors. Additionally, the nongovernment actors were themselves much better funded, staffed, and respected than they had been in the 1970s. It is, therefore, noteworthy that a mere decade later, human rights advocates appear to have become disorganized and weak, and have lost some popular support.

Ironically, part of the movement's new disorganization stems from the fact that the world has changed in directions that the advocates favored. The global spread of democracy, the fall of particular dictators, and systemic changes in countries such as South Africa have lessened abuse, but have also taken away the movement's easy targets. Russia and China continue to face criticism on some issues, but are not the totalitarian dictatorships of the past. Sustaining criticism of and rallying indignation against countries that still have some undesirable traits but that are moving toward democracy have proven difficult. Different groups inside and outside of government have therefore taken opposite positions on which countries should be praised for progress or criticized for slowness. Advocates have also disagreed on which tactics should be employed. For example, during the China MFN debates, business groups maintained a consistent voice for one policy. Within the human rights community, however, some groups supported engagement, whereas others favored punishment. Thus, there was less-strong policy advocacy overall. With so few issues unifying the entire governmental and nongovernmental community,

---

[66] In 1994, the Bureau's name was changed from Human Rights and Humanitarian Affairs to Democracy, Human Rights, and Labor.

supporters of action on a particular country or issue are often isolated voices that are easily overwhelmed by supporters of other concerns.

Human rights concerns also suffer from the continued institutional weakness of their chief governmental supporters. The State Department's Human Rights Bureau has come a long way from its early days, but is still viewed warily by other bureaucrats.[67] Many officials feel that the Bureau simply repeats a mantra of human rights points without considering overall policy calculations or changing conditions. Even when they meet with Human Rights Bureau officials, other officials often tune out the message. Also, many see the Bureau as a mouthpiece for nongovernmental groups rather than as a source for independent analysis. Therefore, the recent access many human rights advocates have enjoyed may actually have hurt their cause by reinforcing the view that they have "captured" the Bureau. The Bureau's overall position is illustrated by looking at its most significant work, the annual reports. These reports have become institutionalized, and likely will continue for years. They also have been given more respect over time. Still, though, there often appears to be little connection between the Bureau's reports and overall policy. Countries are sharply criticized, yet aid is not cut off under 502B or other legislation, trade is continued, and diplomatic relations with violators continue after adjusting for their annual bump in the road. In addition to the Bureau, there are other governmental actors that support human rights, but those in Congress and other executive branch agencies typically push pet projects and particular concerns, not overall policy development.[68]

Given the weakness of governmental actors, human rights policy depends disproportionately on pressure from interest groups and the public. Human rights groups first began to blossom in opposition to President Richard M. Nixon's policy of *realpolitik*. They gained momentum during Carter's presidency, and then came to real prominence during the Reagan era, when they often sharply disagreed with the administration about particular cases and the overall direction of U.S. policy. In some ways, the Reagan years were difficult, but many human rights leaders agree that the groups ultimately benefited from Reagan's opposition.[69] During that era, human rights debates centered on disputes over the facts of who was a human rights abuser. The groups became increasingly professional at gathering and disseminating these facts. Also, during that era, the groups stood out as champions for morality and thus garnered much attention and financial support from those opposed to Reagan's policies. In the post-Cold War era, as the administrations themselves put more focus on human rights, the disputes switched away from facts toward difficult policy choices of how to respond to abuse. Also, the groups were no

---

[67] This and other observations are based on numerous interviews the author has conducted with officials in various State Department bureaus and the NGO community.

[68] Forsythe, "Human Rights in U.S. Foreign Policy," 449.

[69] See the comments of several human rights leaders, in David Rieff, "The Precarious Triumph of Human Rights," *New York Times Magazine*, 8 August 1999.

longer criticizing their ideological enemies, but instead, former colleagues who had entered government service. The groups had better access, but that did not always translate into real policy influence. Additionally, when some government action was taken, the groups were left with the tough decision of whether to celebrate a glass half full, or complain about a glass half empty. Human rights groups also face new challenges, because their major strategy of releasing dramatic reports in the hopes of embarrassing countries into better behavior has lost some of its power over time. The first dramatic report might pressure a country, but years of reports lead many rogue states and others to learn to live with the criticism. Meanwhile, the reports suffer domestically from the problem of "compassion fatigue," a sense that a new problem emerges every time an old one is settled.

Furthermore, human rights issues have not stimulated major grassroots movements, except in unusual cases such as South African apartheid. In polls that ask respondents to rate "promoting and defending human rights in other countries" as a policy goal, significantly fewer than half rate it as "very important."[70] Similar results are found for the goal of bringing democracy to other countries. Notably, these poll numbers have been dropping in the post-Cold War era.

One major problem for both governmental and nongovernmental human rights advocates is the continued U.S. focus on security and economic interests, which makes their views seem of secondary importance. As noted earlier, these other interests are unlikely to recede any time soon, so advocates will continue to fight an uphill battle. A second problem is that few Americans see human rights abuses abroad as directly affecting their personal interests. Americans may support principles of morality, but evidence of human rights abuse can often be ignored simply by turning off the television. On the other hand, tax increases to increase foreign aid, embargoes that risk American jobs, or long-term military interventions do directly impact average citizens. Politicians know that they are unlikely to lose an election by disappointing the human rights community, but they could lose one if the side effects of policies hurt their constituents. Overall, lack of public focus and support for tough policies reinforces the institutional weakness of governmental and NGO human rights advocates. Thus, although human rights supporters are now respected parts of the Washington community and have better access to policymakers, their policy influence will likely remain low for years to come unless they find new tactics or new problems on which to focus.

Overall, the post-Cold War period has seen important new U.S. human rights actions, both bilaterally and multilaterally. Few observers would dispute that a policymaking environment exists now that is sharply different from

---

[70] Chicago Council of Foreign Relations, Foreign Policy Leadership Project, and Times-Mirror Center for the People and the Press polls discussed in Ole Holsti, "Public Opinion on Human Rights in American Foreign Policy" in Forsythe, ed., *The United States and Human Rights*, 131–174.

that of thirty or even a dozen years ago. Still, major structural constraints remain. U.S. power and ability to force change on others is still limited. The United States remains wary of international law and multilateral initiatives that can be applied to U.S. domestic policies or that can constrain foreign actions. Competing national interests, particularly economic growth and anti-terrorism, continue to trump human rights concerns. Domestically, supporters of human rights are still weak actors in the policy-making process. In previous eras, observers often argued that a more effective and consistent human rights policy would come if a few variables were altered. The continued existence of key limits in the very different post-Cold War era shows that, in fact, the limits were never short-term, time- or issue-specific problems, but rather deeper constraints that stem from the realities of global and domestic politics. They did not disappear with the end of the Cold War, and they do not vary significantly by administration.

The Rhetoric of Genocide in U.S. Foreign Policy: Rwanda and Darfur Compared

ERIC A. HEINZE

The world is once again confronting the specter of genocide. Like Rwanda a decade before it, the crisis in the Darfur region of Sudan promises to challenge the moral conscience of those actors who made the sacred promise of "never again." The ceasefire signed in Abuja, Nigeria in May of 2006, while an important step toward ending the bloody conflict in Darfur, has not been signed by all factions to the conflict, is yet to be backed up by adequate force, and to date has had little or no effect on conditions on the ground. Thus, aside from the scarcely armed group of African Union (AU) monitors soon to be assisted by United Nations (UN) peacekeepers pursuant to the Abuja agreement, there has been little forceful action toward stopping the killings in Darfur. The United States, for its part, took the lead in condemning the Darfur atrocities as genocide, and in doing so, departed from the reasoning that informed the American diplomatic rhetorical response to Rwanda 10 years prior. That is, while the administration of Bill Clinton avoided the rhetoric of genocide in reference to the first unequivocal instance of genocide since the Holocaust, the administration of George W. Bush was quick to make this charge in Darfur amidst far more ambiguous circumstances. What accounts for this difference in rhetorical response? This article suggests that prevailing political realities, both domestic and international, account for this discrepancy, thus rendering it politically possible, and even expedient, for the Bush administration to use the rhetoric of genocide over Darfur.

Since the genocide in Rwanda of 1994, a voluminous literature has emerged seeking to explain the origins of that crisis, why the UN and its member states (especially the United States) did not intervene to stop the killing, and exactly

ERIC A. HEINZE is an assistant professor of political science and international studies at the University of Oklahoma. His scholarly articles have most recently appeared in the *Journal of Human Rights*, *Parameters*, the *Journal of Military Ethics*, *Polity*, and the *International Journal of Human Rights*. His book, *Waging Humanitarian War: The Ethics, Law and Politics of Humanitarian Intervention*, is forthcoming with SUNY Press.

when a situation of mass murder is rightly considered "genocide."[1] Owing to the declassification of numerous U.S. State Department memos, Central Intelligence Agency briefings, and other sensitive government materials, it is now well documented that the United States had considerable knowledge of what was happening to Rwandan Tutsis and moderate Hutus in April through June of 1994. There are nevertheless important reasons that the United States did not want to get involved in Rwanda, many of which are in no small part related to the public relations debacle only months prior in Somalia. Thus, when it comes to the political maneuvering involved in "naming the crime" during the Rwanda crisis, conventional wisdom now holds that Clinton administration officials avoided using the "g word" for fear that using it would have obliged the United States to take action under the terms of the 1948 Genocide Convention.[2] The United States did not, after all, want to admit that something was transpiring that would impose a moral, if not legal, obligation to intervene. As a result, U.S. officials did not publicly utter the word "genocide" until well after it had become radically apparent to most observers that genocide had taken place. While the case for classifying the killings in Rwanda as genocide was arguably the most unambiguous since the Holocaust, even in late May of 1994—over six weeks into the killings—U.S. rhetoric on genocide still remained diluted, referring only to "acts of genocide."[3]

Fast forward nearly 10 years to the Darfur region of western Sudan. Since February of 2003, when Darfurian rebels rose up against what they perceived as increasingly heavy-handed and oppressive rule from the Islamic government in Khartoum, a brutal counter-insurgency has been underway that has resulted in hundreds of thousands of civilian deaths and millions more displaced. In this conflict, the specter of genocide was raised amidst findings that Khartoum's strategy in combating the insurgency was essentially to depopulate the countryside of "sympathetic" Darfurian civilians—mostly members of the Fur, Massaleit, and Zaghawa tribes—by arming and providing air support to Arab militias called *Janjaweed*, who would attack villages, kill, rape, and

---

[1] See Alain Destexhe, *Rwanda and Genocide in the Twentieth Century* (New York: New York University Press, 1995); Gérard Prunier, *The Rwanda Crisis: History of a Genocide* (New York: Columbia University Press, 1995); Philip Gourevitch, *We Wish to Inform You that Tomorrow We Will Be Killed With Our Families* (New York: Farrar, Straus, and Giroux, 1998); Mahmood Mamdani, *When Victims Become Killers: Colonialism, Nativism, and the Genocide in Rwanda* (Princeton, NJ: Princeton University Press, 2001); Samantha Power, *"A Problem from Hell": America and the Age of Genocide* (New York: Perennial, 2002); Michael Barnett, *Eyewitness to Genocide: The United Nations and Rwanda* (Ithaca, NY: Cornell University Press, 2002); Linda Melvern, *Conspiracy to Murder: The Rwanda Genocide and the International Community* (London: Verso, 2004); and Romeo Dallaire, *Shake Hands with the Devil: The Failure of Humanity in Rwanda* (New York: Carroll & Graf, 2005).

[2] See Barnett, *Eyewitness to Genocide*, 138–139; Destexhe, *Rwanda and Genocide*, 35; Power, *Problem from Hell*, 359; Dallaire, *Shake Hands with the Devil*, 333, 374, 395, 454; see also David Rieff, *At the Point of a Gun: Democratic Dreams and Armed Intervention* (New York: Simon & Schuster, 2005), 74–75.

[3] See Power, *Problem from Hell*, 362, especially notes 60, 61.

forcibly displace at will.[4] Many of the displaced would starve to death in flight or die slowly of disease and malnutrition in refugee and displacement camps.

By the summer of 2004, amidst utterances of an impending genocide in Darfur by American evangelicals, African American leaders, and human rights advocates, high-level U.S. officials began to openly refer to the situation as genocide—to the delight of humanitarian interventionists, but to the confusion of students of *realpolitik* who believed the United States did not have a dog in that fight.[5] The first official semantical leap was in July of 2004, when the U.S. Congress passed a concurrent, though nonbinding, resolution condemning the violence in Darfur as genocide.[6] Secretary of State Colin Powell followed suit in September of 2004, as did President Bush during an address to the UN General Assembly less than two weeks later.[7] What is remarkable about this willingness to employ the rhetoric of genocide is the extent to which it stands as a radical departure from the reasoning that led the Clinton administration to avoid using such language in 1994. Especially perplexing is that while the Clinton administration sought to deny what (they and) the international community knew about genocide in Rwanda, the Bush White House sought to brand the situation in Darfur as genocide despite significant uncertainty as to whether this was, in fact, the case. Bush continues to do so despite a UN inquiry in January of 2005 that concluded that genocide had *not* taken place.[8] With massive troop commitments in Afghanistan and Iraq, it is no surprise that there would be little appetite in Washington for humanitarian intervention, nation building, or other military involvement in Darfur.[9] The Bush administration would thus seemingly be poorly served by openly referring to the Darfur crisis as genocide if doing so triggers an expectation and obligation to intervene to "prevent and punish" the crime—something the United States has

[4] See Human Rights Watch, *Darfur in Flames: Atrocities in Western Sudan* (New York: Human Rights Watch, 2004); Human Rights Watch, *Darfur Destroyed: Ethnic Cleansing by Government and Militia Forces in Western Sudan* (New York: Human Rights Watch, 2004); see also Alex de Waal, "Briefing: Darfur, Sudan: Prospects for Peace," *African Affairs* 104 (January 2005): 127–135; Alex de Waal, "Who Are the Darfurians? Arab and African Identities, Violence, and External Engagement," *African Affairs* 104 (April 2005): 181–205; Gerard Prunier, *Darfur: The Ambiguous Genocide* (Ithaca, NY: Cornell University Press, 2005); Julie Flint and Alex de Waal, *Darfur: A Short History of a Long War* (New York: Zed Books, 2005).

[5] "'Realism' and Darfur," *The Washington Post*, 1 August 2004.

[6] U.S. House, *Declaring Genocide in Darfur, Sudan,* 108th Cong., 2nd sess., 2004, H. Doc. 467; U.S. Senate, *Declaring Genocide in Darfur, Sudan,* 108th Cong, 2nd sess., 2004, S. Doc. 133.

[7] Steven R. Weisman, "Powell Says Rapes and Killings in Sudan Are Genocide," *The New York Times*, 10 September 2004; address by President Bush to the United Nations General Assembly, *United States Mission to the United Nations*, 21 September 2004, accessed at http://www.usunnewyork.usmission.gov/04gwb0921.htm, 5 July 2005.

[8] Report of the International Commission of Inquiry on Darfur to the United Nations Secretary General (Geneva, United Nations, 25 January 2005), 4, accessed at http://www.un.org/News/dh/sudan/com_ing_darfur.pdf, 18 June 2007.

[9] "Bush and Kerry on the Issue of Sudan," *Associated Press*, 28 October 2004.

not demonstrated the will to undertake. Why, then, were U.S. officials so quick to name the crime absent the political will to intervene to stop it?

This article begins by establishing the Rwandan crisis of 1994 as the paradigmatic example of the crime of genocide since the Holocaust and examining the U.S. response to it. There are, of course, important differences between Rwanda and Darfur, though it is evident in both cases that the United States was not and has not been prepared to put its troops in harm's way to stop the brutality. This begs the question as to what differences between Rwanda and Darfur account for the Bush administration's use of the rhetoric of genocide without an expectation of intervention in Darfur, as contrasted to the Clinton administration's conscious avoidance of such language so as not to impose upon itself this unwanted obligation in Rwanda. Examining events between the spring of 2004 and late 2005, I thus investigate the factors in U.S. politics that led to the official characterization of the Darfur crisis as genocide. Here I highlight the influence of Congress's concern over Khartoum's "other" civil war against rebels in southern Sudan, the roles of the evangelical Christian lobby and the Black Congressional Caucus, and the coinciding of these events with the 10-year anniversary of the Rwandan genocide. Finally, I explore what factors account for the general lack of domestic and international pressure on the U.S. government to follow up its finding of genocide in Darfur by taking forceful action to put an end to it, as the Clinton administration reasoned would be expected of it had it concluded that genocide was occurring in Rwanda. Here I point to the understanding of the obligations under the Genocide Convention, the influence of the Iraq war and the broader war on terrorism, and the desire to not disrupt the peace process in Sudan's North–South civil conflict. I ultimately conclude that once domestic constituencies began pressuring the Bush administration to take action over Darfur, the rhetoric of genocide was pursued *as a substitute* for more forceful action, for which there became less of an expectation because of competing imperatives in the Sudan as well as a general international uneasiness about American military interventionism.

RWANDA AS THE GENOCIDE PARADIGM

Since the story of the Rwandan genocide has been recounted in numerous studies and academic and journalistic accounts,[10] I will not recount that story in

---

[10] In addition to the analyses cited above, see also Arthur J. Klinghoffer, *The International Dimensions of Genocide in Rwanda* (New York: New York University Press, 1998); John A. Berry and Carol Pott Berry, eds., *Genocide in Rwanda: A Collective Memory* (Washington DC: Howard University Press, 1999); Christopher C. Taylor, *Sacrifice as Terror: The Rwandan Genocide of 1994* (New York: Berg, 1999); Bruce D. Jones, *Peacemaking in Rwanda: The Dynamics of Failure* (Boulder, CO: Lynne Reinner, 2001); and Alan J. Kuperman, *The Limits of Humanitarian Intervention: Genocide in Rwanda* (Washington DC, Brookings Institution of Peace, 2001).

detail here, but, rather, briefly outline the politics surrounding U.S. policy. It should be noted, however, that the crisis in Rwanda stands as the first *unequivocal* case of genocide since the Holocaust. The crime of genocide has a precise legal definition, the use of which requires that the victims be members of a "national, ethnical, racial or religious group," and that the relevant acts be committed with the "intent to destroy [the group] in whole or in part."[11] It is now generally accepted in the international legal community that the horrors of Rwanda met this definition.[12] As early as 19 April 1994—just over two weeks into the crisis—non-governmental organizations (NGOs), the popular press, and the commander of the UN peacekeepers in Rwanda, Romeo Dallaire, began using the term "genocide" to describe what was happening in Rwanda.[13] The evidence seemed sufficient to warrant its use: using the radio waves to incite and recruit killers and an anachronistic identity card system to identify ethnic Tutsis, a well-executed plan involving the Hutu-dominated army, civil service, Gendarmerie, and Interahamwe (a Hutu militia) was initiated to destroy Rwanda's Tutsis.[14] In the words of one radio broadcast intended to incite murder, "We have to act . . . wipe them all out."[15] The use of the "g word" to describe the crisis in Rwanda, however, triggered a firestorm of controversy at the UN and in world capitals.

With the failure of Somalia in such recent memory, the Clinton administration had no desire to get bogged down in another conflict in Africa. The doctrinal lynchpin for this policy was presidential decision directive 25 (PDD-25), developed against the backdrop of the Somalia meltdown, that severely circumscribed the conditions under which the United States would participate in peacekeeping. Among other things, PDD-25 required that U.S. participation in any UN operation must "advance US interests," while also limiting U.S. participation in UN missions, as well as U.S. support for other states that intend to carry out UN-sanctioned missions.[16] Though not officially

[11] Convention on the Prevention and Punishment of the Crime of Genocide (Genocide Convention), 9 December 1948, 78 UNTS 277, Article II, accessed at http://www.unchr.ch/html/menu3/b/p_genoci.htm, 18 June 2007.

[12] This is evidenced by the existence of the International Criminal Tribunal for Rwanda (ICTR), the purpose of which is to try individuals for the crimes of genocide, crimes against humanity, and certain war crimes. See Statute of the International Criminal Tribunal for Rwanda (ICTR Statute), 22 February 1995, UN Doc. S/RES/955, Article 2. In 1998, the ICTR issued its first conviction for the crime of genocide in *Prosecutor v. Akayesu* (Case No. ICTR-96-4-T), Judgment, 2 September 1998.

[13] Dallaire, *Shake Hands with the Devil*, 333; Barnett, *Eyewitness to Genocide*, 34; Power, *Problem from Hell*, 357.

[14] See generally Gourevitch, *We Wish to Inform You.*

[15] Organization of African Unity (OAU), *Rwanda: The Preventable Genocide* (Organization of African Unity, 2000), accessed at http://www.africa_union.org/official/_documents/reports/Report_rowanda_genocide.pdf, 18 June 2007.

[16] "Clinton Administration Policy on Reforming Multilateral Peacekeeping Operations, Presidential Decision Directive 25," 3 May 1994, accessed on the website of the Federation of American Scientists at http://www.fas.org/irp/offdocs/pdd25.htm, 14 September 2005.

implemented until 4 May, this directive was used as an informal guide for U.S. policy toward Rwanda and was augmented by a general indifference regarding Rwandan affairs. Some months prior, in response to requests by the African Affairs Bureau in the Pentagon to consider Rwanda a potential trouble spot, high-level administration officials are reported to have responded, "Take [Rwanda] off the list ... US national interest is not involved ... just make it go away."[17] It is thus no surprise that a matter of days after the genocide began, the response of the United States and other Western states was to evacuate their nationals from embassies and diplomatic missions. U.S. Secretary of State Warren Christopher commented that evacuating U.S. nationals was "the prudent thing to do"[18]—a general sentiment of apathy that was echoed by influential members of Congress such as Senator Robert Dole (R-KS), who commented that "the Americans are out, and as far as I'm concerned, in Rwanda, that ought to be the end of it."[19] On 21 April, around the time NGOs and the media began openly entertaining the possibility of genocide, the UN Security Council voted unanimously to reduce the number of UN peace-keepers in the United Nations Assistance Mission for Rwanda (UNAMIR) from an already-anemic 2,100 to a token force of 270, while also further limiting its mandate to the principal task of negotiating a cease-fire between the belligerents.[20]

It was only after the emasculation of UNAMIR—when the signs of geno-cide became increasingly undeniable, with deaths tolls reaching an estimated 200,000—that the UN Security Council began seriously considering whether genocide was actually taking place.[21] While the representatives from the Czech Republic and New Zealand publicly entertained the possibility of genocide, the United States took the lead position in opposing the use of this strong rhetoric, finding no shortage of support from other members of the Council. This was largely because there was no intervention force ready and willing to invade Rwanda to stop the killing, even though the prospect of genocide had caused a moral groundswell of support for action among the advocacy community. As Michael Barnett hypothesizes, "The insinuation was that to make this dis-cursive move would only expand the gap between the moral imperative and the lack of action."[22] Furthermore, there was concern among certain Council members that talking about genocide would not only undermine the UN's neutrality on the ground, it would also dissuade the belligerents from returning to the terms of the negotiated cease-fire, the Arusha Accords.[23]

[17] Cited by Power, *Problem from Hell*, 342.

[18] Ibid., 352.

[19] Ibid.

[20] United Nations Security Council Resolution 912, 21 April 1994, UN Doc. S/RES/912.

[21] Barnett, *Eyewitness to Genocide*, 131.

[22] Ibid., 134.

[23] See Julia Preston, "'This Eerie Calm': The Rwanda Situation Confounds the Security Council," *The Washington Post*, 9 May 1994.

Official thinking in Washington followed a similar logic, with strict adherence to PDD-25. The official U.S. line was that the killings in Rwanda were not genocide, but part of the resumption of hostilities in the civil war, a situation that by definition precludes the use of peacekeepers (as outlined in the Council's own statement on the conditions under which a peacekeeping operation could be established).[24] Pushing ahead with a UN operation, U.S. officials reasoned, would invite a disaster of the kind witnessed in Somalia a few months earlier.[25] After all, the extreme unlikelihood of a ceasefire meant that any potential UN intervention—be it a peacekeeping operation or a Chapter VII enforcement operation—would be thrust into a civil war. U.S. policy was therefore informed by the need to temper the unbridled UN ambitions that U.S. officials believed had brought about the debacle in Somalia. To prevent the UN from dragging the United States into another failed peacekeeping operation, pressure was intense to "pick a winner" and save UN peacekeeping for when it could succeed.[26] But Rwanda had "loser" written all over it *á la* Somalia, so the policy was to reduce, not reinforce, the UN presence. After all, no public official wanted to *again* explain why American soldiers were dying in faraway Africa, where the United States had no compelling security interest.

While some U.S. officials voiced concerns that using the word "genocide," and then being seen as doing nothing, would somehow affect the upcoming congressional elections in November, the overarching concern was that referring to the situation as genocide would cause demands for a U.S. response that the administration was not prepared to undertake.[27] However, virtually no constituencies in the United States gave the Clinton administration the impression that it would pay a political price for failing to rescue the Rwandans; and part of the reason for avoiding the rhetoric of genocide was to keep it this way. Paradoxically, then, U.S. officials "simultaneously believed that the American people would oppose US military intervention [in Rwanda] and feared that the public might support intervention if they realized genocide was underway."[28] This indeed proved to be true, as it was only *after* the revelation of genocide that it became possible to identify a constituency for action in Rwanda.[29]

[24] Paul Lewis, "UN Backs Troops for Rwanda but Terms Bar Any Action Soon," *The New York Times*, 17 May 1994; Barnett, *Eyewitness to Genocide*, 135.

[25] Hearing of the International Security, International Organization and Human Rights Subcommittee of the House Foreign Affairs Committee, 103rd Cong., 2nd sess., 1994.

[26] Barnett, *Eyewitness to Genocide*, 163.

[27] National Security Council official Susan Rice, quoted in Power, *Problem from Hell*, 359; Douglas Jehl, "Officials Told to Avoid Calling Rwanda Killings 'Genocide,'" *The New York Times*, 10 June 1994.

[28] Power, *Problem from Hell*, 373.

[29] Michael R. Gordon, "US to Supply 60 Vehicles for UN Troops in Rwanda," *The New York Times*, 16 June 1994; see also Power, *Problem from Hell*, 374.

U.S. officials went to great lengths in the semantical charade to avoid the rhetoric of genocide. Especially revealing is the now well-known discussion paper on Rwanda, dated 1 May and prepared by an official in the Office of the Secretary of Defense, that read: "1. Genocide Investigation: Language that calls for an international investigation of human rights abuses and possible violations of the genocide convention. *Be Careful. Legal at State was worried about this yesterday—Genocide finding could commit USG* [the U.S. Government] *to actually 'do something.'*"[30] Against this backdrop, one can better understand the maladroit dance around the term "genocide" by the State Department spokesperson when asked to comment on whether the killings in Rwanda constituted genocide:

> As I think you know, the use of the term "genocide" has a very precise legal meaning although it's not strictly a legal determination. There are other factors in there as well. In looking at a situation, to make a determination about that, before we begin to use that term, we have to know as much as possible about the facts of the situation . . . . This is a more complicated issue to address, and we're certainly looking into this extremely carefully right now. But I'm not able to look at all of those criteria at this moment and say, "yes/no." It's something that requires very careful study before we can make a final determination.[31]

It was six weeks into the genocide, on 21 May, before U.S. officials gave the go-ahead to call the killings by their rightful name, and even then Secretary Christopher hopelessly qualified the permission given to U.S. officials, referring ambiguously to "acts of genocide," and refusing to allow characterization of any specific incident in Rwanda as genocidal.[32] Nevertheless, from the point of view of a policy that sought to avoid U.S. involvement in either peacekeeping or enforcement operations in Rwanda, the U.S. decision to consciously avoid the inflammatory rhetoric of genocide makes sense, even if it is morally repugnant. Although it is now understood that the Genocide Convention does *not* require military intervention to halt genocide (even though some in the administration perhaps did not realize this at the time), administration officials were probably correct to assume that both the domes-

[30] Office of the Deputy Assistant Secretary of Defense for Middle East/Africa Region, Department of Defense, "Discussion Paper: Rwanda" (Declassified), 1 May 1994, accessed on the website of The National Security Archive at http://www.gwu.edu/~nsarchiv/NSAEBB/NSAEBB53/index.htm, 20 September 2005. Italics original.

[31] Department of Defense Daily Press Briefing, 28 April 1994, accessed on the website of the Department of State Federal Depository Library at http://dosfan.lib.uic.edu/ERC/briefing/daily_briefings/1994/9404/940428db.html, 20 September 2005.

[32] Action memorandum from Assistant Secretary of State for African Affairs George E. Moose, et al. to Secretary of State Warren Christopher, Subject: "Has Genocide Occurred in Rwanda?" (Declassified), 21 May 1994, accessed on the website of The National Security Archive at http://www.gwu.edu/~nsarchiv/NSAEBB/NSAEBB53/index.html, 20 September 2005; see also Power, *Problem from Hell*, 362.

tic and international public would not bother with legal niceties and would instead focus on the strong moral obligation to "never again" allow genocide to occur. So while the pressure on the administration to name the crime was intense, if it did so, administration officials reasoned, the pressure to intervene would be even more intense, particularly since the United States is one of few states with the assets to execute such an emergency intervention. Thus, if Somalia was any indication, the political risks of not acting were less than the political risks of acting, and the Clinton administration had much to lose and little to gain from an intervention in the heart of Africa. Since naming the crime would have pressured the United States to do just this, the crime was not named.

DARFUR: RETHINKING CONVENTIONAL WISDOM

While the atrocities in Darfur had been raging since February of 2003, it took nearly a year for international activity to reach an effective pitch. The popular press and certain NGOs were the first to characterize the Darfur killings as genocide,[33] but a true sense of international urgency over Darfur only became apparent in April of 2004, when UN Secretary-General Kofi Annan made a direct comparison between the Darfur crisis and the 1994 Rwandan genocide. Speaking at the UN Human Rights Commission on the tenth anniversary of the Rwandan genocide, the Secretary-General stated that "whatever term it uses to describe the situation, the international community cannot stand idle... [but] must be prepared to take swift and appropriate action. By 'action' in such situations I mean a continuum of steps, which may include military action."[34] With the rhetoric of genocide now raised, and with high-profile personalities like the UN Secretary-General drawing comparisons between Darfur and the world's (and the U.S.'s) derelict response to genocide 10 years prior—and even musing about a possible need for military intervention in Darfur—the U.S. foreign policy establishment undoubtedly began to pay closer attention to the events in Darfur.

Despite the considerable attention given to the Darfur crisis by U.S. officials, there are several factors indicative of the Bush administration's desire to avoid military involvement in Darfur, in either a direct or supportive role. First and foremost is the U.S. military commitment in Iraq and Afghanistan. On 22 April 2004, Samantha Power testified before the House

---

[33] See Paul D. Williams and Alex J. Bellamy, "The Responsibility to Protect and the Crisis in Darfur," *Security Dialogue* 36 (March 2005): 27–47; among journalistic accounts, see Eric Reeves, "Unnoticed Genocide," *The Washington Post*, 25 February 2004; Nicholas D. Kristof, "Will We Say 'Never Again' Yet Again?" *The New York Times*, 27 March 2004.

[34] Kofi Annan, Action Plan to Prevent Genocide, Speech Delivered to the UN Human Rights Commission, 7 April 2004, UN Press Release, SG/SM/9197 AFR/893 HR/CN/1077, accessed at http://www2.unog.ch/news2/documents/newsen/sgo4003e.htm, 18 June 2007.

International Relations Committee that it would require 10,000 troops to effectively stop the killing in Darfur.[35] Military realities being what they are, only the United States and possibly a few European states have the lift capacity to rapidly deploy such a force.[36] But with massive troop commitments in Iraq and Afghanistan, it would seem unlikely that U.S. officials would rush to volunteer U.S. forces for such a task. By early July of 2004, Defense Department officials revealed that they had no plans to deploy U.S. forces to Darfur any time soon, not even to support the delivery of humanitarian relief.[37]

Perhaps even more revealing were prior comments by the United States Agency for International Development administrator, Andrew Natsios, in a 27 April press conference. When asked if the United States would support a UN-backed humanitarian intervention if the Sudanese government continued to abet the killings in violation of the negotiated ceasefire (the N'Djamena Agreement, signed between the Sudanese government and Darfurian rebels in Chad on 8 April), Natsios responded that there were "no alternatives" other than a successful implementation of the ceasefire and that "troops are not going to help us right now."[38] It thus seems reasonably clear that from the beginning of the crisis, Bush administration officials had little desire to commit the United States to providing material support for peacekeeping or enforcement action in Darfur, much less take it upon itself to intervene.

Naming the Crime

Members of Congress were the first among U.S. public officials to take the situation in Darfur seriously and thus were the first government officials to characterize the situation as "genocide" in official capacity and public fora. As far as I have been able to ascertain, the first U.S. official to publicly speak of "genocide" in explicit reference to the killings in Darfur was Frank Wolf (R-VA) on the floor of the House on 2 April 2004.[39] Members of the Senate,

---

[35] Committee on House International Relations Subcommittee on Africa, Testimony of Samantha Power, 108th Cong., 2nd sess., 2004.

[36] See John Prendergast, "Sudan's Ravines of Death," *The New York Times*, 15 July 2004; see also the views of Mark Schneider, Senior Vice President of the International Crisis Group, as quoted in Helen Fessenden, "Lawmakers Seek Viable Solution to Sudan's Humanitarian Crisis," *CQ Weekly*, 3 July 2004, 1638.

[37] Fessenden, "Lawmakers Seek Viable Solution," 1638.

[38] "United States Policy in Sudan," remarks of USAID Administrator Andrew Natsios, Special Advisor for Sudan Policy Michael Ranneberger, and USAID Assistant Administrator Roger Winter, 27 April 2004, accessed on the website of the U.S. Department of State at http://www.state.gov/p/af/rls/rm/31856.htm, 27 September 2005.

[39] "Stop the Killing in Sudan," remarks of Frank R. Wolf in the U.S. House of Representatives, 108th Cong., 2nd sess., *Congressional Record* 150 (2 April 2004): E 518.

such as Mike DeWine (R-OH), John McCain (R-AZ), and Jon Corzine (D-NJ), also subsequently invoked the term numerous times in reference to Darfur.[40] By June, members on both sides of the aisle began using this strong rhetoric, and on 25 June, a bipartisan roster of 52 Senators sent a letter to Secretary of State Colin Powell urging an increase in assistance to Darfur, targeted sanctions, a travel ban, freezing of assets, and a UN resolution calling for robust monitoring and peacekeeping.[41] These efforts ultimately led President Bush to dispatch Secretary Powell to Darfur to investigate the killings, where he arrived on 30 June.[42] By this time, however, the Darfur crisis had gained much momentum in Congress, which culminated when both chambers adopted concurrent, nonbinding resolutions on 22 July condemning the atrocities in Darfur as "genocide" and asking the President to do the same and to take action in conjunction with the international community to stop the violence.[43] Two months later, on 9 September, Powell declared to the Senate Foreign Relations Committee that he and his investigative team had concluded "that genocide has been committed in Darfur, and that the government of Sudan and the Janjawid [sic] bear responsibility, and that genocide may still be occurring."[44] This sentiment was echoed by the President as he addressed the UN General Assembly on 21 September.[45]

Sudan's "other" civil war. The politics in Congress that led to the use of the rhetoric of genocide in reference to Darfur have their origins in Congress's preoccupation with other events in the Sudan—namely, the Sudanese government's brutal counter-insurgency against the Sudan People's Liberation Army/ Movement (SPLA/M). The SPLA/M rebels had been fighting the Islamist government since 1983, defending the predominantly non-Arab and non-Muslim populations in the southern provinces (referred to by the media as "Black" or "African" Sudanese) from the government's policies of forced "Islamization" and "Arabization." While this is not the place for a historical treatment of the "North–South" civil war in Sudan, this conflict has frequently been characterized as having certain racial and/or religious undertones. The Islamic regime in Khartoum has for decades pursued brutal policies toward the mostly "African" (contrast "Arab") and Christian and animist (practitioners of

[40] Helen Fessenden, "The Semantics of 'Genocide' and How it Pertains to Sudan," *CQ Weekly*, 3 July 2004, 1639.

[41] Ibid.

[42] Glenn Kessler, "Powell, in Sudan, Presses for Action," *The Washington Post*, 1 July 2004.

[43] House Concurrent Resolution 467, Senate Concurrent Resolution 133.

[44] Hearing of the Senate Foreign Relations Committee on the Current Situation in Sudan and Prospects for Peace, Testimony of Secretary of State Colin Powell, Federal News Service, 9 September 2004.

[45] Bush, *United States Mission*.

traditional tribal faiths) southern populations.[46] The President of Sudan, Omar Bashir, at one point declared this campaign against the southern rebels a holy war and has since directed the armed conflict against civilians, pursuing scorched-earth tactics, forced displacement, enslavement, rape, mass murder, and induced famine.

The fact that Sudan's civil war had elements of religious persecution of Christians and the enslavement of "Blacks" made it of particular concern to evangelical and African American constituencies in the United States. As Allen Hertzke has noted, "The plight of the southern Sudanese people would have remained in the backwater of American concern had not the Christian solidarity movement picked up the case."[47] As a result, numerous influential members of Congress with strong evangelical bases took up what became informally known as the faith-based Sudan coalition, which included the likes of Tom Tancredo (R-CO), Spencer Bachus (R-AL), and Donald Payne (D-MD) in the House, and Sam Brownback (R-KS) and Bill Frist (R-TN) in the Senate.[48] The efforts of the Congress toward alleviating the persecution of Black Christians in Sudan brought about landmark legislation such as the International Religious Freedom Act of 1998, and ultimately, the Sudan Peace Act of 2002.

President Bush, also with a strong evangelical base, strongly supported the initiatives of Congress toward ending Sudan's civil war, proclaiming that his administration would place religious persecution and atrocities in Sudan at the forefront of his foreign policy agenda.[49] The President followed through with his pledge to address Africa's longest running civil war when he appointed John Danforth, an Episcopal minister and former senator from Missouri, as his special envoy. Bush's hometown of Midland, Texas (where several churches have sister congregations in Sudan) even hosted an annual evangelical event in 2001 dedicated to ending the persecution of Christians the world over, wherein Sudan was the focus.[50] It was thanks to this sudden surge of U.S. involvement in the Sudan under the Bush administration that peace talks were allowed to move forward to end the North–South conflict. As I argue below, ending Sudan's civil war, and with it the persecution of Christians in southern Sudan, would be the primary objective of U.S. foreign policy toward Sudan up

---

[46] See generally, Douglas H. Johnson, *The Root Causes of Sudan's Civil War* (Bloomington: Indiana University Press, 2003).

[47] Allen Hertzke, *Freeing God's Children: The Unlikely Alliance for Global Human Rights* (Lanham, MD: Rowman & Littlefield, 2004), 246.

[48] Ibid., 270–271.

[49] "Bush Condemns Suppression of Religious Freedom in Sudan," *The New York Times*, 4 May 2001.

[50] Samantha Power, "Dying in Darfur: Can the Ethnic Cleansing in Darfur be Stopped?" *The New Yorker*, 30 August 2004, accessed on the website of *The New Yorker* at http://www.newyorker.com/fact/content/?040830fa_fact1, 1 October 2005.

until and even after the signing of the final North–South peace agreement on 9 January 2005.[51]

From southern Sudan to Darfur. As a result of evangelical zeal for ending the persecution of Christians in southern Sudan, when the crisis in Darfur erupted in 2003, Sudan already had an unusually attentive constituency in Washington. The timing of the U.S.'s and international community's seizing of events in Darfur is also telling. Congressman Wolf's comments raising the prospect of genocide in Darfur on the floor of the House were almost exactly 10 years after the start of the genocide in Rwanda. What followed on Capitol Hill throughout the months of April and May of 2004 were numerous statements, from members of all political stripes, that made direct comparisons between Darfur and Rwanda 10 years prior. Such proclamations were made by Edward Kennedy (D-MA),[52] John McCain (R-AZ),[53] Jon Corzine (D-NJ),[54] Bill Frist (R-TN), Tom Daschle (D-ND), Sam Brownback (R-KS), and Joe Biden (D-DE),[55] to name just a few. Senator Brownback even broached the possibility of U.S. military involvement, though only as part of a broader effort under UN or North Atlantic Treaty Organization (NATO) sponsorship.[56] In any case, Darfur now had the full attention of Congress, and the concern over the North–South conflict had now spilled over into a concern over events in Darfur. Evangelical personalities such as Franklin Graham played no small part in convincing Congress and the President that Sudan's problems were not over just because progress had been made in peace talks between Khartoum and the SPLA/M.[57] In August of 2004, nearly 50 religious leaders organized by the National Association of Evangelicals called on the President to take "swift action" to stop the genocide in Darfur, including delivering humanitarian aid, considering military options, and working to remove Sudan from the UN Human Rights Com-

---

[51] The Comprehensive Peace Agreement was signed by the government of Sudan and the SPLA/M on 9 January 2005.

[52] "On Sudan," remarks of Edward Kennedy, 108th Cong., 2nd sess., *Congressional Record* 150 (29 April 2004): S 4678.

[53] Executive Session, comments of John McCain, et al., 108th Cong., 2nd sess., *Congressional Record* 150 (6 May 2004): S 4951.

[54] "Sudan Darfur Crisis," remarks of Jon Corzine, 108th Cong., 2nd sess., *Congressional Record* 150 (6 May 2004): S 4945.

[55] "Condemning the Government of the Republic of Sudan," remarks of Bill Frist, Tom Daschle, Sam Brownback, and Joseph Biden, 108th Cong., 2nd Sess., *Congressional Record* 150 (6 May 2004): S 4931.

[56] Fessenden, "Lawmakers Seek Viable Solution," 1638.

[57] The Naivasha Agreement, concluded 26 May 2004, was a preliminary peace agreement that established a ceasefire between the Sudan Government and the SPLA/M. See "Never Again? Genocide in Sudan Tests our Commitment to Justice," *Christianity Today*, 3 August 2004, accessed on the website of *Christianity Today* at http://www.christianitytoday.com/ct/2004/009/0.33.html, 4 October 2005.

mission.[58] Thus, the same evangelical constituency that was so instrumental in persuading Congress and the President to act to end the persecution and enslavement of Christians in southern Sudan was now pushing for action on behalf of non-Christians in Darfur.

The African American leadership was also influential in putting Darfur front and center in U.S. foreign policy circles. By this time, the Darfur crisis was widely portrayed as "Arab on African" violence in the U.S. and other Western media, thus transferring to the Darfur crisis an identity frame similar to that which prevailed in the North–South conflict.[59] In particular, the issue of enslavement, prevalent in both conflicts, served to draw the African American community into a coalition with evangelicals, further contributing to the spill-over of concern from the North–South conflict to Darfur.[60] In July, members of the Congressional Black Caucus demanded an end to the genocide in Darfur, organizing a protest in front of the Sudanese embassy in Washington, wherein Congressmen Charles Rangel (D-NY), Bobby Rush (D-IL), and Joe Hoeffel (D-PA) were among those arrested by police.[61]

Rhetoric Absent Action: The Intervention that Wasn't

Despite the efforts of the peculiar bedfellows of evangelicals, prominent African Americans, and even the human rights advocacy community in raising awareness and concern over the crisis in Darfur—and even despite the sub-sequent rhetoric of genocide by the U.S. Congress, Secretary of State, and President—these efforts did not compel decisive action on the part of the United States to end the suffering in Darfur. Even before Congress approved the genocide resolution, Senators Brownback and Corzine had attempted to qualify the language in the resolution by asserting that the purpose of the resolution was not to oblige the United States to intervene in Darfur, but to "add moral weight to efforts to pass a United Nations resolution."[62] The Sec-retary of State's remarks before the Senate Foreign Relations Committee likewise downplayed any obligation to intervene, as Secretary Powell insisted that despite his finding of genocide in Darfur, "no new action is dictated by [such a] determination" and that "the most practical contribution we can make ... is to do everything we can to increase the number of African Union

---

[58] Alan Cooperman, "Evangelicals Urge Bush to Do More for Sudan," *The Washington Post*, 3 August 2004; statement to President George W. Bush, National Association of Evangelicals 2 August 2004, accessed on the website of the National Association of Evangelicals at http://www.nae.net/images/darfurbush.doc, 4 October 2005.

[59] See de Waal, "Who Are the Darfurians," 199–202.

[60] Allen D. Hertzke, "The Shame of Darfur," *First Things* 156 (October 2005): 16–22.

[61] Brian Naylor, "Lawmakers Arrested at Sudan Protest," *All Things Considered*, National Public Radio Broadcast, 25 July 2004.

[62] Alex Barker, "Bush Faces Pressure on Sudan 'Genocide,'" *Financial Times*, 14 July 2004.

monitors."[63] President Bush likewise danced around the issue of a military response to the discovery of genocide in Darfur. In a presidential debate in September of 2004, Bush downplayed calls for intervention, stating that "we shouldn't be committing troops. We ought to be working with the African Union to do so."[64] So unlike the Clinton administration during the Rwanda crisis, the Bush administration—after some initial hesitancy to use the rhetoric of genocide—did not perceive this semantical move as conferring an obligation to intervene in Darfur. In addition, the political pressure on the Bush administration to actually intervene in Darfur to avert genocide was considerably less than that which the Clinton administration reasoned would have been directed toward it, had it admitted genocide was occurring in Rwanda. The reasons for these developments are several-fold.

Obligations in the Genocide Convention. First is the issue of the precise nature of the legal obligations under the Genocide Convention. During the Rwanda crisis, numerous analysts were of the opinion that a designation of genocide would commit the United States to intervening militarily to stop the killing.[65] Such confusion over the precise obligation conferred by the Genocide Convention is evidenced by the aforementioned Defense Department discussion paper that expressed concern that a finding of genocide in Rwanda might commit the U.S. government to "actually 'do something.'"[66] This, of course, was ostensibly the reasoning that led Clinton administration officials to clumsily dance around using the term in the first place.

In reality, of course, the Genocide Convention confers no obligation on its state parties to physically intervene to stop genocide. The text of the treaty states that "the Contracting Parties confirm that genocide, whether committed in time of peace or in time of war, is a crime under international law which they undertake to *prevent and to punish*."[67] Original and secondary sources on the Genocide Convention now suggest that the treaty does *not* confer an *obligation* to intervene militarily. Rather, Article VIII says that states "*may* call upon the competent organs of the United Nations to take such action . . . as they consider appropriate for the prevention and suppression of acts of genocide."[68] Likewise, reference to the *travaux préparatoires* suggests that the consensus among

---

[63] Senate Foreign Relations Committee, testimony of Secretary of State Colin Powell.

[64] Transcript of the Presidential Debate between President George W. Bush and Senator John Kerry, Commission on Presidential Debates, 30 September 2004, accessed at http://www.debates.org/pages/trans2004a.html, 11 October 2005.

[65] See, for example, Rieff, *Point of a Gun*, 74–75.

[66] Office of the Deputy Assistant Secretary of Defense for Middle East/Africa Region, Department of Defense, "Discussion Paper: Rwanda."

[67] Genocide Convention, Article I, emphasis added.

[68] Ibid., Article VIII, emphasis added; see also William A. Schabas, *Genocide in International Law* (Cambridge, UK: Cambridge University Press, 2000), 448–454.

the negotiators of the Draft Convention was that their objective on the matter of prevention and punishment was to debate whether and the extent to which "states [should] provide for the prevention and punishment [of genocide] in their national legislatures."[69] It is thus highly unlikely that the drafters of the Convention intended to create an obligation to physically intervene to prevent or punish the crime of genocide.

Thus, when Bush administration officials began using the rhetoric of genocide to describe Darfur, accompanied by no intention whatsoever of intervening, they arguably had a better understanding of the precise nature of the legal obligation under the Genocide Convention than had Clinton administration officials during Rwanda. It seems hard to believe, however, that the international legal staff in the State Department in 1994 had never given close examination to the Convention text and were therefore unaware of the escape clauses that the Bush administration would invoke 10 years later. Evidence nonetheless belies this assertion, for if State Department officials had been confident in 1994 that the Convention conferred no such obligation, the concerns expressed in the various declassified memos would have been unfounded. Perhaps these officials were attempting to make the strongest case possible for not invoking the rhetoric of genocide, or were even anticipating the legal reasoning of the press or of other governments that might try to interpret the Convention in a way that would compel U.S. action or otherwise embarrass the U.S. government for reneging on its promise of "never again." In any case, despite claims in the popular press a decade later that a finding of genocide in Darfur "would compel a no-holds-barred intervention,"[70] Bush administration officials knew better. This was demonstrated by Secretary Powell when he proclaimed to the Senate that the United States was fulfilling its obligation to "prevent and punish" genocide under Article VIII of the Convention by "propos[ing] that the next UN Security Council resolution on Sudan request a UN investigation into all violations of international humanitarian law and human rights law that have occurred in Darfur."[71] In addition, in the summer and autumn of 2004, the Bush administration was dealing with both domestic and international constituencies that were much more willing to accept a "strict con-

---

[69] Official Records of the Third Session of the General Assembly, Part I, Summary Records of the Meetings of the Sixth Committee (Paris, United Nations, 1948), 22; see also Eric A. Heinze, "Law, Force, and Human Rights: The Search for a Sufficiently Principled Legal Basis for Humanitarian Intervention," *Journal of Conflict Studies* 24 (Winter 2004): 5–32.

[70] G. Jeffrey MacDonald, "In Sudan Crisis, a Duty to Intervene?" *Christian Science Monitor*, 21 July 2004.

[71] Hearing of the Senate Foreign Relations Committee, Testimony of Secretary of State Colin Powell; Nicholas D. Kristof, "A Wimp on Genocide," *The New York Times*, 18 September 2005; see also United Nations General Assembly, 2005 World Summit Outcome, UN Doc. A/60/L.1, 15 September 2005.

structionist" interpretation of the Genocide Convention because, for reasons explained below, such constituencies were not nearly as enthusiastic about American and/or Western interventionism as they might have been in the spring of 1994.

U.S./UN disagreement over genocide. Before getting to these issues, however, it is important to address the empirical question as to whether the crisis in Darfur actually constitutes genocide as described in international law. To meet the legal definition of genocide under the Genocide Convention, a three-pronged test must be met. First is the *actus rea* of committing certain acts, including killing, causing serious bodily or mental harm, measures intended to prevent births, and the transfer of children. Second, these acts must be committed against a "national, ethnic, racial or religious group." Finally is the *mens rea* requirement that the acts be intended to destroy the said group "in whole or in part."[72]

Without getting into details, the U.S. State Department concluded that these three criteria were met in Darfur, with the *Janjaweed* militias and the Sudanese government committing one or more of the aforementioned actions against a protected group—in this case, the Fur, Massaleit, and Zaghawa tribes—and that these acts were intended to destroy in whole or in part these ethnic groups.[73] A subsequent UN inquiry (which resulted from the U.S. request that the UN Security Council authorize such an investigation) came to a different conclusion. The Report of the International Commission of Inquiry on Darfur concluded that the government of Sudan had *not* pursued a policy of genocide.[74] In addition to some uncertainty as to whether "tribal" groups constitute protected groups for the purposes of the Genocide Convention, the Commission ultimately concluded that there was a lack of genocidal intent—the *mens rea* element. Specifically, "the intent of the attackers was not to destroy an ethnic group as such, or part of the group. Instead, the intention was to murder all those men they considered as rebels, as well as forcibly expel the whole population so as to vacate the villages and prevent rebels from hiding among, or getting support from, the local population."[75] According to the UN Commission, then, the atrocities in Darfur are "only" mass murder and crimes against humanity, but not genocide.

That the UN came to a different conclusion than the United States regarding genocide in Darfur is relevant to the present concern for at least

---

[72] Genocide Convention, Article II.

[73] Hearing of the Senate Foreign Relations Committee, Testimony of Secretary of State Colin Powell; see also U.S. Department of State, *Documenting Atrocities in Darfur*, Bureau of Democracy, Human Rights, and Labor and the Bureau of Intelligence and Research, State Publication 11182, September 2004.

[74] Report of the International Commission of Inquiry on Darfur.

[75] Ibid., 131–132.

two reasons. First, as a circumstantial matter, it is curious, to say the least, that the United States would find it expedient to label the Darfur atrocities "genocide," request a UN investigation only to have its claim challenged, and then continue to use the rhetoric of genocide despite the UN's contradictory findings.[76] While it is impossible to ascertain the extent to which State Department lawyers may have been aware of the uncertainty surrounding a legal determination of genocide, the fact that the UN Commission concluded that genocide had *not* taken place seemingly played into the hands of U.S. interests to the extent that the United States did not want to intervene. In other words, naming the crime plays into U.S. interests; that is, until doing so creates an expectation that it will intervene. So when the UN Commission concluded that genocide had *not* taken place, this assuaged expectations of a U.S. intervention, though the U.S.'s continued use of the rhetoric of genocide paints the picture that the United States is taking a firm stand against this "crime of crimes." The implication is that the United States was employing the rhetoric of genocide *as a substitute* for more-decisive action. After all, at least the Bush administration was "naming the crime," which is far more than could be said of the Clinton administration during the Rwandan genocide.

The second reason that the divergence in the conclusions of the United States and the UN is important has to do with the simple fact that Darfur is not Rwanda. While Darfur has been characterized as "Rwanda in slow motion,"[77] the atrocities in Darfur are qualitatively and quantitatively different from those in Rwanda 10 years earlier. Eight hundred thousand deaths in 100 days are scarcely comparable to an estimated 70,000 in 10 months.[78] Thus, when the United States continued to use the rhetoric of genocide despite the UN's contrary findings, the U.S. attempt to place Darfur in the same category as Rwanda led to charges by several leaders—mainly in the Islamic and Arab worlds—that the United States was employing the rhetoric of genocide as a pretext to invade another oil-rich and predominantly Arab and Muslim state.[79] While such accusations are clearly misguided, if one gives any merit to the reasoning outlined above, these and similar allegations are no small reason why the United States could safely engage in the rhetoric of genocide without much fear of the international public demanding it intervene to stop it.

[76] Jim VandeHei, "In Break with UN, Bush Calls Sudan Killings Genocide," *The Washington Post*, 2 June 2005.

[77] Anthony Lake and John Prendergast, "Stopping Sudan's Slow-Motion Genocide," *Boston Globe*, 20 May 2004.

[78] These figures on Rwanda are well-established. Figures on Darfur are from The World Health Organization between March and December of 2004, as cited by Colum Lynch, "Lack of Access Muddies Death Toll in Darfur," *The Washington Post*, 8 February 2005.

[79] "Sudan Prefers AU Mediation in Darfur Crisis, Says US Stance Isolated," *Global News Wire – Asia Africa Intelligence Wire*, 12 September 2004.

Obstacles to action: Iraq, terrorism, and the Naivasha process. The response of the international community to the U.S.'s finding of genocide in Darfur was profound suspicion and was, at best, mixed. Not surprisingly, Sudan categorically rejected the U.S. finding, and was quick to suggest that the accusation of genocide could severely complicate not only peace negotiations with the Darfur rebels, but also the North–South peace process—the Naivasha Accords.[80] Likewise, the Arab League took the position that the situation in Darfur was neither genocide nor ethnic cleansing and accused the U.S. administration of "exploit[ing] the situation in Darfur for … the US elections campaign [sic] to win black votes," a sentiment echoed by officials from the relief organization Médecins Sans Frontières.[81] AU officials—realizing that U.S. support was key to their efforts to demonstrate the organization's effectiveness in addressing crises in Africa—stopped short of condemning the U.S. finding, though it called on U.S. officials to provide evidence to support their claim.[82] Even before the U.S. administration made its position public, the European Union (EU) made a statement in response to Congress's genocide resolution, saying that the Darfur crisis did *not* meet the legal requirements of genocide.[83] Particularly after the UN Commission of Inquiry released its report on Darfur, the United States thus found itself isolated among its international peers on the issue of genocide. Such international hesitation to ostracize Sudan by accusing its government of genocide in Darfur should also come as no surprise, given the number of actors that have deep economic interests there, particularly China, whose veto has loomed large over any forceful UN Security Council action.[84]

Calls for decisive intervention by American evangelical and advocacy groups were received with equal skepticism in international circles, wherein the issue of U.S. involvement Iraq was difficult to ignore. A widely referenced article in the British newspaper *The Observer* accused the United States of "hyping" genocide in Darfur, despite findings to the contrary not only by the UN Commission of Inquiry, but also the AU, the EU, and importantly, the World Food Programme.[85] The framing of the crisis as "Arab on African" violence was, not surprisingly, opposed by prominent Arabs as yet another

---

[80] Gilbert DaCosta, "Sudan Says UN Genocide Declaration for Darfur Could Hurt Peace Talks," *Associated Press*, 10 September 2004.

[81] "Sudan News Agency on MSF's 'Categorical Rejection' of Powell's Darfur Remarks," *BBC Monitoring Middle East – Political*, 16 September 2004.

[82] "AU Official Asks USA to Provide Evidence of Genocide in Darfur," *Global News Wire – Asia Africa Intelligence Wire*, 13 September 2004.

[83] "US Senate Leader Insists 'Genocide' Underway in Darfur, Despite EU Statement," *Agence France Presse*, 10 August 2004.

[84] Peter S. Goodman, "China Invests Heavily in Sudan's Oil Industry," *The Washington Post*, 23 December 2004; Opheera McDoom, "China's Interests in Sudan Bring Diplomatic Cover," *Reuters*, 17 December 2005.

[85] Peter Beaumont, "US 'Hyping' Darfur Genocide Fear," *The Observer*, 3 October 2004.

selective and unfair vilification of Arabs as *génocidaires*, particularly in a context in which the Western media routinely identify them as the instigators of terrorism.[86] Likewise, notable voices from the developing world—such as Indian-born senior vice-rector of the UN University in Tokyo, Ramesh Thakur—openly disparaged Western "humanitarians clamoring for another war," particularly in light of Iraq, arguing that any Western intervention in Darfur would "be exploited as yet another assault on Arabs and Muslims."[87] As Human Rights Watch's Michael Clough put it, "The fact that the US was waging a globally unpopular war in Iraq without a UN mandate inevitably affected how other UN member states responded [to the U.S.'s genocide finding], particularly once the graphic images of . . . Abu Ghraib were broadcast around the world."[88]

The United States could scarcely afford the international political ramifications of military involvement in another predominantly Arab and Muslim (not to mention oil-rich) state at a time when the rest of the world was exceedingly suspicious of U.S. ambitions in the Middle East and of American interventionism in general. While the United States has indeed been part of military efforts genuinely intended to alleviate human suffering in other countries—such as in Kosovo in 1999—in the case of Iraq, "most actors in international and world society believed that humanitarian justifications were used to mask the exercise of hegemonic power."[89] If U.S. troops set foot in Darfur, the argument went, the United States would again be perceived as using humanitarianism as a pretext for otherwise neo-imperial ambitions, not to mention opening up a new front for jihadist attacks against U.S. and accompanying forces.[90] With the U.S. military already spread thin in Iraq and Afghanistan, at least some administration officials—probably more in the Pentagon—were no doubt relieved when the UN Commission announced that there was *not* genocide in Darfur. Ironically, it was the lack of U.S. credibility abroad and fear of exploitative U.S. motives that served to provide political cover for the Bush administration's non-intervention in the face of its own conclusion of genocide in Darfur.

In addition to concerns over the Iraq factor, one cannot ignore the connection of U.S. Sudan policy to the overall global war on terrorism. That is,

---

[86] De Waal, "Who Are the Darfurians," 200–201.

[87] Ramesh Thakur, "Western Medicine is No Cure for Darfur's Ills," *Financial Review*, 31 August 2004; see also "Sudan Can't Wait," *The Economist*, 31 July 2004, 11.

[88] Michael Clough, "Darfur: Whose Responsibility to Protect?" in *Human Rights Watch World Report, 2005* (New York: Human Rights Watch, 2005), 34.

[89] Williams and Bellamy, "Responsibility to Protect," 36–37; see also Hugo Slim, "Dithering over Darfur? A Preliminary Review of the International Response," *International Affairs* 80 (October 2004): 811–828.

[90] See John Laughland, "The Mask of Altruism Disguising a Colonial War," *The Guardian*, 2 August 2004; see also Susan E. Rice, "Why Darfur Can't be Left to Africa," *The Washington Post*, 7 August 2005.

in the past few years, the Sudanese government has emerged as a very reliable partner and source of intelligence for the United States in the war on terrorism.[91] Given the high priority placed on terrorism in Washington, it is no surprise that a forceful response to "genocide" in Darfur would have to be weighed against the increasing need to befriend regimes like the one in Khartoum for purposes of anti-terrorism, despite its miserable human rights record. The United States scarcely allows human rights concerns to hazard its security and anti-terrorism ties with states like Pakistan and Egypt, so it would make sense that the United States would be extremely careful about potentially damaging a similarly beneficial relationship with Sudan.

The point remains that there was little desire for U.S.-led intervention in Darfur among international constituencies, though it was ultimately U.S. constituencies—namely, evangelical Christians—whose calls for intervention in Darfur would need to be assuaged. Recall that is was the evangelical lobby that was largely responsible for putting Sudan's North–South conflict high on the administration's agenda, which as I argued above, spilled over into a concern for Darfur. In fact, much later, it was revealed by the former U.S. representative to the UN, John Danforth, that the use of the term "genocide" to describe Darfur was intended for "internal consumption," mainly by the Christian right.[92] One must wonder, therefore, to what extent the United States would have reacted to Darfur at all had it not already been paying close attention to the events concerning Sudan's "other" civil war.

In any case, in November of 2004, about the time the administration was deflecting calls for more-decisive action in Darfur, it returned the focus of its Sudan policy from Darfur back to the stalled North–South peace negotiations—the Naivasha Accords.[93] Whether this shift in U.S. policy resulted from Khartoum's veiled threats that the U.S.'s rhetoric of genocide was endangering the Naivasha process is unknown. What is known is that the United States had invested considerable diplomatic capital in the Naivasha process and was eager to see it implemented, as were many in the faith-based Sudan coalition. Ending the North–South conflict was, after all, the original promise of President Bush to his evangelical base, so it made political sense to not let the Darfur crisis spoil the entire process, especially in an election year. The Bush administration thus returned to the tactic employed prior to the Darfur crisis of trying to use economic carrots to induce Khartoum to sign the Naivasha Accords.[94]

---

[91] Suzanne Goldenberg, "Ostracised Sudan Emerges as Key American Ally in 'War on Terror,'" *The Guardian Weekly*, 6 May 2005; see also Ken Silverstein, "Official Pariah Sudan Valuable to America's War on Terrorism," *Los Angeles Times*, 29 April 2005.

[92] "White House Described Darfur as 'Genocide' to Please Christian Right," *The Independent* (London), 2 July 2005, 26.

[93] "US Shift on Darfur Policy," *The Washington Post*, 27 December 2004; see also Clough, "Darfur: Whose Responsibility," 34–35.

[94] Williams and Bellamy, "Responsibility to Protect," 38.

In doing so, the administration disabused observers of any notions that it would be willing to risk wrecking three years of intense diplomacy toward ending Africa's longest running civil war in favor of outright confrontation with Khartoum over Darfur. Referring to Darfur as genocide was one thing, inasmuch as it was for "internal consumption," to placate a restive evangelical Christian constituency; but at least President Bush would not go down in history as the president who refused to recognize genocide, unlike his predecessor. Going any further than this—say, pushing hard for economic sanctions in the Security Council or even intervening militarily—would have sacrificed the hard-won Naivasha process, which would have alienated American evangelicals even more than failing to intervene in Darfur. Thus, when important domestic constituencies put pressure on the administration over Darfur, the administration was effectively able to deflect such calls by raising the possibility that intervening or otherwise confronting Khartoum would jeopardize the very goal that these constituencies were fighting for in the first place: an end to the North–South conflict and the religious persecution that accompanied it.

Importantly, the U.S. administration found allies in the international community to support the position that the Darfur crisis was essentially secondary to securing a permanent peace deal between Khartoum and the SPLA/M. In a report by the UN Secretary-General's Special Representative for Internally Displaced Persons, Francis Deng explicitly linked the Darfur crisis to the North–South conflict. According to Deng's report, deploying protection forces to Darfur under Chapter VII of the UN Charter would provoke armed resistance by Khartoum, "turn Darfur into a threatre for another layer of conflict," and "fundamentally undermine the [Naivasha] peace process and lead it to collapse and plunge the whole country into an even greater crisis."[95] Thus, in a fortuitous convergence of interests, both U.S. and UN officials preferred an "African solution" to this problem that was to involve the AU.[96] Furthermore, several analysts argued that the best chance of securing a political solution to Darfur was through implementation of the Naivasha Accords, which involved a power-sharing deal that would allow the late SPLA/M leader, John Garang, to serve as Vice President in Khartoum to President Bashir. Once Garang was seated as the Vice President, it was argued, "Garang's desire to represent all of Sudan's non-Arab peoples, including Darfurians, would make it politically impossible for him to endorse a war there."[97] A confrontation with Khartoum that risked bringing about the downfall of President Bashir would also risk

---

[95] UN Economic and Social Council, Report of the Representative of the Secretary-General on Internally Displaced Persons: Mission to Sudan—the Darfur Crisis, UN Doc. E/CN.4/2005/8, 27 September 2004, ¶¶ 35, 36.

[96] Ibid., ¶ 37.

[97] Williams and Bellamy, "Responsibility to Protect," 39; see also Alex de Waal, "Darfur's Deep Grievances Defy All Hopes for an Easy Solution," *The Observer*, 25 July 2004; Ulrich Mans, "Sudan: The New War in Darfur," *African Affairs* 103 (April 2004): 291–294.

the power-sharing arrangement that was thought to be the best chance of a peaceful settlement of the Darfur crisis.[98] This concern over the success of the Naivasha process in both domestic and international circles, in tandem with general international trepidation about American interventionism as a result of the Iraq war, thus contributed to a political atmosphere wherein U.S. officials could engage in the rhetoric of genocide without an expectation of intervention.

CONCLUDING REMARKS

The Bush administration's use of the rhetoric of genocide in reference to the crisis in Darfur stands as a radical departure from the reasoning that led the Clinton administration to avoid such language in reference to Rwanda. The reasons for this ultimately have to do with prevailing political realities, both domestic and international. Domestic constituencies' attention to events in Darfur cannot be understood without reference to Sudan's North–South conflict, which already had a formidable following in Washington. Nevertheless, when the already-significant attention given to this conflict shifted to Darfur at a time when the world was remembering the 10-year anniversary of the Clinton administration's failure to acknowledge reality in Rwanda, pressure was great to "do something," or at least "say something," about Darfur, which was more than Clinton officials had done about Rwanda. After all, in 1994, there was no Rwandan equivalent to the faith-based Sudan coalition in the United States, no Rwandan lobby in Washington, and no significant Rwandan expatriate community to put pressure on the Clinton administration. Thus, after some hesitation, Bush administration officials found it politically expedient to engage in the rhetoric of genocide to appease mainly evangelical constituencies, at least to the extent that such rhetoric would not create an expectation that the United States would participate in military intervention.

Whether U.S. officials were aware of it, hoping for it, or whether it was entirely accidental, prevailing political conditions in the summer and fall of 2004 were such that the expectation for intervention was mollified, despite a pronouncement of genocide. In the legal community, it had become clear that a finding of genocide did not trigger a legal obligation to physically intervene in Darfur, whereas the same cannot necessarily be said of the Rwandan crisis of 1994, at least, evidently, as far as some State Department lawyers were concerned. Likewise, even though some evangelical and human rights advocacy groups were calling for intervention on ethical grounds, the deployment of U.S. military assets to another far-away conflict would have been a tough sell to the American public at a time when the United States was fighting expensive counter-insurgencies in Afghanistan and Iraq. And, of course, even calls for decisive action by the main advocates of the Darfur cause—the evangelical and

---

[98] Slim, "Dithering over Darfur," 822.

African American lobbies—were muted once it was realized that a confrontation with Khartoum would jeopardize efforts to end the "other" civil war that
had brought about religious persecution of Christians and a revival of the slave
trade. Thus, the Bush administration was able to mitigate calls for intervention
despite its acknowledgement of genocide by essentially framing other interests
as more important—namely, the Naivasha process. According to this logic,
then, the Clinton administration in 1994 should have been able to assuage
calls for intervention in Rwanda—even if it had admitted that genocide was
transpiring—by reminding the American public of what had happened in
Somalia. Again, differing political circumstances precluded this being the case.

First, in the spring of 1994, the U.S. military was not committed to the
extent that it was in the summer and fall of 2004. As such, the argument that
U.S. forces were spread too thin was not as plausible for Clinton to make as a
reason not to intervene to avert genocide. The argument that the crisis required an "African solution" was likewise not as available to Clinton officials
during Rwanda. The Bush administration, by contrast, could more plausibly
pass any peacekeeping or other military burden to the AU, which was founded
in 2002 and whose charter specifically authorizes it to intervene to prevent
humanitarian crises.[99] And while the United States was itself among those
likely—if not *the* most likely—to veto Security Council action over Rwanda,
the virtual certainty of a Chinese veto of action in Darfur has given the United
States ample political cover to refrain from forcefully pursuing decisive Security Council action over Darfur. In addition, one cannot ignore the empirical
differences between Rwanda and Darfur in terms of the sheer scale and speed
at which the killings took place. The fact that Darfur was "Rwanda in slow
motion" suggests that there would have been more of an imperative to quickly
intervene in Rwanda and less time for deliberation, whereas the slower and
more drawn-out suffering and dying of Darfurians would not seemingly neces-
sitate the same sense of urgency, particularly when most deaths were due to
starvation and disease as opposed to a machete blade.

Other aspects of international politics played equally important roles. As
argued above, U.S. involvement in places like Afghanistan and Iraq led to
significant skepticism and mistrust by the international community concerning
the motives and desirability of American military interventionism. Thus, calls
for U.S. military intervention in Darfur, not surprisingly, were not well received in many other countries. This international sentiment is very much
in contrast to that which prevailed during the Rwanda crisis. While certainly
not uncontroversial, during the 1990s, the idea of humanitarian intervention
gained some acceptance as a legitimate use of military force.[100] Even the 1999
U.S.-led NATO intervention over Kosovo—which was not authorized by the

---

[99] Constitutive Act of the African Union, 26 May 2001, OAU Doc. CAB/LEG/23.15, Article 4(h).

[100] International Commission on Intervention and State Sovereignty, *The Responsibility to Protect*
(Ottawa: International Development Research Centre, 2001), 7.

Security Council and was thus technically illegal—was widely viewed as a legitimate use of military force.[101] Had Clinton come forth with an admission of genocide in Rwanda, officials reasoned that the international public would have demanded that the United States take the lead in stopping it, as it did to stop human suffering in northern Iraq, Somalia, and Bosnia, and as it was considering doing in Haiti. The Clinton administration was arguably more responsive to the views of the international public than the Bush administration, and thus would have taken international calls for action more seriously and would have been more moved by charges of selective indignation. While the degree of legitimacy possessed by the United States as a global enforcer of human rights during the 1990s would have facilitated international demands for it to intervene in Rwanda, it was, *inter alia*, the precise *lack* of such legitimacy that contributed to the absence of such pressure regarding Darfur.

It is a matter of legal hairsplitting that separates genocide from "mere" mass murder or "simple" crimes against humanity. But the word "genocide" undoubtedly has entailments that these other atrocities do not: it is more inflammatory, more reproachful, and entails at least a moral (if not legal) obligation to stop such acts. This is why Clinton administration officials danced around the word in 1994, and it is why the Bush administration's characterization of the Darfur crisis as genocide created a groundswell of controversy in world capitals in 2004. The implications of its use, however, are undoubtedly affected by the prevailing political milieu as well as the perceived political interests of states and their leaders. For the Clinton administration during the Rwanda crisis, the power of the rhetoric of genocide was that it would have obligated it to "do something." Whereas for the Bush administration during the Darfur crisis, its emotive and condemnatory attachments led to its use *as a substitute* for more-decisive action. It may indeed be a truism to say that the United States and those elites who represent it will only use the rhetoric of genocide if they stand to gain something by doing so. But instead of simply relegating such an insight to the grand tautology that "states behave in accordance with their national interests," we can try to understand—although always incompletely—the precise conditions that led the state to behave in the way it did or to use the rhetoric it did (or did not), particularly when such (lack of) action or rhetoric contributes to the suffering and death of so many innocent people. Examined in this light, the rhetoric of genocide in U.S. foreign policy, while not being excused, must at least be explained and better understood if we are to come to grips with its consequences.*

[101] Independent International Commission on Kosovo, *The Kosovo Report* (Oxford, UK: Oxford University Press, 2000), 4.

*The author would like to thank Ken Rutherford, Mutuma Ruteere, Dave Forsythe, and the anonymous referees at *PSQ* for helpful comments on this article. All views and any mistakes remain mine alone.

Tragic Choices in the War on Terrorism: Should We Try to Regulate and Control Torture?

JEROME SLATER

What should be done about the problem of torture in the war on terrorism? Which is better—or worse: the continuation of a principled but ineffective "ban" on torture, or an effort to seriously regulate and control torture, at the price of its partial legitimization?

Until 11 September 2001, the issue scarcely arose. Since the end of the eighteenth century, nearly every civilized society and moral system, certainly including the Judeo-Christian, or Western, moral system, in principle (although not always in practice) has regarded torture as an unmitigated evil, the moral prohibition against which was to be regarded as absolute.[1] Since September 11, however, many Americans—not just government officials, but a number of moral and legal philosophers, as well as media commentators—are far from sure that torture must be excluded from our defenses against truly catastrophic terrorism. In any case, there no longer can be any question that since September 11, agencies of the American government, particularly the armed forces and the Central Intelligence Agency (CIA), have systematically used various forms of physical and psychological coercion, beatings, or even outright torture (especially "waterboarding," or near-drowning) on suspected terrorists, both directly, as in Afghanistan, Iraq, and Guantanamo Bay, or indi-

---

[1] For a brief history of the use of torture in European judicial systems and practice, see James Ross, "A History of Torture" in Kenneth Roth, Minky Worden, and Amy D. Bernstein, eds., *Torture: Does it Make Us Safer? Is It Ever OK?: A Human Rights Perspective* (New York: Human Rights Watch, 2005), 3–17.

JEROME SLATER, a frequent contributor to *Political Science Quarterly*, is a university research scholar at the State University of New York at Buffalo. He is working on a history of U.S. policy in the Arab-Israeli conflict.

rectly, by turning over suspected terrorists to allied states that are known to torture.[2]

To be sure, in some cases, lower-level soldiers have apparently gone beyond what was authorized, or at least tacitly condoned. However, various reports and investigations have left no serious doubt that the overall use of methods that have long been considered to amount to torture, or something close to it, have been either authorized, defended as legal, or, at a minimum, condoned at the highest levels of the American government, apparently including Secretary of Defense Donald Rumsfeld, if not beyond him.[3]

Assuming that this assessment is accurate, what can be done about it? Even more pointedly, what *should* be done about it? I will address these issues in the framework of traditional just-war analysis, a very useful perspective that often has been neglected in the recent discussions about torture. My premise is that the war on Islamic terrorism is indeed legitimately regarded as a war, however untraditional; if so, I will argue, the issues raised by torture should be regarded as simply a special case of the issues raised by any normally unjust means that may or may not be employed in a just war.

There are essentially three positions that can be taken about the problem of torture. The first is the traditional moral position: torture is categorically (that is, absolutely) prohibited, and there are no exceptions.

---

[2] These practices have been revealed in reports by the International Red Cross, Human Rights Watch, and Amnesty International; by a number of investigative reporters; and even by internal American military investigations that have been leaked to the press. The most detailed and authoritative works are Amnesty International, "Guantanamo and Beyond," May 2005; Mark Bowden, "The Dark Art of Interrogation," *Atlantic Monthly*, October 2003, 51–76; Mark Danner, *Torture and Truth: America, Abu Ghraib, and the War on Torture* (New York: New York Review of Books, 2004); Seymour M. Hersh, *Chain of Command: The Road from 9/11 to Abu Ghraib* (New York: HarperCollins, 2004); Human Rights Watch, "Torture in Iraq," 25 September 2005; Joseph Lelyveld, "Interrogating Ourselves," *New York Times Magazine*, 12 June 2005, 36–69; Jane Mayer, "The Experiment," *New Yorker*, 11 and 18 July 2005; PBS *Frontline* Special Report, "The Torture Question," 19 October 2005. See also Carlotta Gall, "Rights Group Reports Deaths of Men Held by U.S. in Afghanistan," *New York Times*, 14 December 2004 and 19 December 2005; David Johnston and James Risen, "The Reach of War: The Interrogations," *New York Times*, 27 June 2004; David Johnston, "Rights Group Cites Rumsfeld and Tenet in Report on Abuse," *New York Times*, 24 April 2005; Warren Hoge, "Investigators for UN Urge U.S. to Close Guantanamo," *New York Times*, 17 February 2006; Douglas Jehl, "Report Warned on CIA's Tactics in Interrogation," *New York Times*, 9 November 2005; Anthony Lewis, "Making Torture Legal," *New York Review of Books*, 15 July 2004; Eric Schmitt and David Rohde, "About 2 Dozen GIs to Face Trial or Other Punishment in Deaths of 2 Afghan Prisoners," *New York Times*, 2 September 2004.

[3] For a summary of the evidence that torture and actions "tantamount to torture" (in the language of a report by the International Red Cross) are "a direct product of an environment of lawlessness, created by policy decisions taken at the highest levels of the Bush Administration," see Kenneth Roth, "Justifying Torture" in Roth, Worden, and Bernstein, eds., *Torture; Does It Make Us Safer?*, 191. For a similar assessment, charging that the Bush Administration had made "a deliberate policy choice" to employ abusive interrogation in the interrogation of terrorism suspects, see the 2005 Annual Report of Human Rights Watch, summarized in "Rights Group Assails the U.S. Over Abuse of Terror Suspects," *New York Times*, 19 January 2006.

The second position is that the legal and moral norm of categorical prohibition must be maintained in principle, law, and rhetoric—even as we recognize and tacitly accept that there might be certain exceptional circumstances in which there is a strong case for overriding the norm. Thus, although we should not provide the authorities with any institutionalized or advance authorization for torture, in the exceptional cases we may rightfully decide not to punish those representatives of the state who have violated the norm. "We'll do what we have to do," as Joseph Lelyveld puts it: "Don't ask, don't tell."[4]

The third position is that terrorism—especially but not necessarily limited to terrorism with weapons of mass destruction (WMD)—is likely to be a long-term if not permanent threat and is so grave that "exceptional circumstances" have become the norm. Consequently, the task today is to create some type of legal and institutional framework for the regulation and control of torture, to ensure that it is resorted to in the war on terrorism *only* when the consequences of not doing so are so terrible as to outweigh the terrible nature of torture itself.

I shall defend the third position, arguing that the question of means in just wars must be considered from two different perspectives (sometimes complementary, but sometimes in conflict): that of national security, and that of morality or justice. Proceeding from that premise, I shall argue that in the war on terrorism, physical or psychological coercion and, in especially exceptional circumstances, even outright torture may be defensible from both of those perspectives, certainly from the perspective of national security, and even—as a lesser evil—in terms of moral consequences. At the same time, however, the risks that torture will be used—indeed, is already being used—when it is *not* defensible from either perspective are so great that serious institutional controls over torture must be established.

Perhaps I should add this: in making this admittedly painful argument, it is not my intention to be polemical. The torture issue is no longer considered to be beyond—or beneath—debate. My purpose here is to join this emerging debate, both at the analytical level and to make explicit the arguments and policy suggestions that seem to follow from the analysis. However, inasmuch as we are still at an early stage in this debate, those who are participating in it may well make logical, moral, or empirical errors; if these occur, they can be corrected only by further debate.

DEBATING TORTURE: THE RECENT LITERATURE

Until quite recently, there has been considerable doubt among moral, legal, and political philosophers about whether there ought to be any public debate about torture. Most of these thinkers believed that torture should be regarded as simply beyond the pale; public discussion or debate might have the perverse consequence of legitimating it. Indeed, even the few scholars who argued that

---

[4] Lelyveld, "Interrogating Ourselves," 69.

torture could sometimes be seen as a lesser evil sometimes conceded that the risk of legitimation precluded public discussion. Whatever the validity of this concern, the issue is now moot. In the last few years, there have been a number of discussions of the torture issue in leading media, as well as in academic conferences and, especially, in the recent publication of major works by some of America's leading political, legal, and moral thinkers.[5] Thus, the meta debate (that is, should there be a debate?) is effectively over, and the substantive debate has begun.[6]

The main issues in this debate are these: What constitutes torture? Should all forms of physical or mental coercion be considered torture? If so, should all of them be unconditionally prohibited? If, on the other hand, it is legitimate to make distinctions, where is the line to be drawn? Are there real-world cases in which some kinds of coercion—or perhaps, in extreme cases, *any* kind of coercion, including torture by any definition—are morally justifiable, if only by a lesser-evil argument? If so—and in the context of the existing realities, this may be the most important question of them all—how can coercion or torture be limited to only those cases in which it is indeed a lesser evil?

What Is Torture?

Surprisingly, the very definition of torture has become more controversial in the last few years, and efforts to clarify it for both legal and moral purposes have created a dilemma: if it is defined too broadly, it fails to make morally relevant distinctions, but if it is defined too narrowly, it opens the door to various euphemisms that may seem to condone many forms of severe prisoner abuse that fall outside the definition.

According to all the major dictionaries, torture means more than the infliction of physical duress, stress, or even mere pain; it consists of the infliction of "intense," "excruciating," "great," or "severe" pain.[7] Similarly, the UN

[5] The major works that will be examined here are Karen J. Greenberg, ed., *The Torture Debate in America* (New York: Cambridge University Press, 2006); Philip B. Heymann and Juliette N. Kayyem, *Protecting Liberty in an Age of Terror* (Cambridge, MA: MIT Press, 2005); Michael Ignatieff, *The Lesser Evil: Political Ethics in an Age of Terror* (Princeton, NJ: Princeton University Press, 2004); Sanford Levinson, ed., *Torture: A Collection* (New York: Oxford University Press, 2004); Roth, Worden, and Bernstein, eds., *Torture: Does It Make Us Safer?*; Michael Walzer, *Arguing About War* (New Haven, CT: Yale University Press, 2004).

[6] A useful discussion of the meta debate can be found in Oren Gross, "The Prohibition on Torture and the Limits of the Law" in Levinson, ed., *Torture: A Collection*, 249–250. Gross concludes that public debate on torture is critical: "The alternative to no debate ... (or, indeed, to discussion that merely consists of repeating the mantra that torture must be absolutely prohibited) is not the disappearance of the practice of torture. ... By not discussing [torture] ... we do not make it go away; we drive it underground. ... We may as well make ... choices in as informed a manner as possible, taking into account the widest panoply of relevant moral and legal considerations."

[7] See Webster's Third New International Dictionary, the Oxford English Dictionary, and Cambridge International Dictionary.

Convention Against Torture (to which the United States is a party) distinguishes between torture ("any act by which severe pain or suffering, whether physical or mental, is inflicted") and "other acts of cruel, inhuman, or degrading treatment or punishment which do not amount to torture." Although both are legally prohibited, only "torture" is done so in absolute terms: "No exceptional circumstances whatsoever, whether a state of war...or any other public emergency, may be invoked as a justification of torture."

Pentagon officials and legal advisers to the administration of George W. Bush have relied on these dictionary and UN definitions to deny that recently revealed U.S. interrogation measures—such as hooding prisoners, keeping them naked, binding them in painful "stress" positions, threatening them with dogs, subjecting them to sustained loud noises as well as heat and cold, or depriving of them sleep—constitute torture. In their initial position (the Bybee memorandum), Bush legal advisers sought to narrow the definition even further, taking advantage of the UN language in order to distinguish interrogation methods that were "merely" cruel, inhuman, or degrading from outright torture, defined as actions that "produce pain and suffering...equivalent in intensity to the pain accompanying serious physical injury, such as organ failure, impairment of bodily function, or even death."[8] However, after severe criticism, the Justice Department formally retreated from the Bybee memorandum in late 2004; the Bush administration now officially accepts that any "severe" physical and mental pain and suffering constitutes torture and is therefore prohibited by U.S. as well as international law.[9]

In some recent discussions of the torture issue, the varying administration distinctions have been regarded as meaningless or hypocritical, mere euphemisms that are designed to conceal the harsh reality that "at the highest levels of the Pentagon there was an interest in using torture as well as a desire to evade the criminal consequences of doing so."[10] Yet, although lawyers for the Bush administration are hardly disinterested parties in the debate over torture, it is undeniable that most of the other major participants in the ongoing debate are agreed on the need to distinguish torture from lesser abuses, suggesting

[8] Memorandum from Assistant Attorney General Jay Bybee, 1 August 2002, reprinted in Danner, *Torture and Truth*, 115, 141.

[9] On the revised administration position, see a statement of Secretary of State Condoleeza Rice, in Joel Brinkley, "U.S. Interrogations Are Saving Lives, Rice Says," *New York Times*, 6 December 2005, and Neil A. Lewis, "U.S. Spells Out New Definition Curbing Torture," *New York Times*, 1 January 2005. However, a number of investigations have established that the administration has used "waterboarding" in its interrogations of captured high-level al Qaeda officials. Waterboarding—forcing a person's head under water until he almost drowns, or at least fears drowning—is torture by any reasonable definition; nonetheless, Porter Goss, the head of the CIA, has defended it as "a professional interrogation technique." Roth, "Justifying Torture" in Roth, Worden, and Bernstein, eds., *Torture: Does It Make Us Safer?*, 194.

[10] James Fellner, director of U.S. programs for Human Rights Watch, quoted in "The Reach of War: Legal Opinions," *New York Times*, 8 June 2004.

names like "coercion," "physical or mental abuse," "torture lite,"[11] or "highly coercive interrogation."[12]

The case for drawing distinctions is a strong one. If we were to insist that torture must be understood as comprising all forms of interrogation that go beyond the noncoercive, we would then have to invent other words to capture the morally relevant distinctions between, say, sleep deprivation and other kinds of nonfatal physical and mental pressures and the more truly fiendish, nearly unimaginable forms of torture or murder that fanatics, sadists, or psychotic autocrats have inflicted on their victims throughout history.

That said, the rather odd distinctions in the UN Convention Against Torture will not do; the distinction between torture and "cruel, inhuman, or degrading" treatment does not seem morally compelling. Similarly, it is not clear that the distinction between "highly coercive interrogation" and "torture" is meaningful—at least not sufficiently meaningful that the former may sometimes be acceptable but the latter must always be categorically prohibited. Perhaps the best solution is to distinguish between "torture," which should continue to be defined as the infliction of severe physical or mental pain, and "coercion," defined as significantly less-severe measures than torture (as already mentioned, stress binding, sleep deprivation, exposure to heat and cold, and the like)—although such measures, if sufficiently intense and sustained, might well become indistinguishable from outright torture. In short, in order to maintain the dictionary and everyday usages as well as to facilitate the making of morally relevant distinctions, it is important to distinguish between torture and coercion, even though sometimes the line between them may be thin.

Is Torture or Coercion Ever Morally Allowable?

At least among lawyers and legal scholars who are not working for the Bush administration, there is no serious doubt that not merely outright torture but all forms of "cruel, inhuman, or degrading practices" or physical coercion are illegal under American law, whether derived from the Constitution, from congressional legislation (such as the recent McCain amendment), or from international treaties to which the United States is legally bound. Thus, the central issue in the current debate is—or should be—whether the terrorist threat has made current law outmoded, considered from the perspectives of both national security and morally acceptable consequences.

As is widely understood, the most extreme case that would test the existing categorical prohibitions on torture—so far hypothetical, but one that may not be remote in the foreseeable future—would be an apparently imminent terrorist attack against cities, using biological or nuclear weapons that could kill hundreds of thousands of innocents. Less extreme are the already-existing

---

[11] Bowden, "The Dark Art of Interrogation," 4.
[12] Heymann and Kayyem, *Protecting Liberty*, 12.

cases, which are highly likely to reoccur—non-WMD terrorist attacks that do not destroy entire cities but do kill large numbers of innocents, as in the terrorist attacks on the World Trade Center and on the passenger trains in Madrid.

Just-war Theory and the Torture Issue

The most useful, systematic, and sophisticated framework in which to examine the moral issue of torture in the war on terrorism is just-war theory. A good place to begin is with a reexamination of the writing of Michael Walzer, the most authoritative contemporary just-war thinker,[13] following with an assessment of two recent major philosophical books that analyze, either explicitly or inferentially, the torture issue in just-war terms: Michael Ignatieff, *The Lesser Evil: Political Ethics in an Age of Terror* (Princeton University Press, 2004), and Sanford Levinson, ed., *Torture: A Collection* (New York: Oxford University Press, 2004).

Both Walzer and Ignatieff consider the age-old but still perplexing issue of whether "the end justifies the means": is it morally allowable to use unjust means if the use of them is necessary to reach a just end or realize a just cause? In broad terms, there are two different philosophical or ethical systems or traditions that consider this issue: consequentialism (or utilitarianism) and categorical morality. Consequentialist moral reasoning holds that we may morally judge actions only in terms of their practical consequences; categorical morality holds that there are certain rules or principles that must never be violated, regardless of the circumstances—or, as the Catholic moral tradition holds, evil may never be done so that good can come of it.

In general, Walzer is a categorical moralist, for he insists that we must make separate moral evaluations of the causes for which wars are fought (*jus ad bellum*) and the means by which wars are fought (*jus in bello*). Even just wars, then, are absolutely prohibited from employing unjust means, which principally means that innocent civilians or noncombatants may never be deliberately attacked. The same reasoning, it would appear, would preclude the use of torture—surely an unjust means.

There is, however, one critically important exception to Walzer's application of categorical morality to warfare: "supreme emergency," which "exists when our deepest values and our collective survival are in imminent danger."[14] Walzer examines the British bombing of German cities early in World War II, when Britain's defeat seemed imminent, no other means of defense was working, and the bombing of cities seemed to have some chance of dissuading Hitler

---

[13] Michael Walzer, *Just and Unjust Wars* (New York: Basic Books, 1977); Michael Walzer, *Arguing About War* (New Haven, CT: Yale University Press, 2004). Although Walzer does not directly address the issue of torture, it seems reasonable to infer his position, both from his overall moral philosophy as well as his decision to allow the reprinting of his famous essay, "Political Action: The Problem of Dirty Hands" in Levinson, ed., *Torture: A Collection*, 61–75.

[14] Walzer, *Arguing About War*, 33.

from attacking. In these circumstances of "supreme emergency," Walzer becomes a consequentialist:[15] there are no longer any prohibitions on methods that are genuinely necessary to win a just war, not even indiscriminate bombing of cities. In his recent work, Walzer puts it this way: "When our deepest values are radically at risk, the constraints lose their grip, and a certain kind of utilitarianism reimposes itself. I call this the utilitarianism of extremity, and I set it against a rights normality. ... No government can put the life of the community itself and of all its members at risk, so long as there are actions available to it, even immoral actions, that would avoid or reduce the risk."[16]

To be sure, not everyone accepts Walzer's supreme emergency argument, but for those who do (like this author), the same logic must hold true for torture. That is, if it is not categorically prohibited to deliberately attack many thousands of innocent civilians if and when no other means in a just war are available to ensure the literal survival of entire societies, then it is hard to see why it should be absolutely forbidden to torture terrorist combatants if it is necessary to do so to save cities—or even, perhaps, when the stakes in terms of innocent lives are very high but short of constituting a supreme emergency. I shall return to this argument below.

It is an observable and unsurprising fact that in this debate, there is a direct relationship between how seriously one takes the threat of mass-casualty terrorism and the position one takes on the torture issue. Some of those who are participating in the recent debate seem to implicitly or even explicitly minimize the threat.[17] That is not the view, however, of the National Commission on Terrorist Attacks Upon the United States (hereinafter, 9/11 Commission), which cited the evidence that Osama bin Laden and al Qaeda have been actively seeking to acquire WMD, nor of most academic specialists in international security—particularly those who have some governmental experience in either defense or intelligence agencies.[18]

---

[15] But *only* in these circumstances, as opposed to the later British and American city bombings of Germany and Japan, when the allied victory was already assured.

[16] Walzer, *Arguing About War*, 40, 42.

[17] For example, the journalist and commentator William Pfaff writes that to most of the democratic world, the American claims about the threat of terrorism seem grossly exaggerated, and therefore U.S. behavior is disproportionate. William Pfaff, "What We've Lost: George W. Bush and the Price of Torture," *Harper's Magazine*, November 2005, 50–56. Similarly, the General Counsel for Human Rights Watch clearly minimizes the dangers of WMD terrorism when she denies that "we live in an entirely different world than has ever existed at any time or place." (Dinah Pokempner, "Command Responsibility for Torture" in Roth, Worden, and Bernstein, eds., *Torture: Does It Ever Make Us Safer?*, 171. The lawyer Joshua Dratel, the law professor Stephen Holmes, and the legal philosopher David Luban also tend to dismiss the WMD threat as exaggerated, not "realistic," or not "representative." Greenberg, ed., *The Torture Debate*; see especially 114, 127.

[18] On the September 11th Commission's finding, see its *Final Report*, 4 August 2004. See also the authoritative work by a leading academician and former high government official, Graham Allison, *Nuclear Terrorism: The Ultimate Preventable Catastrophe* (New York: New York Times Books, 2004). Stephen Van Evera of MIT, another leading national security expert, points out that Osama Bin

Thomas Kean, chairman of the 9/11 Commission, has summed up the consensus of the governmental and academic specialists: "We have no greater fear than a terrorist who is inside the United States with a nuclear weapon. The consequences of such an attack would be catastrophic for our people, for our economy, for our liberties."[19] Indeed, if anything, this formulation *understates* the threat: why just one nuclear weapon in one city? If organized terrorist groups succeed in acquiring and detonating one nuclear weapon in one city, what will prevent them from acquiring other nuclear weapons and detonating them in other cities?

In short, a review of the literature suggests that the more seriously one takes the threat of terrorism—especially, but not necessarily exclusively, the threat of WMD terrorism—the less persuasive are the arguments against coercive interrogations, "torture lite," or even, in some instances, outright torture. One of the few exceptions is Michael Ignatieff, whose credentials in national security are not in doubt. Ignatieff argues for a categorical or absolute prohibition against not only torture but also physical (although not "nonphysical") coercion. Presumably, then, he would hold to these prohibitions even in the case of a genuine supreme emergency, such as an imminent WMD attack against a city.[20] Leaving aside, for the moment, whether this is a morally persuasive position, it would seem to be quite anomalous in light of Ignatieff's overall consequentialist argument that in the war on terrorism, it will be necessary to choose lesser evils to avoid even greater ones, and that included among these necessary and justified lesser evils are various forms of violence, assassinations, and perhaps even preemptive war.

Laden has explicitly said that "to kill Americans ... civilian and military—is an individual duty for every Muslim" and that al Queda's press spokesman, Suleiman Abu Ghaith, "has claimed the right to kill four million Americans, including two million children." Van Evera further notes that the leaders of al Qaeda "seek to acquire weapons of mass destruction and may also have the opportunity: enough nuclear materials remain poorly secured in Russia to make tens of thousands of Hiroshima-sized atomic bombs. Many Soviet nuclear and biological weapons scientists also remain underpaid or unemployed, ripe for hiring by terrorists." Stephen Van Evera, "Why U.S. National Security Requires Mideast Peace," MIT Center for International Studies, May 2005, 1–2.

[19] Quoted in Philip Shenon, "Sept. 11 Report Card Assails U.S. Progress Against Terror," *New York Times*, 15 November 2005.

[20] To be sure, Ignatieff does concede that "when we have to face terrorists who control weapons of mass destruction ... most bets—and gloves—would be off." Ignatieff, "The Lesser Evil," 10. But this is not his judgment of what, morally speaking, should or at least must be done, but only his prediction of what realistically will happen. In a more recent essay, Ignatieff similarly hedges his argument a bit, conceding that most Americans will not agree with him, and that in a crisis they will "privilege security over liberty and thus reluctantly endorse torture in their name." Michael Ignatieff, "Moral Prohibition At a Price" in Roth, Worden, and Bernstein, eds., *Torture: Does It Ever Make Us Safer?*, 27. Although this concession is not inconsistent with his normative position, it does suggest that categorical prohibitions against not merely torture but all forms of coercive interrogation are wholly impractical.

In the recent literature, a number of eminent lawyers, as well as political, moral, and legal philosophers, examine in forthright fashion the arguments for and against continuing to treat torture as categorically and unconditionally prohibited. Surprisingly, only a minority seem to hold to the traditional position that torture should be both defined broadly and totally banned (among them, the playwright and novelist Ariel Dorfman; Joshua Dratel, a defense attorney; the legal philosopher David Luban; and Kenneth Roth, Executive Director of Human Rights Watch).

Several other powerful condemnations of torture nonetheless end by reluctantly seeming to accept—either directly (Henry Shue) or by implication (Elaine Scarry)—that in some extreme circumstances, torturers might be able to plausibly argue that torture was necessary to avoid catastrophe. Still others would ban torture more narrowly defined, but accept "torture lite" or "highly coercive interrogation" in extreme circumstances.[21] Several other essayists even more explicitly argue that torture should be regarded as a lesser evil in extreme cases, and still others—in particular, Jean Bethke Elshtain, John T. Parry, and Judge Richard A. Posner—suggest (either explicitly or by unavoidable implication) that even in some situations short of supreme emergency, torture might legitimately be regarded as a lesser evil.

Only a few writers, however, notably Alan Dershowitz,[22] Andrew C. McCarthy (a former Federal district attorney),[23] and Heymann and Kayyem, argue that because torture (or only great coercion, for the latter writers) is sometimes necessary, the law should be changed and torture/coercion brought within the U.S. legal system, so that they can be regulated and controlled. In particular, Dershowitz argues, the security services must be required to apply to judges for "torture warrants," in which they must present evidence that torture is required in each case in which it is contemplated. Only judges, trained to evaluate evidence and to balance competing values, such as "the needs for security against the imperatives of liberty," should decide—openly and under the law—whether torture is (literally) warranted.

The Dershowitz proposals have been widely rejected, often with anger and contempt—a "stunningly bad idea," in Elshtain's words[24]—even by those who (like Elshtain herself) accept that in some cases, torture may be the lesser evil.

---

[21] See especially Heymann and Kayyem, *Protecting Liberty*, 12–13. However, given the emphasis that these authors place on protecting national security against very real threats, including the threat of WMD attack, and their willingness to countenance "highly coercive interrogation" in extreme situations, it is not easy to understand why they draw the line at torture. The explanation is probably that they give great weight to not violating the law of the land, which indeed prohibits torture—but if the threat is great and the line between highly coercive interrogation and torture is very thin, then why not simply argue for a change in the law?

[22] Alan Dershowitz, "Tortured Reasoning" in Levinson, ed., *Torture: A Collection*, 257–280.

[23] Andrew C. McCarthy, "Torture: Thinking About the Unthinkable" in Greenberg, ed., *The Torture Debate*, 98–100.

[24] Jean Bethke Elshtain, "Reflection on the Problem of 'Dirty Hands'" in Levinson, ed., *Torture: A Collection*, 83.

Hard cases make not only bad law but also bad ethics, it is often said. Rather than normalizing, institutionalizing, or legitimizing torture, it is argued, it is far better to continue the formal and official prohibition—even if an after-the-fact necessity defense might be available to those who authorize or engage in torture. In extreme circumstances, the consensus position holds, military and security professionals must be prepared to do what must be done, while later seeking to avoid punishment by convincing the courts or public opinion that there was no other choice.

Confronting the Arguments against Torture

Let us suppose that the security services capture someone who (on the basis of substantial evidence) is almost surely a member of a terrorist cell that is on the verge of carrying out a major attack against a city. Should this situation occur, we might ask ourselves three questions: In all likelihood, what *would* the authorities do? What *should* the authorities do? And, if torture or coercion cannot or should not be ruled out in this situation, then how can they be limited to only those situations in which they are the lesser evil?

Surely there can be no doubt about what the authorities would do in those circumstances—and in practical terms alone, that suggests the need for serious consideration of how to prevent abuses. Further, because there is an increasingly widespread understanding that the stakes are so high in the war on terrorism, especially but not limited to WMD terrorism, it seems evident that most Americans—including, as we now know, many eminent moral philosophers—would also agree that the authorities should do whatever it takes to prevent catastrophe.[25]

It does not necessarily follow, of course, that the opinion of the public or of a number of philosophers is persuasive; the moral issue must be examined on the merits. My central argument is that the moral issue raised by torture in the war on terrorism should be regarded as no different in principle from the broader moral issues inherent in war, generally. We do not absolutely proscribe war if the cause is sufficiently just—indeed, as WMD spread, it is possible (at least in principle, although not necessarily in practice) that in some circumstances, even preemptive war might be justified. Moreover, no matter how accurate the weaponry and how hard we may try to avoid it, it is inevitable that there will be civilian casualties. If wars that will surely result in the killing of hundreds or thousands of innocent noncombatants cannot be morally prohibited if the stakes are high enough, then how can it be morally prohibited to inflict non-fatal and reversible pain on a few anything-but-innocent terrorists,

---

[25] See Oren Gross: "Most of us believe that most, if not all, government agents, when faced with a genuinely catastrophic case, are likely to resort to whatever means they can wield, including ... torture. ... *And most of us hope they will do so.*" Gross, "The Prohibition on Torture," 249, emphasis added.

if that is the only way to save hundreds, thousands, or even hundreds of thousands of innocent lives?

Even so, before we can conclude that torture may sometimes be justified, we must first confront several practical arguments that challenge the "lesser evil" defense. First, it is often argued that torture does not work, for people will tell the torturers anything they want to hear. Although this argument has a certain surface plausibility, on closer scrutiny it is not persuasive: the historical evidence leaves no serious doubt that torture has often produced information that otherwise would not have been revealed, especially about the organization and location of members of resistance or insurgency groups. To be sure, in the overwhelming majority of such cases, the torturers had no just cause and therefore no moral right to such information, but that is another matter altogether.

Thus, leaving aside for the moment the issue of whether torture is ever justifiable, the strictly empirical issue of whether it "works" is not difficult to ascertain. There is little doubt, for example, that in the 1950s, the French torture of Algerian captives temporarily succeeded in destroying the underground revolutionary movement; similarly, there is evidence that in Ireland, British torture or coercion succeeded in gaining useful information.[26] More recently, there is evidence that in 2002, Sri Lanka tortured three terrorists into revealing the location of a bomb set to explode later that day,[27] and it is known that in "ticking-bomb" cases, Israel tortures—or, at least, inflicts physical and mental coercion upon—captured Palestinian militants, who have sometimes apparently revealed information that has prevented terrorist attacks against civilians.

Elsewhere as well, torture appears to be producing valuable information in the current war on terrorism. Dershowitz and others have cited cases in which Jordanian and Philippine torture resulted in the breaking up of terrorist plans and networks, including a plot to bring down a number of airplanes,[28] and both the Schlesinger and 9/11 Commission reports stated that interrogation of captured al Qaeda officials—widely known to include severe coercion and probably outright torture—has provided important information about that organization's structure and plans.[29]

---

[26] Heymann and Kayyem, *Protecting Liberty*, 165.

[27] Ibid., 166.

[28] Alan M. Dershowitz, *Why Terrorism Works: Understanding the Threat, Responding to the Challenge* (New Haven, CT: Yale University Press, 2002), 136–138.

[29] See Douglas Jehl, "Captured Terrorists Hint at New Plan, Officials Say," *New York Times*, 13 July 2004; Douglas Jehl and David Johnston, "CIA Expands Its Inquiry into Interrogation Tactics," *New York Times*, 29 August 2004; Bowden, "The Dark Art of Interrogation," especially 55–56. Although the Schlesinger Report, *Final Report of the Independent Panel to Review DOD Detention Operations*, reprinted in Danner, *Torture and Truth*, 329–399, does not say that the useful information was the result of torture; in fact, it is widely known that the interrogation methods of leading suspects includes severe coercion and waterboarding. According to widespread reports, almost no one can hold out against waterboarding; for example, Joshua Dratel—a severe critic of torture—reports that a CIA station agent told him that because everyone succumbs to torture, if he were captured, he would avoid pointless suffering and simply talk immediately. Greenberg, ed., *The Torture Debate*, 21–22.

A second practical argument against torture is that in the long run, it backfires and ends by being self-defeating: it engenders implacable hatreds, hardening the terrorists in their hostility and creating new ones. The usual case cited is Algeria in the 1950s and 1960s, when despite French torture, the revolutionary movement was reconstituted and soon succeeded. "The use of torture may have won the battle of Algiers for the French, but it cost them Algeria."[30]

It is important, however, to notice the differences between the Algerian situation and the present one. First, the perpetuation of French colonialism in the face of the nationalist demand for liberation and independence was not a just cause, so of course, the French use of torture was not justified; there is no moral or practical dilemma if an unjust method is used to pursue an unjust cause. Secondly, it may be rhetorically effective to say that it was torture that caused the French to ultimately lose in Algeria, but it is not accurate; they resorted to torture precisely because they feared defeat if they did not—and it is hardly implausible that they indeed would have been defeated even sooner had it not been for the temporary success of torture in destroying the revolutionary movement. In other words, the French may well have lost in Algeria despite their use of torture, not because of it.

Even so, it cannot be denied that the use of torture has already had a variety of costs, including international costs. It is only too plausible that the American torture in Afghanistan and Iraq will engender new acts of terrorism—and not only in those countries, but elsewhere, including against the United States itself. Moreover, it is certainly possible that the international backlash against torture in the war on terrorism—especially torture that is clearly illegitimate by *any* defensible criteria, as in Afghanistan and Iraq—will lead some otherwise friendly countries to refuse to cooperate or to minimize their cooperation with American intelligence efforts.

Still, in the final analysis, if torture and coercion are confined—as they should be—to protecting large numbers of innocent human lives, then it is not necessarily convincing to argue that in the long run, the political costs will be too high. To begin with, long-run political costs are inherently difficult to predict, and might well be minimized if torture was seriously controlled and plausibly necessary to save many innocent lives. Beyond that, the immediate stakes may be so high that they preclude guesswork about long-run consequences. And in the limiting case of WMD terrorism, the classic rejoinder to the long-run consequences argument—in the long run we'll all be dead—is redundant: if we fail to prevent WMD terrorism, by whatever action it takes, in the *short* run we'll all be dead.

Perhaps the most troubling of the arguments against torture in extreme circumstances is the innocence problem. Undoubtedly, there cannot be complete certainty that the person being tortured really has useful knowledge of an impending terrorist attack, but we do know that almost inevitably, errors will be

---

[30] Donald P. Gregg, "Fight Fire With Compassion," *New York Times*, 10 June 2004.

made—indeed have already been made in Afghanistan, Guantanamo, and Iraq, where a number of investigative reports have concluded that many innocent civilians have been abused by American forces.[31]

Given the stakes, however, in this writer's reluctant judgment, the innocence problem, tragic though it is, cannot be regarded as a decisive argument for a categorical prohibition of torture—after all, the criminal justice system also suffers from less than 100 percent reliability, but we do not abolish prisons on that account, even though we know that many innocents inevitably will pay a very high cost. Moreover, painful as it is to contemplate, it is hard to avoid the conclusion suggested by Alan Dershowitz and Richard Posner: "The dogma that it is better for ten guilty people to go free than for one innocent person to be convicted may not hold when the guilty ten are international terrorists who, moreover, are seeking and may succeed in obtaining weapons of mass destruction."[32]

What does follow, however, is that we must take the innocence problem very seriously, and take whatever steps we can to minimize it. Indeed, it is the very possibility of error that strengthens the argument for serious institutional controls over torture, to ensure that the evidence requiring it is very strong, or that it is stopped if it becomes increasingly likely that the victim either is innocent or has no further information that we are entitled to have.

SHOULD TORTURE BE REGULATED AND CONTROLLED?

I have argued that torture (or coercion) in the war on terrorism is both inevitable, and in some circumstances, justifiable as a lesser evil than unchecked terrorism. If that is persuasive, it would seem to follow that torture should be minimized, regulated, and controlled by subjecting it to the rule of law. On the other hand, there are powerful arguments against seeking to do so, so we must first address these arguments.

The Price for Ending Hypocrisy Is Too High

Some skeptics about the need for or desirability of institutionalizing controls over torture concede that torture in the war on terrorism is inevitable—and perhaps even in some circumstances, a lesser evil than otherwise-unsuccessful efforts to prevent the mass murder of innocents—and that therefore it is true that our professed absolute rejection of torture is hypocritical. Even so, their argument is that total consistency is not truly necessary; occasional hypocrisy

---

[31] For brief discussions of the innocence problem, see Elaine Scarry, "Five Errors in the Reasoning of Alan Dershowitz" in Levinson, ed., *Torture: A Collection*, 281–290; and Ross, "A History of Torture," 9–10.

[32] Richard A. Posner, "Torture, Terrorism, and Interrogation" in Levinson, ed., *Torture: A Collection*, 295.

may be a tolerable price for a political order to pay, especially if the alternative price—abandoning long-held norms prohibiting torture—is too high.

On the other hand, hypocrisy also may have serious costs. As McCarthy has argued, "By imposing an absolute ban on something we know is occurring, we promote disrespect for the law in general."[33] In any case, the ending of hypocrisy is not the main argument for institutionalizing controls over torture as well as less-intense kinds of coercion. Rather, it is that the price we pay for the current situation—uncontrolled, unregulated, unaccountable, and typically unpunished torture that cannot be justified by a lesser-evil argument—is higher than the undoubted price we would pay by abandoning the fiction that torture can *never* be justified by a lesser-evil argument.

The Legitimization Problem

A second argument against seeking to control torture is that the effort to do so will "legitimize" torture and thus, presumably, make it even more prevalent. Some writers have drawn an analogy between torture and the development of the absolute prohibitions against slavery or genocide. Not so long ago, they argue, slavery was also thought to be "inevitable," and it would appear that genocide is still inevitable, yet we do not say that because slavery and genocide are inevitable, we should try to minimize and regulate them.

This argument is surely right about slavery and genocide, but it ignores the crucial distinction between those unconditional evils and the evil of torture: slavery and genocide are *never* a necessary (but evil) means to a desirable end. Thus, there can be no consequentialist argument to be made on behalf of slavery or genocide. Put differently, because there is no conceivable end that would justify slavery or genocide, these cannot be "lesser evils" to anything. Tragically, in the world in which we now live, we cannot say that about torture.

In any case, to say that a formerly banned practice has become "legitimized" can be understood in two senses. First, it may be understood as an empirical statement: as a matter of fact, like it or not, the practice has become widely accepted. Second, it may be understood normatively, meaning that what was previously thought to be categorically wrong in a moral sense is no longer so regarded.

If this deconstruction of the term "legitimize" is correct, then, the argument against controls may be becoming moot. Understood in its empirical sense, torture is well on its way to be becoming "legitimized" in the United States, for scarcely a week goes by without new revelations of American torture—directly, by American soldiers or CIA personnel and indirectly, through "rendering" suspects to foreign collaborators. To be sure, recently, there has been growing congressional concern over the torture issue, but there is reason to be skeptical about whether this concern will be sustained and result

[33] Greenberg, ed., *The Torture Debate*, 108.

in real controls over torture. Beyond a handful of courts martial prosecutions of soldiers near the bottom of the chain of command, as of early 2006, very little had been done by the armed forces, the administration, or Congress to seriously investigate, let alone punish, those guilty of ordering, condoning, or acquiescing in the American torture or outright killing of alleged terrorist suspects in Afghanistan, Iraq, or Guantanamo.[34]

Moreover, it is evident that most of the cases of torture are not in response to "ticking-bomb" situations—even of conventional bombs, let alone WMD; nor has the practice been limited to torture of high-level officials of terrorist organizations, who presumably know of plans for mass-murder terrorism. Indeed, according to newspaper reports and several international non-governmental organization investigations, some 70–90 percent of Iraqis rounded up by American soldiers were neither terrorists nor insurgents.[35] Consequently, it appears that most of the actual cases of torture or coercion cannot be defended as necessary in the war on terrorism; they remain greater evils, not lesser ones. Under these circumstances, the argument here is that on balance, the need for effective controls over torture outweighs the not-unreasonable concern that controls will succeed only in legitimizing and perhaps even increasing torture.

Judicial Controls Are Often Ineffective

A similar set of arguments point to the well-known problems of judicial control of state authorities. For example, a number of critics of Dershowitz's call for advance judicial authorization—"torture warrants"—point out that the existing criminal warrant system is frequently abused by the police, who may either gather evidence illegally or plant evidence even after getting warrants.

Indeed, for that matter, we cannot assume that the judges themselves are immune from politics, ideology, or simple error—Luban argues that "politicians pick judges, and if the politicians accept torture, the judges will as well," and tellingly observes that Jay S. Bybee (of the infamous Bybee memorandum) is now a federal judge.[36] In the same vein, other critics have noted that judges are not the voice of pure law or reason, but rather actual people operating within a particular (and fallible) institutional structure. Moreover, where will they come from? Will they be elected, or chosen—and if so, by whom? For these and other reasons, it cannot be simply assumed that judges will be either independent or wise.

These are all legitimate and cogent observations and criticisms, but in my judgment, they are not decisive. Of course, the judicial system is flawed in a

---

[34] For an impressive marshalling of the evidence, see Roth, "Justifying Torture," 184–201.

[35] Even the semi-official Schlesinger Report conceded that American soldiers had rounded up "any and all suspicious-looking persons—all too often including women and children," and that "some individuals seized the opportunity provided by this environment to give vent to latent sadistic urges." Reprinted in Danner, *Torture and Truth*, 344.

[36] Greenberg, ed., *The Torture Debate*, 51.

variety of ways, and undoubtedly any efforts to control and regulate the use of torture by means of that system would be difficult and would sometimes fail. But compared to what? Compared to the current system, in which torture is largely uncontrolled, especially when ordered or tolerated by officials at the top of the system, who are not held accountable for their behavior? Is justice more likely to emerge from a system of no accountability, or one that demands accountability and the adherence to the rule of law, however short of perfection that system falls?

In any event, it should not be beyond our capacity to improve the existing system, and to devise effective principles, procedures, and institutions to control torture, in order to ensure that it is resorted to only when an overwhelming emergency leaves no other rational or, indeed, morally defensible choice. A good place to begin is by ending the current practice of "rendition"—turning over suspects to allied governments that have no compunction about torture. In this case, for several reasons, categorical prohibition is appropriate. First, on its face, rendition is particularly sleazy, designed as it is to evade U.S. legal prohibitions against torture. Moreover, it is widely *seen* to be sleazy, and it has been so widely exposed that it has defeated the purpose of giving the U.S. government "plausible deniability" that it uses torture in the war on terrorism; indeed, in the eyes of much of the world, including the West, hardly any accusations against the American government—probably even those that are false—are any longer plausibly deniable.

Further, although torture in general entails the risk that false confessions will result, rendition is especially likely to do so, for governments who are anxious to demonstrate their value to the United States have much less incentive to be skeptical and to verify all such "intelligence."[37] Finally, rendition is obviously inconsistent with the need to develop a system of executive, legislative, and judicial controls over torture and coercion.

An institutionalized process for controlling torture would begin with some kind of system of advance authorization—something like Dershowitz's "torture warrants," perhaps, but one that would be less likely to suffer from the problems (police evasions, dishonesty in gathering evidence, and other abuses) that sometimes occur in the existing judicial warrant system. In any case, judicial control of coercion and torture should not be limited to an authorization

---

[37] For example, there have been a number of reports that the Bush administration based its claim that the Saddam Hussein government in Iraq was linked to al Qaeda on a "confession" made by a high-level operative captured by American forces and turned over to Egypt for interrogation under torture, a statement later recanted when the al Qaeda leader was no longer in Egyptian custody. Douglas Jehl, "Qaeda-Iraq Link U.S. Cited is Tied to Coercion Claim," *New York Times*, 9 December 2005. See also a television interview of Craig Murray, the former British Ambassador to Uzbekistan, another U.S. ally that cooperates with American rendition policy. Murray states that many "confessions" obtained under particularly horrible forms of torture by the Uzbekistan government have been demonstrably false, producing dangerous misinformation in the war on terrorism. (Murray's testimony is in *Torture*, a British documentary televised on the Sundance channel, 12 December 2005.)

process, but must also encompass post-facto judicial review, sanctions when appropriate, and judicial remedies for those wrongly tortured.

How, precisely, would a system of judicial control operate? Andrew C. McCarthy, a former Assistant U.S. District Attorney and currently a law professor, has suggested the creation of a single federal "national security court." Such a court—perhaps similar to the existing special federal court that decides whether U.S. intelligence agencies can engage in domestic spying—would allow the judges to develop expertise in matters of national security.[38] Any violations of the legal norms, rules, and procedures—at any level, in principle up to and including the Commander in Chief—must be treated as impeachable offenses or outright crimes, and if serious enough, punishable by jail terms.

Moreover, controlling coercion and torture in the war on terrorism should be the responsibility not only of the judiciary, for Congress could and should also play a much greater role, not only through legislation, but also by more vigorous use of its investigative and oversight powers, to ensure that the executive branch is complying with the law.

Other than these general suggestions, it is beyond the scope of this paper—and certainly beyond this author's competence—to provide a detailed prescription for how the current system can be improved.[39] My premise is that a recognition of the problem, together with a serious will to deal with the torture issue in a manner that both protects national security and is morally defensible, could find institutional expression.

Even so, in the final analysis, it cannot be denied that any system of institutionalized controls over torture must rely to a certain extent on trust that the authorities—especially at the top of the political system—will not seek to evade and bypass them. In this context, it is instructive to consider the McCain Amendment, now the law of the land, and President Bush's reaction to it. In signing McCain—which purports to categorically prohibit not merely torture but also the "cruel, inhuman, or degrading treatment" of any terrorists captured by the United States—Bush issued a statement in which he reserved the right to interpret it according to his own judgment of the constitutional authority of the president, especially in his capacity as Commander in Chief of the armed forces.

In view of the administration's overall record, then, there is every reason to suspect that in some circumstances, it will seek to avoid the McCain prohibi-

---

[38] Greenberg, ed., *The Torture Debate*, 109–110. To be sure, it is ominous that the Bush administration chose to bypass this court in certain circumstances, but its actions have generated a number of lawsuits and a considerable uproar in public opinion and in Congress. Perhaps, then, the existence of the special court may yet prove to be an effective constraint on executive overreaching. Once again, though: whatever the outcome, it would hardly follow that a system of no judicial authorization and review would be better.

[39] However, for a number of detailed suggestions on how all three branches of the government can improve the institutions and procedures for controlling "highly coercive interrogation," see Heymann and Kayyem, *Protecting Liberty*, especially 35–39.

tions. Moreover, even McCain himself has conceded that his legislation would not (should not?) apply to a "million to one" extreme ticking-bomb situation, in which the "the president will authorize whatever techniques he thinks will work," but should take responsibility for doing so.[40]

In short, it is not yet knowable whether the McCain amendment, the first serious effort to assert legislative control over the executive branch on how the war on terrorism may be fought, will be effective or indeed *should* be effective in extreme circumstances—even, apparently, in the eyes of its architect. But it does not follow that this early effort to institutionalize controls over torture demonstrates the futility of trying to do so. For one thing, the McCain amendment could well prove to be a significant constraint when it should be, if not on Bush, then perhaps on future presidents, as well as on the professionals in the CIA, the Pentagon, and the armed forces.

Beyond that, once again we must ask: compared to what? If a genuine, total, and unconditional ban on coercion or torture in the war on terrorism is neither practical nor wise, serves neither the requirements of national security nor of morally acceptable consequences, then it is hard to see why the present, largely uncontrolled system should be regarded as more trustworthy.

The Criteria Governing Torture

What moral criteria or principles should guide a system of judicial controls? Just-war theory provides the appropriate guidelines: just cause, last resort, and proportionality.

Just Cause

As in decisions to go to war, an unambiguously just cause is a necessary precondition of resorting to either severe coercion or outright torture—otherwise, of course, torture could never meet the lesser-evil criterion. Because of the terrible nature of this method, just cause should be interpreted particularly narrowly to exclude any purpose other than clear self-defense against terrorist attacks on civilian populations.

To be sure, as already noted, a common objection to making just cause a criterion for justifying torture is that it may be abused by untrustworthy governments. For example, Levinson asks: "Why in the world would we necessarily trust a highly politicized state elite, with its own potential political interests in creating a perception of danger," to decide when a genuine catastrophe exists?[41] A legitimate concern, certainly—but no different from allowing states to go to war on the basis of "self-defense," or, for that matter, on humanitarian

---

[40] Associated Press, "McCain Makes Exception on Torture," *Buffalo News*, 20 December 2005; David E. Sanger and Eric Schmitt, "Bush Says He's Confident that He and McCain Will Reach Agreement on Interrogation Policy," *New York Times*, 13 December 2005.

[41] Sanford Levinson, "Contemplating Torture" in Levinson, ed., *Torture: A Collection*, 33.

grounds. Both self-defense and humanitarian intervention can be abused (as some observers would argue was the case in Iraq), providing pretexts rather than convincing justifications for the use of force. Nonetheless, we do not throw out the principles. In short, as in the broader principle of self-defense, an argument justifying torture in catastrophic circumstances is just that—an argument, and one that may or may not be persuasive, or even honest. There is no way around the problem, but the alternative—no limiting criteria—is worse.

That said, it is important to make a number of distinctions, even within the framework of self-defense. There are at least three possible scenarios, unfortunately all, to one degree or another, realistic ones, in which the issue of torture is certain to be—and must be—considered: the capture of terrorists at the field level who are about to engage in WMD attacks on cities, the capture of terrorists about to engage in non-WMD attacks on cities, and the capture of terrorist leaders who are planning or who know about the plans for future major terrorist attacks.

Let us begin with consideration of the easiest case: preventing the destruction of entire cities. Assume, in the usual fashion, that the authorities have captured a member of a terrorist cell and that the evidence is very strong that he has information that could prevent an imminent WMD attack. As discussed earlier, preventing such an attack constitutes a supreme emergency (in Walzer's terms) or "an ultimate catastrophe," in the terminology of several contributors to the Levinson book. To repeat an earlier point: if early in World War II, a genuine supreme emergency (avoiding defeat at the hands of Nazi Germany) allowed Britain to legitimately override the principle of noncombatant immunity by deliberately killing (through bombing of cities) tens of thousands of German civilians—some of them, undoubtedly, strongly opposed to Hitler—then it is hard to see why torture of a few non-innocent terrorists in a different but genuine supreme emergency should be regarded as beyond the pale.

The case for torture to prevent more-limited attacks is obviously less overwhelming. Even so, non-WMD attacks can also kill thousands of innocents, as on September 11, or perhaps "merely" hundreds, as in the Madrid railroad bombing. Although short of constituting supreme emergencies, such conventional attacks may well be sufficiently catastrophic to justify torture if there is no other way to avert them. Suppose, for example, that on 10 September 2001, the authorities, learning of an impending massive attack in the United States but not knowing where or by what means, had captured Mohammed Atta or one of the other leaders of the attack on the World Trade Center, and all other efforts to gain the necessary information had failed? Who would have wished to argue that torture would have been illegitimate even if it had succeeded in preventing the attack?

To be sure, it is certainly the case that this is a troubling line of thought. As one internal critic of U.S. government torture asked: "How many lives [have] to be saved to justify torture? Thousands? Hundreds? Where do you draw the line?"[42] A cogent and disturbing question indeed, and one that is impossible to answer in the abstract. Yet, in actual and specific cases, such as September 11, the answer may be reasonably apparent.

The ticking-bomb cases aside, the third scenario in which torture or at least "highly coercive interrogation" must be considered is the capture of high-level al Qaeda leaders (already a reality, as we now know)—or, perhaps eventually, Iraqi terrorist leaders, like Abu Masab al-Zarqawi—who, after some period of regular interrogation, are refusing to talk about their organization or plans for future attacks. Because large numbers of innocent lives are genuinely at stake in such cases, as well as in obvious ticking-bomb situations, it is hard to see why torture (when both normal interrogation and coercion short of torture had failed) should be ruled out. Indeed, such cases might also constitute ticking-bomb situations—for all we know, major attacks might well be imminent.

Put differently, because the key to winning the war on terror is accurate intelligence, it is not evident that there is a compelling national security *or* moral distinction between using methods genuinely necessary to extract tactical intelligence to prevent imminent attacks and using those necessary to extract strategic intelligence (information about the organization, finances, membership, and location of terrorist groups) in order to prevent future attacks.

Last Resort

As has been already suggested, it is morally obvious that torture can be legitimately resorted to only in order to extract information that is crucial to save innocent lives, and then only when other methods of gaining the necessary information have been tried and failed: that is, normal methods of interrogation or even various forms of physical or psychological coercion, short of outright torture.

Moreover, neither coercion nor torture can ever be resorted to—and this *is* a categorical prohibition, one for which it is impossible to imagine any exceptions—for any purpose other than an urgent need to avert a catastrophe: not to humiliate, not to punish, not to take revenge. It is now evident that the U.S. armed forces violated this prohibition in Afghanistan and, especially, Iraq. Under a system of serious controls, any torture that was not a last resort and was for illegitimate purposes would be severely punished. And that would include anyone in the chain of command—right to the top—who ordered, authorized, or merely acquiesced in torture for such purposes.

Proportionality, or the Sliding Scale

As discussed earlier, it is a well-established principle in Western morality—or, more accurately, one to which we give lip service—that "the end doesn't justify

---

[42] Jane Mayer, "Annals of the Pentagon: The Memo," *New Yorker*, 27 February 2006, quoting Alberto Mora, the former general counsel of the U.S. Navy.

the means." Given the current realities, however, it would appear that we can no longer afford to insist that the moral judgments we make about means (*jus in bello*) be entirely separate from the judgments we make about ends (*jus ad bellum*).

Philosophers generally agree that moral constraints on behavior cannot be impossible of realization—that is, so demanding that they are antithetical to human nature itself. In that sense, then, it would appear that it is beyond human nature to truly live by an unconditional principle that a just end never justifies unjust means, even if the end is overwhelmingly just (the prevention of mass murder) and the means (torture) are genuinely imperative to achieve it. That is, in certain circumstances the end *does* justify the means.

The argument can be put even more strongly. It is not only beyond human nature but morally unpersuasive on the merits to have an absolute ban on torture that is necessary to prevent human catastrophes. It would be both irrational, in terms of national security, and morally incoherent to place a higher value on not inflicting temporary pain on one or several terrorists than on doing what is necessary to protect both national security and innocent human lives—in the most extreme case, perhaps hundreds of thousands of innocent lives.

The guiding principle concerning torture, then, must be proportionality, or the sliding scale, in which all actions are judged by their consequences for both justice and national security. The greater the evil to be averted, the fewer the restrictions on the means that are required to do so. And if the fate of an entire city, or indeed *many* cities, hangs in the balance—and some day that may well be the case—then there can be no limits at all. When what is at stake is, for all practical purposes, an infinite evil, the guiding principle of the authorities seeking to prevent it will be, must be, and should be: whatever it takes.[43]

CONCLUSION

If we are to succeed in the war against terrorism, we surely must do much more than defend ourselves against terrorist attacks. The broader task is to do whatever can be reasonably and legitimately done to address the causes of terrorism, as well as the motivations of terrorists to target the United States. In my view, such measures must include great changes in American foreign policy—a far more balanced policy in the Israeli–Palestinian conflict, for example, as well as a general policy of military noninterventionism, except in those few cases in which truly vital national interests are at stake. Meanwhile, though, we need to prevent attacks on American cities.

In attempting to do so, we confront a terrible dilemma. On the one hand, of course torture violates a central moral command of any civilized society;

[43] For a similar argument, see Posner, "Torture, Terrorism, and Interrogation," 293.

as a number of recent writers have emphasized—as if there were contrary views that needed refuting—torture is evil, antithetical to the values for which America stands, and destructive of the souls of the torturer as well as the tortured. Similarly, it has often been said that the war on terrorism is a war to preserve American values, so that if we resort to torture "the terrorists will have won," and the like.

On the other hand, the rhetoric does not do justice to the complexity of the problem and it will not do to simply dwell on the undoubted horrors of torture without consideration of the even greater horrors entailed in the mass murder of innocents. The crisis is unprecedented, the stakes are catastrophically high, and values are in conflict. Self-defense and the protection of innocent lives are also important values, and the terrorists will have "won" even more decisively if they succeed in destroying cities, the national economy, and possibly, the entire fabric of liberal democracy. Indeed, it should be regarded as instructive that it is not merely the United States but also some of the most civilized European liberal democracies that have evidently found it necessary to sometimes effectively condone or at least acquiesce in the torture of terrorist suspects.[44]

Put differently, so long as the threat of large-scale terrorist attacks against innocents is taken seriously, as it must be, it is neither practicable nor morally persuasive to absolutely prohibit the physical coercion or even outright torture of captured terrorist plotters—undoubtedly evils, but lesser evils than preventable mass murder. In any case, although the torture issue is still debatable today, assuredly the next major attack on the United States—or perhaps Europe—will make it moot. At that point, the only room for practical choice will be between controlled and uncontrolled torture—if we are lucky. Far better, then, to avoid easy rhetoric and think through the issue while we still have the luxury of doing so.

As I have argued, there are three general positions on the problem of torture in the war on terrorism. The first we can call "absolute prohibition": even in the present circumstances, we must retain and enforce a categorical prohibition against torture. The second we can label (perhaps not too unfairly) "absolute prohibition, except when absolutely necessary": retain the norm and the laws that torture is categorically prohibited, but expect that the authorities will disregard the law—and *rightfully* disregard the law—if torture is the only means to prevent catastrophic terrorist attacks. The third is "legalize in order to control," in which the fiction that torture is categorically prohibited is abandoned so that we may create laws, procedures, and institutions to ensure

---

[44] Kenneth Roth of Human Rights Watch points out that a number of European governments, including those of Sweden, Germany, Austria, the Netherlands, and the United Kingdom "seem to be toying with emulation" of the United States by becoming "complicit in torture"—for example, by sending terrorist suspects to countries known to torture or, in the case of Britain, refusing "to rule out information extracted from torture in court proceedings." Roth, "Justifying Torture," 199–200.

that torture is resorted to only when the evidence—presented *before* the fact—strongly indicates that coercion, and perhaps even torture, is indeed the necessary last resort to prevent mass-murder terrorism.

All of the choices have substantial defects. As I have argued, a categorical prohibition of torture today fails all the important tests: that of national security, that of moral consequences, and (because it has no chance of being observed under certain circumstances) that of practicality, a necessity in any meaningful system of moral constraint. For these reasons, many moral and legal philosophers, as well as political leaders (like John McCain), explicitly or in effect choose the second option: ban coercion but allow for exceptions, after the fact. In essence, this position concedes that in extreme circumstances, torture may be unavoidable, but nonetheless argues that our society would be better off if we continued to act *as if* torture were categorically prohibited. However, this choice also has major defects. First of all, of course, it is clearly hypocritical. As argued earlier, although one can concede that civilized and stable societies must often live with useful hypocrisies, in this case, the price may be too high. Aside from encouraging general cynicism about the rule of law, more particularly we are likely to forfeit our ability to control torture if we do not explicitly recognize it and treat it as a necessary evil under some circumstances.

Put differently, the second option, a compromise between absolute prohibition and control through partial legalization, reflects an empirical judgment as much as or more than a moral norm, for it is premised on the assumption that the fiction of categorical prohibition will lead to less torture, especially less clearly illegitimate torture, than if torture (even in extreme circumstances) were to become "legitimized." However, the historical record demonstrates that when torture is formally banned in principle but unregulated in practice, it almost always becomes an instrument of governmental police thugs or outright sadists, not only when the end does not justify the means but also when the end itself—such as punishment, intimidation, revenge against political dissidents, or even the amusement of sadists—is unjust.

That the United States is not immune from that danger is already all too clear. Indeed, we could end up with the worst of all worlds: uncontrolled torture that violates every morally necessary constraint, undermines national security by turning the world against us, produces little or no useful information, and precipitates rather than diminishes terrorism. In Iraq, Afghanistan, and probably Guantanamo, the use of torture by American soldiers and intelligence personnel is, from all the evidence now available (and who can doubt that more will be forthcoming), widespread and, indeed, not confined to stopping terrorism. Yet, it appears unlikely that in the end much is going to be done about it, at least at the top of the chain of command. Nor is this new. A convenient amnesia about the Vietnam War has triumphed in the United States; American soldiers engaged in coercion, torture, murder, and other war crimes in Vietnam, and in most cases, little or nothing was done about that either.

This history, past and present, demonstrates that we should not continue to leave the decision on whether to order, condone, or acquiesce in the torture of captured terrorists to unregulated and unaccountable political and military leaders who have already abundantly demonstrated that they are not to be trusted with this terrible power. For these reasons, there is a strong argument for developing laws, institutions, and procedures to authorize, monitor, and control torture, as well as, when necessary, to severely punish unauthorized and illegitimate torture.

To be sure (as I have already discussed), this course also has significant defects: judicial and institutional controls will not always work, imperial presidents may simply disregard the law, and an explicit acknowledgment of torture is likely to harm the image of the United States throughout the world. On the other hand, we have already suffered enormous damage as a consequence of our resort to uncontrolled and unaccountable torture, so it is not unreasonable to expect that an acknowledgment of the problem, accompanied by an honest and sustained effort to fix it as best we can, would make things better. Anyway, the operative question remains: compared to what? Because torture cannot, will not, and, in some catastrophically bad circumstances, should not be banned, on balance a system of controls would seem to best serve this country's national interests as well as have acceptable—or, perhaps better said, least evil—moral consequences.

If this conclusion is accepted, the task becomes to institute controls that are as powerful as we can devise, in order to ensure that torture is resorted to only when there is no other rational or morally defensible choice. We must devise a judicial system that meets three criteria: it must be independent of the government, the armed forces, and the intelligence services; it must be capable of continuous and sustained authorization, observation, and control of torture; and it must have the authority to impose severe criminal sanctions against anyone—no matter at what level of government—who authorizes, engages in, or acquiesces in illegitimate torture. As indicated above, several measures that could meet these criteria have already been proposed, and assuredly more would be forthcoming once a decision in principle was made to move in this direction.

I have argued that there are no good choices in the war on terrorism, only tragic ones. It cannot be denied that any legitimization of torture is a morally painful and historically dangerous step. In some circumstances, though, our only real choice, in terms of both national security and moral consequences, will be between controlled and uncontrolled torture. We gain nothing by pretending differently. In the struggle against deadly terrorism, some of world's most civilized democracies are themselves unwilling to shrink from doing what they think is necessary. Such are the times in which we live.